Bernhard Tauchnitz

The Physiology of Common Life by George Henry Lewes

Bernhard Tauchnitz

The Physiology of Common Life by George Henry Lewes

ISBN/EAN: 9783741162978

Manufactured in Europe, USA, Canada, Australia, Japa

Cover: Foto ©Thomas Meinert / pixelio.de

Manufactured and distributed by brebook publishing software
(www.brebook.com)

Bernhard Tauchnitz

The Physiology of Common Life by George Henry Lewes

COLLECTION

OF

BRITISH AUTHORS

TAUCHNITZ EDITION.

VOL. 519.

THE PHYSIOLOGY OF COMMON LIFE BY LEWES

IN TWO VOLUMES.

VOL. 2.

LEIPZIG: BERNHARD TAUCHNITZ.

PARIS: C. REINWALD & CIE, 15, RUE DES SAINTS PÈRES.

UCHNITZ EDITION.

Each volume ½ Thlr.

ADAMS: Sacred Allegories 1 v.
.UILAR: Home Influence 2 v. The
.ecompense 2 v.
.lta 1 v. Carr of Carrlyon 2 v. The
. v.
ORTH: Windsor Castle 1 v. Saint
. v. Jack Sheppard (w. portr.) 1 v.
.ashire Witches 2 v. The Star-Cham-
. The Flitch of Bacon 1 v. The Spend-
tariff 1 v. Mervyn Clitheroe 2 v. Ovingdean
Grange 1 v. The Constable of the Tower 1 v.
The Lord Mayor of London 2 v. Cardinal Pole
1 v. John Law 2 v. The Spanish Match 2 v.
The Constable de Bourbon 2 v. Old Court 2 v.
Myddleton Pomfret 2 v. South-Sea Bubble 2 v.
Hilary St. Ives 2 v.
"ALL FOR GREED," author of: All for
Greed 1 v. Love the Avenger 2 v.
MISS AUSTEN: Sense and Sensibility 1 v.
Mansfield Park 1 v.
NINA BALATKA 1 v.
REV. R. H. BAYNES: Lyra Anglicana 1 v.
CURRER BELL: Jane Eyre 2 v. Shirley
2 v. Villette 2 v. The Professor 1 v.
E. & A. BELL: Wuthering Heights, and
Agnes Grey 2 v.
LADY BLESSINGTON: Meredith 1 v.
Strathern 2 v. Memoirs of a Femme de
Chamber 1 v. Marmaduke Herbert 2 v. Coun-
try Quarters (w. portr.) 2 v.
BRADDON: Lady Audley's Secret 2 v.
Aurora Floyd 2 v. Eleanor's Victory 2 v. John
Marchmont's Legacy 2 v. Henry Dunbar 2 v.
Doctor's Wife 2 v. Only a Clod 2 v. Sir Jasper's
Tenant 2 v. Lady's Mile 2 v. Rupert Godwin
2 v. Dead-Sea Fruit 2 v. Run to Earth 2 v.
BROOKS: The Silver Cord 3 v. Sooner or
Later 3 v.
BROWN: Rab and his Friends 1 v.
TOM BROWN'S School Days 1 v.
BULWER (LORD LYTTON): Pelham (w.
portr.) 1 v. Eugene Aram 1 v. Paul Clifford 1 v.
Zanoni 1 v. Pompeii 1 v. The Disowned 1 v.
Ernest Maltravers 1 v. Alice 1 v. Eva, and the
Pilgrims of the Rhine 1 v. Devereux 1 v. Godol-
phin and Falkland 1 v. Rienzi 1 v. Night and
Morning 1 v. The Last of the Barons 2 v. Athens
2 v. Poems of Schiller 1 v. Lucretia 1 v. Harold
2 v. King Arthur 2 v. The New Timon: Saint
Stephen's 1 v. The Caxtons 2 v. My Novel 4 v.
What will he do with it? 4 v. Dramatic Works
2 v. A Strange Story 2 v. Caxtoniana 2 v. The
Lost Tales of Miletus 1 v. Miscellaneous Prose
Works 4 v. The Odes and Epodes of Horace 2 v.
SIR HENRY LYTTON BULWER: His-
torical Characters 2 v.
BUNYAN: The Pilgrim's Progress 1 v.
BURIED ALONE 1 v.
MISS BURNEY: Evelina 1 v.
BURNS: Poetical Works (w. portr.) 1 v.
BYRON: The Works (w. portr.) compl. 5 v.
T. CARLYLE: The French Revolution 3 v.
Frederick the Great 13 v. Oliver Cromwell 4 v.
The Life of Friedrich Schiller 1 v.

"THE LAST OF THE CAVALIERS,"
author of: The Last of the Cavaliers 2 v.
The Gain of a Loss 2 v.
S. T. COLERIDGE: The Poems 1 v.
WILKIE COLLINS: After Dark 1 v. Hid
and Seek 2 v. A Plot in Private Life 1 v. The
Dead Secret 2 v. The Woman in White 2 v. Basil
1 v. No Name 3 v. Antonina 2 v. Armadale 3 v
The Moonstone 2 v.
"COMETH UP AS A FLOWER," author
of: Cometh up as a Flower 1 v. Not wisely
but too well 2 v. Red as a Rose is She 2 v.
FENIMORE COOPER: The Spy (w. portr.
1 v. The Two Admirals 1 v. Jack O'Lantern 1 v
THE TWO COSMOS 1 v.
MISS CRAIK: Lost and Won 1 v. Faith
Unwin's Ordeal 1 v. Leslie Tyrrell 1 v. Wini
fred's Wooing and other Tales 1 v. Mildred 1 v
MISS CUMMINS: Lamplighter 1 v. Mabel
Vaughan 1 v. El Fureidis 1 v. Haunted Hearts 1 v.
DE-FOE: Robinson Crusoe 1 v.
CHARLES DICKENS: The Pickwick Club
(w. portr.) 2 v. American Notes 1 v. Oliver Twist
1 v. Nicholas Nickleby 2 v. Sketches 1 v. Mar-
tin Chuzzlewit 2 v. A Christmas Carol; the
Chimes; the Cricket 1 v. Master Humphrey's
Clock 2 v. Pictures from Italy 1 v. The Battle
of Life; the Haunted Man 1 v. Dombey and
Son 3 v. Copperfield 3 v. Bleak House 4 v.
A Child's History of England (2 v. 2° 27 Ngr.).
Hard Times 1 v. Little Dorrit 4 v. A Tale of
two Cities 2 v. Hunted Down; the Uncom-
mercial Traveller 1 v. Great Expectations 2 v.
Christmas Stories 1 v. Our Mutual Friend 4 v.
Somebody's Luggage; Mrs. Lirriper's Lodg-
ings; Mrs. Lirriper's Legacy 1 v. Doctor Mari-
gold's Prescriptions; Mugby Junction 1 v. No
Thoroughfare 1 v. Edwin Drood v. 1.
B. DISRAELI: Coningsby 1 v. Sybil 1 v.
Contarini Fleming (w. portr.) 1 v. Alroy 1 v.
Tancred 2 v. Venetia 2 v. Vivian Grey 2 v.
Henrietta Temple 1 v.
DIXON: Lord Bacon 1 v. The Holy Land 2 v.
New America 2 v. Spiritual Wives 2 v. Her
Majesty's Tower 2 v.
MISS A. B. EDWARDS: Barbara's History
2 v. Miss Carew 2 v. Hand and Glove 1 v. Half
a Million of Money 2 v. Debenham's Vow 1 v.
MRS. EDWARDS: Archie Lovell 2 v. Steven
Lawrence 2 v.
ELIOT: Scenes of Clerical Life 2 v. Adam
Bede 2 v. The Mill on the Floss 2 v. Silas
Marner 1 v. Romola 2 v. Felix Holt 2 v.
THE STORY OF ELIZABETH 1 v.
ESSAYS AND REVIEWS 1 v.
FRANK FAIRLEGH 2 v.
"PAUL FERROLL," author of: Paul
Ferroll 1 v. Year after Year 1 v. Why Paul
Ferroll killed his Wife 1 v.
FIELDING: Tom Jones 2 v.
FIVE CENTURIES of the English Lan-
guage and Literature 1 v.
FOUND DEAD 1 v.
LADY FULLERTON: Ellen Middleton 1 v.
Grantley Manor 2 v. Lady-Bird 2 v. Too Strange
not to be True 2 v. Constance Sherwood 2 v.
A Stormy Life 2 v. Mrs. Gerald's Niece 2 v.

COLLECTION

OF

BRITISH AUTHORS.

VOL. 519.

———————

THE PHYSIOLOGY OF COMMON LIFE BY G. H. LEWES.

IN TWO VOLUMES.

VOL. II.

THE

PHYSIOLOGY OF COMMON LIFE.

BY

GEORGE HENRY LEWES,

AUTHOR OF "SEASIDE STUDIES," "RANTHORPE," &c.

WITH NUMEROUS WOODCUTS.

COPYRIGHT EDITION.

IN TWO VOLUMES

VOL. II.

LEIPZIG

BERNHARD TAUCHNITZ

1860.

The Right of Translation is reserved.

CONTENTS

OF VOLUME II.

CHAPTER VIII.

FEELING AND THINKING.

CHAPTER IX.

THE MIND AND THE BRAIN.

SECTION I. — THE CEREBRUM.

CHAPTER IX.
(Continued).
THE MIND AND THE BRAIN.

SECTION II. — THE CEREBELLUM AND MEDULLA OBLONGATA.

CHAPTER IX.
(Continued.)
THE MIND AND THE BRAIN.

SECTION III. — THE SPINAL CHORD AND ITS FUNCTIONS.

CHAPTER X.

OUR SENSES AND SENSATIONS.

THE PHYSIOLOGY OF COMMON LIFE.

VOL. II.

CHAPTER VIII.

FEELING AND THINKING.

Object and scope of the inquiry — Psychology and Physiology two separate sciences — The Brain not the exclusive organ of the Mind: the two established doctrines — What is Nerve-force? — Structure of the Nervous System — Are nerves conductors only, and what do they conduct? — Error of likening nerves to the conducting-wires of a battery — Independent action of nerves — Neurility the property of a nerve — Sensibility the property of a nerve-centre — The distinction between property and function — Refutation of the supposed distinction between sensory and motor nerves — Where is the Sensorium? — Opinions of elder writers; modern opinions — Proof that Sensibility depends on histological, not on morphological structure, and that all nerve-centres possess it — Sensibility, Sensation, and Consciousness — Ambiguities of language: different meanings of "consciousness" — Can there be sensations of which we are unconscious? — Sensation and Perception — Unperceived sensations — The Law of Sensibility — Reflex actions and Reflex feelings — Sensations unattended to in reverie and sleep — Illustrations of sleepers being conscious of sensations — General consciousness: Systemic Sensations: the feeling of existence — Systemic-consciousness, Sense-consciousness, and Thought-consciousness.

In the mighty web of things there are no threads more wonderful than Sensation and Thought; nor have any more constantly solicited the attention of philosophers, from the earliest dawn of speculative inquiry to the angry contests of to-day. They have been problems ever-alluring and ever-baffling: one moment the threads seemed to be within the easy grasp of an outstretched hand, only to vanish again into the inextricable confusion of tangled mystery.

Feeling and Thinking are of too profound an interest, and too closely allied with all vital phenomena, not to find a large place in the "Physiology of Common Life." But what place must we give them? How must these difficult subjects be treated? Their very depth and extent of interest oblige us to select only those aspects which fall strictly within the scope of this work. They have psychological aspects, and physiological aspects, both of great importance; but as our business here is not to discuss any but physiological problems, we must leave untouched the discussion of the many vexed questions of Psychology, and confine ourselves to what are strictly the physiological aspects of Thought and Sensation.

Psychology is the science of Mind; Physiology is the science of Life. All who recognise the former as a science, declare its aim to be the elucidation of the laws of Thought, the nature of the Soul, and its prerogatives. This science may seek — and I follow those who think it *ought* to seek — important means of investigation in the laws of Physiology; just as Physiology itself must seek important aids in Chemistry and Physics. But as an independent branch of inquiry, its results cannot be held amenable to physiological canons; their validity cannot be decided by agreement or disagreement with physiological laws. To cite an example: Psychology announces that the mind has different faculties, and that each of these faculties may have a temporary exaltation, or a temporary suspension. This fact seems established on ample evidence, and is valid in Psychology, although hitherto no *corresponding* fact in Physiology has been discovered — neither the anatomy of the brain, nor any knowledge of the brain's action, can be adduced as furnishing the *evidence;* and if Psychology were absolutely amenable to the conclusions of Physiology, we should here have to doubt one of the most indisputable of psychological facts. On the other hand, it is no less certain that the physiology of the Nervous System must be studied free from all control on the part of psychologists. If we do not prescribe conclusions for them, neither must they prescribe conclusions for us. To them we leave the laws of thought. To us they must leave the difficult task of ascertaining the relation between Sensation and the various parts of the Nervous System. After this explicit statement of the object and scope of the following chapters, I trust no psychologist will object to my conclusions if they fall short of, or run counter to his. He must consider himself out of court. Our science does not pretend to cope with the mysteries of his. Those mysteries will most probably for ever remain unsolved; meanwhile the labours of physiologists have made it possible that there should be at least a science of those vital phenomena connected with the Nervous System; and "thus," to use the fine expression of Professor Huxley, "from the region of disorderly mystery, which is the domain of ignorance, another vast province has been added to science, the realm of *orderly mystery*."

The reader will have remarked that the Nervous System is mentioned, and not simply the Brain; although, inasmuch as the Brain is universally held to be the organ of the Mind, the sole centre of Sensation and Thought, there might seem to be no reason for our treating any other part of the Nervous System in this inquiry. My reason is simple: I do not agree in this opinion respecting the Brain as "the organ" of the mind. One of the principal conclusions to which fact and argument will direct us in these pages will be, that the Brain is only *one* organ of the Mind, and not by any means the exclusive centre of Consciousness. I am aware of the paradoxical air such a statement must have in these days; because the hypothesis that the Brain is the sole organ of Consciousness, after having been execrated as a heresy, and having had to battle through a stormy period of illiberal opposition, has now settled down among the respectable and respected conclusions of philosophy. If I venture to dispute, and disprove, this conclusion, it is because, after having for many years devoutly believed it, I have been gradually led, in the course of very various researches, not only to a different conception, but also to understand the source of the original error.

It will be understood that by the word Mind we do not designate the intellectual operations only. If the term were so restricted, there would be little objection to our calling the Brain the organ of the Mind. But the word Mind has a broader and deeper signification; it includes all Sensation, all Volition, and all Thought: it means the whole psychical Life; and this psychical Life has no one special centre, any more than the physical Life has one special centre: it belongs to the whole, and animates the whole. The Brain is a part of this whole, a noble part, and its functions are noble; but it is only the organ of special mental functions; as the liver and the lungs are organs of special bodily functions. It is a centre, a great centre, but not *the* centre. It is not the exclusive Sensorium. Its absence does not imply the absence of *all* consciousness, as I shall prove by experiment. It cannot therefore be considered as *the* organ, but only as *one* organ of the Mind.

The ancients seem to me to have been nearer the truth than the moderns; they made Mind one form of Life. Their *animus*, mind, was but a form of *anima*, soul or life.* In the Greek writers, the word soul (ψυχή) is used to express a Vital Principle. And this use of the word has become traditional; but is discarded by the physiologists and psychologists, who not only separate Mind from Life, but give Mind a special centre — the Brain.

This doctrine of the Brain is understood in two different ways by two contending schools. The one regards the Brain as the *original agent;* the other regards it as the intermediate *instrument.* According to the one, the Brain thinks as the stomach digests. According to the other, the Brain is the instrument of Thought, played upon by the Mind, as a piano is played upon by a musician. These two schools, however opposed, meet on neutral ground when they come to Physiology. It matters little which side we take: the observed phenomena are the same, whether the brain be regarded as an organ, or an instrument. A piano out of tune will yield discordant music, let the performer be never so skilful. A penny-whistle can never have the clang of a trumpet. It is obvious, therefore, that on the structure and state of the instrument will depend the quality of the sounds produced. This conclusion is the only one which concerns the physiologist; he is not bound to decide between the two contending schools; he is only bound to ascertain, if possible, what functional relation exists between Mind and Brain. As far as I have been able to see into this matter, the Brain is the most important organ in a complex apparatus of organs — the Nervous System;

* "Nunc animum atque animam dico conjuncta teneri
Inter se, atque unam naturam conficere ex se."
LUCRETIUS, III. 137.

and this Nervous System has one general property—Consciousness. There are various special forms of Consciousness, but
they are all intimately allied. Those forms of Consciousness which
we class under the head of Intelligence and Emotion, are mainly,
if not wholly, dependent on the Brain; but there are other forms
of Consciousness besides these, there are other centres of Sensation and Volition besides the Brain.

The evidence on which I venture to depart so widely from the
established doctrine, will be brought forward in the course of the
following pages; meanwhile this explicit statement of the point
of view adopted will keep the attention alert, and will also explain why the Nervous System in general, and not the Brain
only, must occupy us. It is a system eminently deserving of
study. By its agency we are brought into those relations with
the external world which give rise to Sensation. It also regulates
and co-ordinates all the processes of life. It gives unity to the
wondrous multiplicity of organs and their actions, making each
depend on each, and all co-operate to one end. It bestows on
animals their respective rank in the scale of beings: the more
perfect development of this system is the invariable index of a
more complex and effective organisation, since by it a multiplicity of different organs is reduced to unity.

I. THE NATURE OF THE NERVE-FORCE. — What is the force
which acts in the nerves, and which brings various parts of the
organic mechanism into union? From the earliest days of Science
there have been hypotheses explaining the nature of this force.
The hypothesis of "Animal Spirits" reigned undisturbed for
centuries. These spirits were said to be secreted by the grey
surface of the Brain; then, descending down the Spinal Chord
to the nerves, they returned back the same way. When a nerve
was tied, or divided, the passage of the animal spirits was prevented. This hypothesis is dethroned; but let no one insult it:
erroneous it may have been, but it served its purpose as an hypothesis, and helped to explain the observed facts quite as well as
any succeeding hypothesis has done. The "nervous fluid" which
replaced it was not a whit more scientific; and the hypothesis
that Electricity is the nerve-force, although having more evi-

dence in its favour, is open to still more serious objections, because it inevitably tends to confuse and mislead both theory and
practice. Whether nerve-force be, or be not, identical with
Electricity, must for the present be considered an open question.*
But we must bear in mind that even should the evidence finally
turn out to be in favour of the electrical hypothesis, the physiologist would still have to consider nerve-force as something special
— if it be electricity, it is electricity under certain special conditions, which give it a distinctive character, *only* found in the
living nerve. It will always be nerve-force for him; as light will
always be light to the student of optics, although the philosopher
may prove light to be correlated with heat and motion.

For reasons presently to be adduced, it will be of great advantage to have a particular name for this nerve-force; and as I
shall show that what is commonly expressed by the term "nerve-
force" is really decomposable into *two* very different forces, corresponding to two very different nerve-tissues, I propose two
names: *Sensibility* (already in use, although restricted to the
Brain), as the property of ganglionic substance; and *Neurility*,
as the property of nerve-fibre. If the etymology of the latter
term is open to exception, the advantage of its being readily
intelligible, and of going well with Sensibility and Contractility,
may be a compensation. Of course, no stress is laid on this inno-
vation: it is simply suggested as a convenient term, requisite to
give precision to our language when talking of complex nerve-
actions.

When a nerve-fibre is stimulated, its Neurility is called into
play. If the fibre be in connection with the Brain, or Spinal
Chord, the effect is a *sensation*. If the fibre be in connection
with a muscle, the effect is *contraction*. If the fibre be in connection with a gland, the effect is *secretion*.

But before this can be fully appreciated, we must describe
the general characters of the Nervous System.

II. Structure of the Nervous System. — The nervous
system is composed of, I⁰, nerves, and, II⁰, ganglia, or centres.

---

* See the arguments pro and con in LUDWIG: *Lehrbuch der Physiol.*
TODD and BOWMAN: *Physiological Anatomy.* LONGET: *Traité de Physiologie.*
FUNKE: *Lehrbuch der Physiol.*

The nervous *tissues* (for there are two) are composed of nerve-fibres and nerve-cells. Fig. 34 represents a spinal ganglion with nerve-trunks: the ganglion is seen to be composed chiefly of cells; the nerve-trunks of fibres.

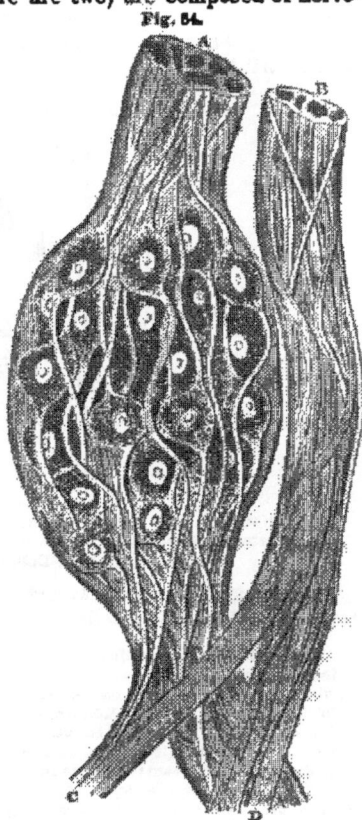

Fig. 84.

These *nerve-fibres*, which, when arranged in bundles, and enveloped in a sheath of connective tissue, form nerves and nerve-trunks, are, strictly speaking, cylinders, containing a more or less liquid substance.

The appearances represented in fig. 35 differ from those of the fibres in fig. 34. They are, however, what is always seen under the microscope, after the tissue has been subjected to pressure. The fibres present a varicose aspect, which arises from the semi-liquid contents being displaced. The size of the fibres varies considerably.

Whether nerve-fibres are *fibres*, or *tubules*,[*] is a question we cannot pause to consider here, since it is one which at present can have but an anatomical interest. For the sake of

A SPINAL GANGLION, with its two roots — posterior A and anterior B.
(After Leydig.)

* LEEUWENHOEK (*Select Works*, II. 305) was the first to describe them as tubules; and EHRENBERG subsequently revived that opinion. It is, however,

convenience we may speak of them as fibres. In bundles of greater or smaller calibre they form nerves; and isolated, or united, they have one constant property, which I propose to name Neurility.

Fig. 35.

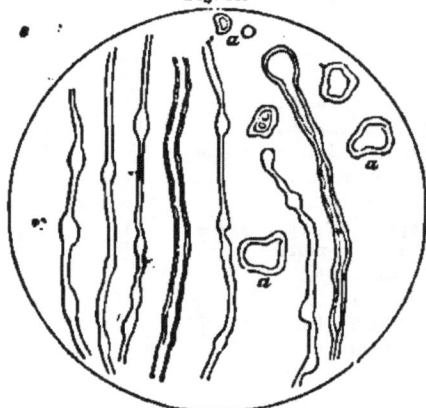

NERVE-FIBRES FROM WHITE SUBSTANCE OF THE BRAIN.
a a a the semi-liquid contents pressed out and floating as irregular drops.
(After Dalton.)

The ganglia, or centres, are characterised by a very different tissue; namely, cells and granules. Of the granules I

a delicate and difficult question, and turns upon whether the thread which we find forming the central axis or the nerve-fibre is normal, or the product of coagulation. Comp. BIDDER und KUPFFER: *Untersuchungen über die Textur des Rückenmarks*, p. 28; and KÖLLIKER: *Gewebelehre*, 1859, p. 278. Indeed, on this as on most questions connected with the histology of the nervous system, the student will find an immense mass of material, the following being the most important: — KÖLLIKER: *Mikros. Anat.* and *Gewebelehre*, LEYDIG: *Lehrbuch der Histologie*. GERLACH: *Gewebelehre*. STILLING: *Über den Bau der Nerven-primitiv-faser*. BIDDER und KUPFFER (as above). LENHOSSEK: *Mémoire sur la Structure intime de la Moëlle épinière* in the *Annales de Sciences*, 1857, tome vii. FAIVRE: *Histologie du Système Nerveux*. TODD and BOWMAN: *Physiological Anatomy*. Unhappily everybody differs from everybody on more than one point; and the student, if sincere, will often find himself differing from them all.

can here say nothing, except that they are too often neglected
as of no account. The cells are peculiar, and often readily
distinguishable from all other animal cells. In size they vary from
the 300th to the 4000th of an inch. In shape they also vary.
Here are two from the grey matter of the spinal chord. They
are seen to send off prolongations of their substance in various
directions, and *sometimes* one of these forms the union between
two cells, as in *c*, fig. 36. It is also taught by most writers that

Fig. 36.

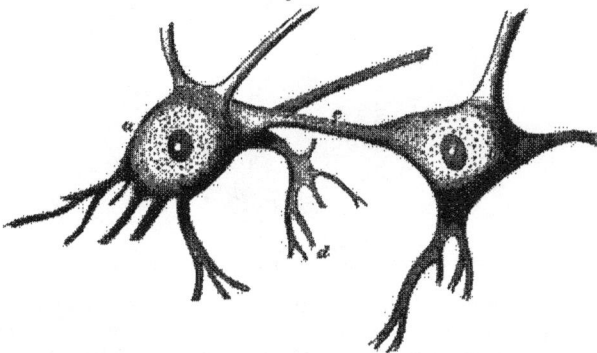

NERVE-CELLS FROM SPINAL CHORD. — (After Gratiolet.)

these prolongations are the beginning, or the ending, of nerve-
fibres; in other words, that the connection between fibres and
cells is always of this direct kind.* In fig. 34 we have this theo-
retical view represented. Without disputing the statement that
fibres are sometimes traced thus in connection with cells, I have
to declare that, in more than a thousand preparations, I have
only seen it half-a-dozen times; therefore, to make this supposed
connection between cells and fibres the basis of any physiological
inferences, will be in the highest degree incautious. Yet this is
what many German and French writers are now doing. The

* For the literature of this subject see STILLING: *Nerven-primitiv-faser*,
p. 101-3; or SCHRÖDER VAN DER KOLK: *Bau und Functionen der Medulla Spinalis und Oblongata*, 1859, pp. 5 et seq.

ordinary aspect of cells and fibres in a ganglion is more like
fig. 37.

Fig. 37.

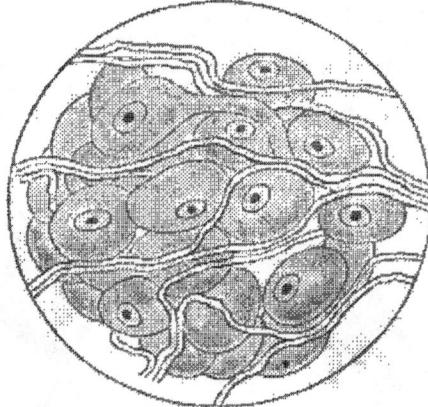

GANGLIONIC STRUCTURE. — (After Dalton.)

These cells, and the granules in which they are imbedded,
have a greyish colour; and it is to them that what is called the
grey or "cineritious" matter of the Brain and Spinal Chord
owes its name. There are, however, certain grey fibres very
abundant in the sympathetic system. Nevertheless it may be
understood that when the *grey matter* is spoken of, the cellular
or ganglionic substance is meant; when the *white matter* is
spoken of, nerve-fibres are meant.

A nerve-centre is a ganglion, or mass of ganglia fused together. It has everywhere the the same property, which is Sensibility. The chief centres are congregated together within the
skull and spine, forming what is called the cerebro-spinal axis.
A general idea of this axis, and the principal nerves which issue
from it, may be seen in fig. 38, on the opposite page.

III. ARE THE NERVES CONDUCTORS ONLY? AND WHAT DO THEY
CONDUCT? — Nerves are very generally likened to telegraphic

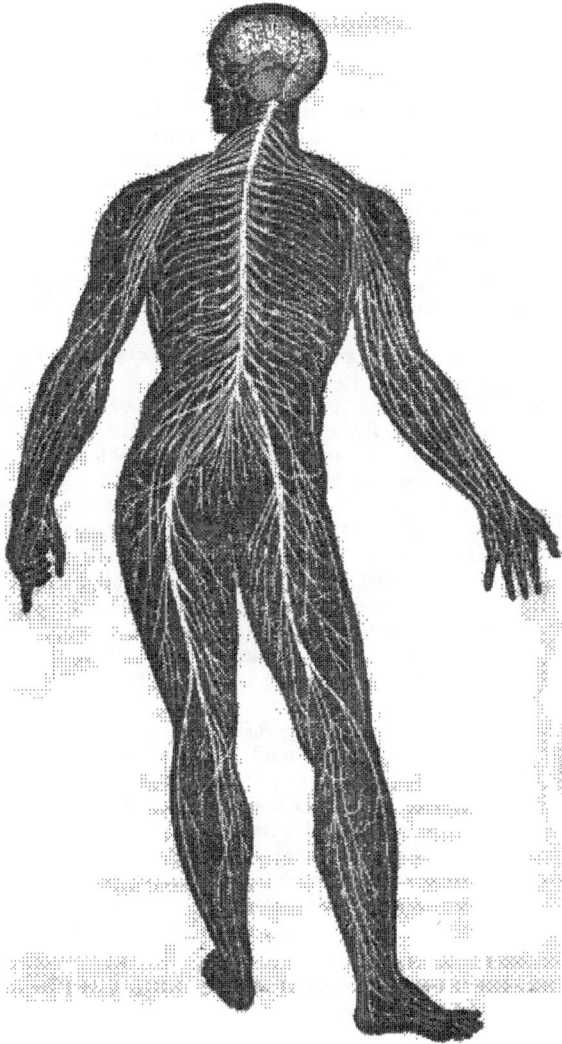

Fig. 38.

wires, carrying messages to and from the centres, or to the conducting wires of a galvanic battery.* But, except as a loose and superficial analogy, this is not acceptable; and it is based on a misconception so important that we must pause a moment to consider it. The misconception is, that the centres *produce* a force which the nerves, as passive conductors, *transmit.* The analogy is to the plates of a battery producing the electricity, which the wires conduct. I think there is ample and decisive evidence to show that the nerves have a force of their *own*, the property of their tissue, which is far from being the product of nerve-centres, and is wholly *unlike* that produced by the centres.

If we cut off the leg of a frog recently killed, and dissect out a portion of its sciatic nerve, as in fig. 39, N, it will be easy to show that this nerve, although separated from its centre, has still its peculiar force; for no sooner are the two poles of a galvanic battery brought in contact with this nerve (as at *a* and *b*), than the muscles of the leg are contracted, as they would be contracted during life, when the centre stimulated the nerve.

Fig. 39.

Nor must it be supposed that this contraction occurs because the nerve conducts electricity to the muscles. The same effect will follow, under proper conditions, if the nerve be simply pinched or pricked. Anything which stimulates the nerve, causes the muscles to contract. But if the nerve be *dead*, electricity fails to cause a contraction. Claude Bernard found that the *woorara* poison had the effect of destroying the irritability of the nerves, and leaving the muscles unaffected: when, therefore, he had poisoned a frog with woorara, the galvanic battery applied to the nerve no longer made the muscles contract; but applied directly to the muscles, it made them contract. Indeed, one of the earliest experiments was

* In many cases this metaphor has been an hypothesis. The Italian anatomist Rolando claims the merit of not only having, before Sir. Charles

enough to show that the force in the nerve does not come from the centre, but is excited in the nerve itself. Willis tied the phrenic nerve, and found that the diaphragm was moved when the nerve was irritated *below* the ligature — that is, below the point where its separation from the centre was effected — but no motion could be caused in the diaphragm when the nerve was irritated *above* the ligature.

But, it may be asked, did not this nerve which we see acting when separated from a centre, *originally receive* its force from that centre? and is not the force which we excite in it, the remains of what has been produced in the centre, and accumulated in the nerve? The answer is an unequivocal, No. If the nerve were merely a reservoir, and not a spring, it could never *recover* its force after having once been exhausted; but exact experiment has determined that while a nerve separated from a centre may be so exhausted by repeated irritations, that it ceases to produce any contractions; yet if it now be allowed repose, under proper conditions, it recovers its activity, and, on being irritated, will again cause muscular contractions.* Schiff found that a frog's nerve, which had been separated from its centre, but not otherwise disturbed, retained its power of exciting contractions as long as thirteen weeks. It is therefore impossible to regard the force in the nerves as a *residue* of what was produced in the centres, seeing that the nerve itself has the power of *restoring* its wasted force.

When the conducting wire is separated from the battery it loses at once all galvanic power: it is a bit of wire, and it is nothing more. All its galvanism came from the battery, and this it could only conduct, not create. But the nerve, when separated from its centre, still retains its force: any irritation of such a nerve will excite that force, just as the stimulus from its centre

Bell, distinguished the two kinds of nerves, but also of having asserted each to be conductors of two kinds of electricity, positive and negative. ROLANDO : *Ricerche anatomiche sulla struttura del Midolo spinale*, 1824, p. 4. The conception of the Brain as a galvanic battery of which the nerves are the conducting wires, is often attributed to Sir John Herschel. It was an obvious conception when once the nerve-force was supposed to be identical with electricity; and it has been very misleading.

* Comp. Schiff: *Lehrbuch der Physiol.*, 1. 112.

would excite it. The battery is removed, and lo! the wire is found to be galvanic.

That the nerve itself, even during absolute repose, is the work-shop of a development of force, of chemical and electrical changes, has been demonstrated by Dubois-Reymond. That the nerve, so long as it is *living*, so long as the necessary nutritive changes can be kept up, has a property not derived from the centre, but belonging exclusively to the nerve itself, is no less de-monstrable. Without implying any hypothesis as to the nature of this force, I have called it Neurility (in the sense of *excitability*, but without the misleading suggestions of that word). Numerous physiologists have noticed the facts which prove that the nerves are something more than passive conductors, but I am not aware that any one has seen the full significance of these facts, and has proposed to connect them with a property inherent in nerve-fibre, and essentially differing from the property inherent in ganglionic substance, or nerve-cells. In a paper read at the meeting of the British Association in Aberdeen* I suggested the desirableness of a new nomenclature to replace the very lax expressions now in use; and as an example, the old term "nerve-force," which con-founds together the activity of the nerves and that of the centres, was shown to need two distinct substitutes, one expressing the activity of the nerves — *Neurility*; and one expressing the activity of the centres — *Sensibility*.

Neurility simply means the property which the nerve-fibre has, when stimulated, of exciting *contraction* in a muscle, *secre-tion* in a gland, and *sensation* in a ganglionic centre.

IV. WHAT IS SENSIBILITY. — This very interesting and im-portant question has become involved in a cloud of obscurities which would vanish if that strictness of nomenclature, to which I have just alluded, were adopted in physiology, as in chemistry and physics. The philosophic reader will learn with surprise that many eminent men are at present disputing whether the seat of sensation is itself sensitive, whether the seat of intel-ligence is also the seat of consciousness, and whether there are not separate parts of the spinal chord devoted to the *transmission*

* *On the Necessity of a Reform in Nerve Physiology.*

of sensibility — as if Sensibility were a thing to be carried from one part of the body to another!

It is found that cutting, pinching, tearing, or galvanising the grey matter of the brain and spinal chord produces no sensation whatever. The fact is doubtless surprising at first. We know that the brain is a seat of sensation, that impressions made on the nerves going to the cerebro-spinal centres produce no sensation unless those centres are affected; yet we see a man or an animal submit without the slightest wincing to have a slice of his brain cut off, or the grey matter of his spinal chord pricked and cut. The explanation is easy. Sensibility is the inherent property of the ganglionic tissue forming the grey matter of the nerve-centres. This property is stimulated into activity by the Neurility of the nerves, but is *not* stimulated by those mechanical irritations which suffice to stimulate the nerves. The pinch, or prick, which awakens the activity of the nerve-fibre, leaves the nerve-cell dormant. You are not surprised if the pistol hangs fire when the percussion-cap is removed, or spoiled. In vain the hammer falls, no explosion takes place; because, to produce an explosion of the gunpowder, a spark is necessary, and that spark is received from the percussion-cap. It is the same with Sensibility. The hammer first acts on the cap; the cap does not transmit the *blow*, it produces a spark, and the spark makes the powder explode; the irritation acts on the nerve, the nerve does not transmit this irritation, it has its own Neurility excited, and *this* awakens the Sensibility of the centre — when the nerve goes to a centre; when it goes to a muscle it awakens Contractility.

It is absolutely indispensable that we should bear distinctly in mind this fundamental position: that Sensibility is the *property inherent in ganglionic tissue* — the one peculiar "force" belonging to all nerve-centres, as Neurility belongs to all nerves. But in order to a right comprehension of this position, as well as to a philosophical investigation of the many problems which assail us, it is necessary that we make another reform in our phraseology, and cease to confound the idea of *property* with that of *function*.

The property of a nerve, for instance, is that which belongs to it as a nerve, and not that which arises from its connection with any other organ: it depends on *structure*, as the elasticity of steel depends on the structure of steel, or the transparency of crystal depends on the structure of the crystal.

The function of a nerve is very different: it is the *use* to which that property may be applied; and depends on the connections established between the nerve and other parts.

Property is invariable so long as the structure remains.* Functions are as variable as the varying nature of organic connections.

These principles are elementary. They lead at once to a most important axiom: *Identity of structure everywhere implies identity of properties.*

No matter how different the *uses* to which a given substance, say iron, may be applied, it always and everywhere retains its properties *as* iron: we may fashion it into nails, anchors, windlasses, anvils, or cannon, and get very different results; but the properties of iron remain persistent through all these differences of use. This, you will perhaps remark, is a truism. It is so; and yet I do not recall a single writer on the nervous system who has not, on important occasions, entirely overlooked it. Two examples will suffice to show this. Physiologists have established a distinction between sensory and motor nerves, which distinction many of them refer explicitly, and others implicitly, to a difference in the *properties* of these nerves: one set of nerves are said to have the property of conducting sensitive impressions, and the other set of conducting motor stimuli — one having a centripetal and the other a centrifugal conductibility. We shall presently examine the validity of this supposed distinction; for the present it is enough to say that although both nerves are identical in all fundamental characters — although their structure is identical — physiologists have no misgiving in attributing to them different properties; which is like saying that of two bars of iron forming a crank, one is capable of being rendered magnetic, and the other not. .

The second example is more directly to our present purpose. Sensibility is ascribed to the ganglionic substance of the Brain,

* Under identical conditions, of course: the same substance under different conditions will manifest very different properties. Hence allotropism.

or some portion of the Brain, and denied to other masses of ganglionic substance, absolutely identical in all the fundamental characters. Nevertheless no physiologist, to my knowledge, has been aware of this violation of a first principle. No one has seen that to rescue this opinion from such a contradiction he must prove the ganglia themselves to have a structural distinction, corresponding with this supposed distinction of property. Nor could this be proved. The contrary is demonstrable. There is no fundamental difference: similar cells, similar granules, similar fibres, and similar connective tissue are found in the one and in the other: nothing is found in the one that is not in the other: they are identical. The differences, such as they are, are *morphological*, not *histological* — differences of form, not of *structure* — and it will hereafter appear that these accessory differences do not affect fundamental characters.

It is simple logic, therefore, to conclude that there being one *common tissue*, there must be one *common property*, in Brain, Medulla, and Chord, however various the *functions*, or uses, to which this property may in each case be applied. Experiment clearly verifies what logic thus deductively concludes, namely, that the Spinal Chord is in all animals a seat of Sensibility; and in some animals the all-important seat. This will be demonstrated in a future chapter. The only escape from the logic of this argument is to deny that Sensibility is a property at all; and to call it the function of certain nerve-centres. But against such an issue, two obstacles are placed: First, if we refuse to consider Sensibility as the property of ganglionic tissue, we shall have to declare what *is* the property of that tissue, manifest wherever the tissue is in activity, and common to all nerve-centres; Secondly, I shall hereafter show that all the phenomena we indicate by the term Sensibility are exhibited when those nerve-centres, generally supposed to be its exclusive organs, are removed.*

* Until the reader has considered this experimental evidence which proves Sensibility to belong to all the centres, I must ask him to suspend judgment on this important point. Indeed I may say, once for all, that inasmuch as the new views advocated in these chapters belong to a system related in all its parts, they cannot always be judged without reference to the whole.

Contractility is the property of muscular fibre; and however various the uses, or functions, of the muscles — extensors, flexors, sphincters, voluntary or involuntary — this fundamental property is found in all.

Neurility (*i. e.* the power of exciting a muscle, a gland, or a nerve-centre) is the property of the nerve-fibre; and however various the uses, or functions, which various nerves may serve — as, for example, those of sight, hearing, and taste, those of locomotion and those of secretion — the same fundamental character is found in all.

Sensibility is the property of ganglionic substance, and however various the uses, or functions, which different centres may serve — those of Respiration being very different from those of facial Expression, and these again from those of Perception, and so on — the same fundamental character is found in all.

The only known stimulus which will excite Sensibility in a centre, is that of the active nerve-fibre. By this means impressions on the skin become sensations in the centres. By this means one centre plays on another and awakens its Sensibility; an impression on the skin not only excites a sensation in the spinal chord, but runs up the brain, and there excites another sensation. While Sensibility seems capable of being awakened only by this one stimulus, Neurility seems capable of being awakened by a variety of stimuli; and among these we must reckon the activity of a centre, for no sooner is a centre excited, than the nerve-fibres in connection with it are excited also.

V. ARE THERE TWO KINDS OF NERVE: SENSORY AND MOTOR? — Before proceeding further into the interesting question of Sensibility, it is necessary to notice another application of those logical canons which ought to direct our investigations, but which here also have been strangely overlooked.

It is the universal opinion of physiologists, that there are two distinct kinds of nerve, named respectively the sensory and motor, the one being capable of exciting sensations, but no motions; the other of exciting motions, but no sensations. This doctrine dates from Hippocrates and Galen, and has received continual support from the frequent cases of paralysis in which there was a loss of sensibility in a limb without loss of motion, or a loss of motion without loss of sensibility. A terrible case came to my knowledge some years ago. The patient had a complete, though temporary, paralysis of motion, while preserving his sensibility unaffected. He lay motionless, and had the horror of hearing with painful distinctness all that was said about his condition, and of feeling with painful distinctness all the stimulants which were applied to awaken his sensibility. He was tortured in the belief that he felt nothing, because he could not by any movement, or cry, express the pain he felt. Fortunately this condition was not of long duration, and he recovered sufficiently to indicate the suffering to which he had been exposed.*

Early in the present century Sir Charles Bell made an anatomical discovery which has immortalised him, and which seemed to furnish the final scientific confirmation of the long-suspected distinction between the two sets of nerves. It would lead us too far were we to enter upon the history of this famous discovery; enough for the present if a brief statement of what is now the doctrine of the schools be laid before the reader.

There are nerves which, on being stimulated, excite muscular contractions: these are the *motor* nerves, and we can follow them into the very substance of the muscles, where they end, we know not how. There are nerves which, on being stimulated, excite sensations: these are the *sensory* nerves, and we can follow them into the skin, or the organs of sense. Finally, there are *mixed nerves*, which excite both contractions and sensations: but these, although their fibres are contained in a common trunk, are really two different nerves, having different *origins* in the centres, and different *endings* in the muscle and skin. For the sake of simplicity, we will confine ourselves to the sensory and motor nerves which issue from the spinal chord in thirty-one pairs, and which, shortly after their issue, unite to form trunks.

The Spinal Chord is formed of two halves, much as the cere-

---

* In the French translation of Sir Charles Bell's *Nervous System of the Human Body* there is an interesting record of a man who from a fall had entirely lost his sensibility on the right side, though preserving his power of movement; and had entirely lost the power of movement on the left side, though preserving his sensibility.

brum is formed of two hemispheres. Each half sends forth its
own pairs of nerves; and each pair has a double root—one root
issuing from the *anterior* columns of the chord (in animals the
under part), and the other root from the *posterior* columns (in
animals the *upper* part). In fig. 40 the anterior and posterior

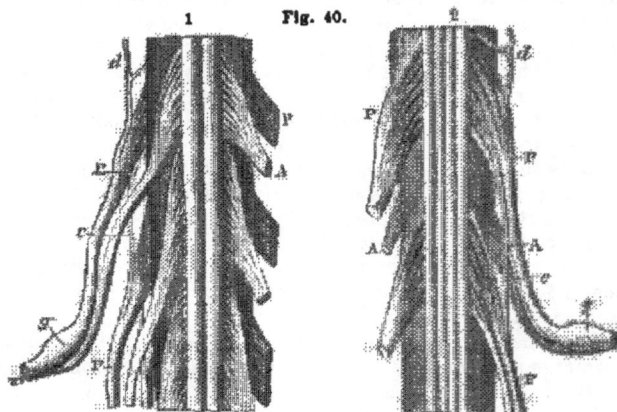

SPINAL NERVES AND SPINAL CHORD. — (After Barnard.)

1, Anterior view; 2, posterior view. A is the anterior root of the
nerve, and P the posterior root. One pair in each figure is represented
with the division made below the ganglion (*g*). The other pairs are
divided above the ganglion. At *c* and *d* are filaments connecting two
posterior roots.

columns are represented with two pairs of roots. The anterior
root A is seen to join the posterior P just below the ganglion *g*,
after which the two become one trunk, to divide and subdivide
like the branches of a tree. The following diagram of a *transverse* section through the Chord will render the arrangement more
intelligible. These posterior and anterior roots (fig. 41, *a* and *d*)
are called respectively the sensory and motor roots. It is maintained that the fibres furnished by the one root have the power
of transmitting impressions only *to* the Brain, whereas the fibres
furnished by the other root have the power of transmitting impressions *from* the Brain to the muscles: the posterior root is *afferent*,

and awakens sensation, but never motion; the anterior root is *efferent*, and awakens muscular contraction, but never sensation.

Fig. 41.

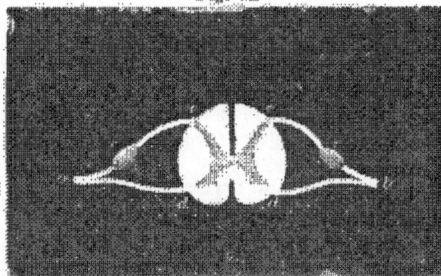

TRANSVERSE SECTION OF SPINAL CHORD WITH NERVE ROOTS.
(After Dalton.)

The assumed proof of this important position is as follows: If the posterior root be divided (as at *a b*, fig. 42, A) before the union

Fig. 42.

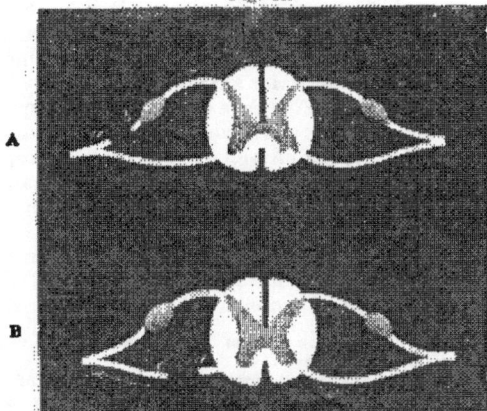

with the other root, no amount of irritation of the cut end, *a*, will produce muscular contraction, but the slightest irritation of the

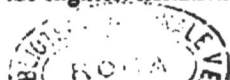

cut end, *b*, will produce sensation. This shows that the posterior root is the channel for sensitive impressions, and not for muscular contractions.

If, on the other hand, the anterior root be divided (as at *c d*, fig. 42, B), the reverse is noticed—the cut end, *d*, may be irritated without producing the slightest sign of sensibility, whereas irritation of the cut end, *c*, is instantly followed by contraction of the muscles to which the nerve is distributed. This shows that the anterior root is the channel for muscular stimuli but not for sensitive impressions.

It was incumbent on me to expound the views held by all the physiologists of our day respecting the two kinds of nerves. Having discharged that duty to the public, there is another which remains. I believe that the view just expounded is erroneous, founded on a misconception, and in open contradiction with first principles. In two papers read before the Aberdeen Meeting of the British Association,* I pointed out the source of the misconception, and the evidence which destroyed the supposed distinction.

The anatomical discovery of Sir Charles Bell is now unimpeachable.** As far as demonstration can go, it has been demonstrated that the anterior nerves move the muscles to which they are distributed; and the posterior nerves convey sensory impressions from the skin, to which they are distributed. The opponents have long been silenced. Europe is convinced. But this discovery has been supposed to imply a physiological distinction respecting the properties, or functions, of the two nerves; and against this interpretation Professor Arnold, of Zurich, many years ago raised his voice, declaring that Bell and his followers had made the initial mistake of confounding *muscle*-nerves with *motor*-nerves.*** But Arnold's voice was lost in the chorus of Bell's followers. Indeed, neither the state of anatomical knowledge, nor the pos-

---

* *On the Supposed Distinction between Sensory and Motor Nerves;* and, *A Demonstration of the Muscular Sense.*

** While these sheets are passing through the press, M. AMÉDÉ PICHOT has published the history of this discovery in his brief but very agreeable biography: *Sir Charles Bell: Histoire de sa Vie et de ses Travaux.*

*** ARNOLD: *Über die Verrichtung der Wurzeln der Rückenmarksnerven,* 1844.

session of a general doctrine, permitted him to give his arguments and experiments their full value; and I have not met with a single physiologist who has embraced his views. Nevertheless I think Arnold was right; and having reached the same conclusion by a different route, I feel it a duty not to shrink from opposition to the teachers who most claim respect.

Referring to the distinction already established between property and function (p. 15), our first effort must be to ascertain whether the supposed difference between the two nerves is one of property, or one of function. It cannot be one of property, because the structure of the two nerves is identical,* and identity of structure, we know, implies identity of property. Moreover, it has been proved experimentally by Dubois-Reymond and Schiff, that both nerves conduct in both directions.

Is the difference one of function? There are doubtless many who never believed it to be one of property, but conceived that it arose simply from the fact that the anterior nerves played upon muscles only, and therefore only awakened Contractility; and that the posterior nerves played upon the centre only, and therefore only awakened Sensibility. This was the opinion I formerly held. But if this has been the opinion held by some physiologists, they have not given it precise and scientific statement — they have not urged the necessity of founding the idea of function on *anatomical distribution*. Had they done so, Anatomy would speedily have convinced them, as it convinced me, of the error of regarding the nerves as essentially distinct in function.

---

* It is unnecessary here to enter on the detailed proof. I have done so in the paper read before the British Association, and will only add that Schiff rests the structural distinction on the fact shown by his experiments, that although nerves which have been divided grow together again, a motor-nerve will not unite with a sensory nerve. The fact is valuable; but as we are at present utterly in the dark respecting the nutrition of nerves, we can found no conclusion as to their properties on any differences they may exhibit in nutrition. Schiff has himself proved that motor nerves conduct *both* ways — centripetally and centrifugally; and for my purpose that is all the proof necessary. The want of some recognised doctrine could alone permit so eminent a man as Kölliker to write as follows: "In respect of nerve-fibres, Anatomy is unable to discover any difference between sensory and motor; but this can in nowise furnish Physiology with a ground for supposing that the nerves have similar functions!" — *Gewebelehre*, 1859, p. 363.

Messrs. Todd and Bowman, in their valuable work, remark
that it is not necessary to suppose any *intrinsic* difference of
structure in the nerves capable of producing effects so manifestly
different. "The actions of a nerve depend upon the nature of
its *central and peripheral connections.*"* Very true. But what
does Anatomy teach us respecting these connections? It teaches
that as regards the *centre*, the two nerves *agree;* and so far they
must agree in function. It further teaches that as regards the
periphery, the two nerves *differ;* and so far they must differ in
function. Both are directly connected with the ganglionic substance of the Spinal Chord, and both must therefore have a similar
functional relation to it: but as one is directly connected with the
muscles, and the other with the skin, their functional relations
to muscle and skin will of course be different. Nothing can be
plainer; yet by an oversight which will one day appear astound-
ing, physiologists have one and all disregarded the very important fact that both anterior and posterior nerves are similarly
connected with the Spinal Chord, and consequently must exercise a similar influence on it.** Surely if one nerve can excite
the ganglionic centre with which it is connected, a similar nerve,
similarly connected, must also similarly excite that centre? To
assume that of two nerves having the same property and similar
connections, one only should exercise that property, and the
other be utterly powerless, is a license of imagination which
Logic must reprove.

Observe, I say the relation is *similar*, not the *same*. It requires but a moderate acquaintance with microscopic anatomy
to be aware that the anterior and posterior roots differ in their
distribution over the Spinal Chord; indeed, it is partly upon
this difference of distribution that I explain to myself the different *forms of sensibility* excited by each root. But underlying

---

* TODD and BOWMAN: *Physiol. Anat.*, L 231.
** Thus SCHRÖDER VAN DER KOLK, in his important work, maintains
that the Medulla Oblongata is the seat of Perception, because *there* the sensory
fibres terminate in nerve-cells; yet he denies that the motor fibres, which *also*
terminate in nerve-cells (according to him), can have any sensory function.
See *Bau und Functionen der Medulla Spinalis* in several places. He also explicitly says that the grey matter of the Chord is only concerned with co-
ordinating movements; whereas the same grey matter in the Medulla Oblongata is sensitive! — pp. 73, 83.

this diversity there is a fundamental agreement: both are in
direct connection with the ganglionic substance, and both must
excite its activity. Hence they may be called similar, though
not the same. The form of sensibility excited by the anterior
root is as unlike the form of sensibility excited by the posterior
root, as the sensation of Sound is unlike the sensation of Light,
which are nevertheless similar, in being both sensations.

Thus does Anatomy, philosophically interpreted, teach the
sensory function of both nerves. The same aids will make clear
to us wherein the nerves differ. It has already been stated that
the difference in their peripheral connections necessarily brings
about a corresponding difference in their functions. The function of moving a muscle is assigned to the nerves distributed to
muscles; the function of conveying impressions of touch, temperature, tickling, &c., is assigned to the nerves distributed to
the skin, where alone these impressions can be made. So intimately is function dependent upon anatomical distribution,
that the very nerve which is sensitive to touch and temperature,
if the stimulus reach it through the skin, is *not* susceptible to
either (but only to pain), if the stimulus be *directly* applied to
the nerve.*

The posterior nerves, being distributed to the skin, can, it
is obvious, only exercise a motor function in as far as they are
related to moving organs, or muscles. Now *in* the skin there
are such organs, insignificant enough, it is true, and only discovered within the last few years: these are muscular fibres surrounding the hair-follicles; and it is these which the posterior
nerves cause to contract. If there were no muscular fibres in the
skin, the posterior nerves would have no motor function; but
they would have the possibility of exercising such a function. As,
however, there are such fibres, the nerves have this function —

* I found that pinching or cutting one of the sensory nerves of a frog
under the skin of the back, produced no sign of sensibility whatever; whereas
pricking the skin to which this nerve was distributed immediately caused the
frog to leap. VOLKMANN many years ago drew attention to the great differences in the sensibility of a nerve when irritated at its periphery, or at the
trunk; and Professor SCHIFF of Berne, to whom I mentioned the experiment
just alluded to, assured me that it was quite consonant with all he had observed — and few have had larger experience.

not a very energetic or striking one, perhaps, but the same in
kind as that of the anterior nerves.

Thus does Anatomy assure us that both nerves are sensory,
and both nerves motor. With this torch in our hands, let us
enter the otherwise obscure path of experimental inquiry. It is
unnecessary to prove the motor function of the muscle-nerves;
let us inquire into their sensory function. If the muscle-nerves
can excite any Sensibility at all, it must be that of what we call the
Muscular Sense, by which we adjust the manifold niceties of
contraction required in our movements.* In a future chapter
(Our SENSES AND SENSATIONS) this muscular sense will be examined in detail, and the proof furnished that this form of sensibility persists when all *external* stimuli fail to awaken any sensation whatever. For the present we must be content with the fact
that there is a peculiar sensibility derived through the muscles,
and that this must have for its channels either the posterior, or
the anterior nerves. So much is beyond question. Now it has
been proved by the experiments of Arnold, Brown-Séquard,**
and the present writer, that the posterior nerves may be divided
without destroying this muscular sensibility. Indeed Brown-
Séquard divided *all* the sensory roots of the four extremities of a
frog, yet not only did this frog execute its ordinary muscular
adjustments, but when its nose was irritated with acid, the
fore-leg was employed to rub the acid away. Perhaps you think
that this frog moved its limbs by an effort of the will? To anticipate such an objection, I etherised a frog, removed its
brain, and skinned it: the animal was thus rendered insensible
to all *external* stimuli, and without a brain to direct its movements; yet it adjusted its muscles, and rubbed away the acid
from its irritated nose (the only spot sensitive to external irri-

* That muscles communicate with centres and awaken sensations (which
can only be done through their nerves) is thus admitted by TODD and Bow-
MAN: "A continued or violent irritation of a motor nerve in some part of its
course, causing spasm or convulsive movement of the muscles it supplies,
may be propagated along its whole length to the centre, and may there give rise
to irritation of neighbouring fibres, whether motor or sensitive, exciting more
convulsion and pain." — Physiol. Anat., I. 232.

** ARNOLD: Rückenmarksnerven, p. 111-113. BROWN-SÉQUARD's Lectures
in the Lancet, 3d July 1858.

tations, because the only spot which retained its skin) as perfectly as an uninjured frog would have done.*

The conclusion seems irresistible, that the muscular sensibility is derived through the anterior, or muscle-nerves. What is to oppose such a conclusion? Nothing but the negative argument, which is furnished by the experiment of dividing the roots of the nerves (see p. 21). If the reader who has followed the exposition thus far will consider this experiment attentively, he will see that, instead of being the victorious experiment it is commonly believed to be, it does not touch the question at all. I admit, without reservation, the fact that, when the anterior root is irritated, the animal gives no sign of sensation. But I affirm that those who demand such a sign, demand a kind of evidence which *cannot*, in the nature of things, be given, let the anterior root be never so unequivocally sensitive. Simple logic assures us that the sensibility excited by the muscle-nerves cannot be the *same* as that excited by the skin-nerves, any more than the sensibility excited by the optic nerve can be the same as that excited by the auditory nerve. The argument I am combating would, if admitted, serve to prove that the optic nerve was not sensory; for the optic centre will not respond to odours,

* I seize this opportunity to defend myself, and other experimentalists, from the charge of cruelty, in performing experiments on live animals. The question is too large to be argued here; but as a purely personal matter I may say, that all my friends know my great fondness for animals of every kind, and the almost excessive shrinking from the sight of pain which renders it unendurable for me to see animals suffering. Had it not been for the discovery of ether and chloroform, I should never have pushed my investigations to the length of experiment on live animals, where great pain could be supposed to follow. But it is now becoming almost universal, not simply out of tenderness to animals, but out of regard for accuracy, to render animals *insensible* before performing any serious operation. A frog or salamander, after being etherised, remains utterly insensible for more than two hours; and dogs leap upon the operating-table on which they have before been etherised, with as much alacrity as if they had been fed there. It is the *wounding*, and not the *wound*, which causes pain. Cut a rabbit's spine in two, and you may see him in a few minutes quietly eating, as if nothing had been done to him. That some experimenters put animals to great pain, and sometimes do so with unjustifiable thoughtlessness, is true; but cruelty is never their motive: they inflict pain, not for the sake of exercising power, but for the sake of gaining that scientific knowledge which is to lessen the pain of future men and women.

sounds, heat, or cold; and when it does respond to a stimulus, will only respond as a sensation of light — that is to say, its own special form of sensibility — whatever stimulus awakens it. Cut the optic nerve in two — pinch it, prick it, burn it, and you produce no pain, nothing like it, nothing but the sensation of a flash of light. Now, if we are justified in attributing muscular sensibility to the anterior nerves, it is obvious that these nerves when irritated can only excite muscular sensations, and no others. It is further obvious that the signs of such sensations must be very different from those of other sensations. Let us suppose that an irritation of the anterior root, by pricking or galvanism, *does* awaken this muscular sensibility, by what sign *could* the fact be known? The irritation produces no *pain;* it can only produce that sensation which accompanies, or precedes, adjustment of the muscles, or one of the vague but diffusive sensations which muscular sensibility contributes to the general consciousness. The direct *response* to such a sensation would be an adjustment of the muscles to which the particular nerves were distributed; but this cannot take place, because the connection between these nerves and muscles is cut off. What sign could be manifested? Evidently none at all. The negative argument, therefore, which this experiment was supposed to furnish, does not touch the question; and the positive proof that the anterior nerves minister to muscular sensations, remains unaffected.

Having proved the sensory function of the anterior nerves, it is not difficult to prove the motor function of the posterior nerves. They cannot move the muscles, simply because they are not distributed to the muscles; but they move the muscular fibres of the skin, and cause the contractions of the skin. Claude Bernard, seeing the necessity of explaining the existence of sensibility in the muscles and contractility in the skin, boldly assumed — and has stated it as if it were a fact — that the posterior nerves sent off filaments to the muscles, and the anterior nerves sent off filaments to the skin. But anatomy will not support that assertion.

There has been no collection of facts to throw light on the movements of the muscular fibres in the skin; but it is worth inquiring what share they have in the erection of quills upon the fretful porcupine, or the hairs on the back of an irritated dog. Division of the posterior roots would, I should anticipate, prevent the quills of the porcupine from rising up. But there is no experimental evidence on this subject at present.

The conclusions to which we are thus led are as follows: There is no fundamental distinction between the two nerves; both are sensory, and both are motor; but they are so in different degrees. They are, strictly speaking, distinguishable as muscle-nerves and skin-nerves: the muscle-nerves being the channels for muscular-sensations and muscular-movements; the skin-nerves being the channels for skin-sensations and skin-movements. But inasmuch as the muscle-nerves have an energetic motor function, far surpassing that of the others, the name of *motor* may continue to designate the anterior nerves; and further, as the skin-nerves are channels of more *intense* and more *various* sensations than the muscle-nerves, the name of *sensory* may continue to designate the posterior nerves — it being understood that these are merely verbal distinctions employed for convenience.[*]

We have now gone over the chief points needful to be remembered respecting the structure and properties of the Nervous System, and it is hoped the reader's patience has not been too severely taxed. To have passed more lightly over these points would have rendered our future progress less secure, and we should have been less able to grapple with those questions of more general interest, which cluster round Feeling and Thinking. Something like a scientific basis has been laid down; let us now see to the superstructure.

VI. Where is the Sensorium? — The Sensorium means the seat of sensation, or consciousness. The term *sensorium commune* means that there is one particular seat for all sensations whatever. Where is that important seat?

[*] Some experimenters have endeavoured to prove that one half of the gray-matter of the Spinal Chord is devoted to motion, and the other half to sensation; but the decisive experiments of Schiff have shown that both halves are motor and both sensory; and I regard this as a final proof of the double function of each nerve-root connected with each half.

According to the principles laid down in these pages, Sensibility is the fundamental property of ganglionic tissue, and inherent in this living tissue, as Contractility is inherent in the living muscular tissue. It is therefore clear that we must make the Sensorium, or seat of Sensibility, coextensive with the nervous centres.

This is by no means the opinion of Physiologists. They aver that there is only one centre, or one group of centres, which is endowed with Sensibility. As they have no logical basis for this position, we need not be surprised to find them by no means agreed respecting the centre, or centres, which are thus arbitrarily selected for the Sensorium. It seems a matter of fancy with the majority; and as one man's fancy is as good, or bad, as another's, we find one stoutly affirming that the Sensorium is *not* where another positively places it. Boutekoe, Lancisi, and others, placed it in the *corpus callosum*; why not, since the selection seems arbitrary? Willis placed it in the *corpora striata*; Descartes in the *pineal gland*; Vieussens in the *centrum ovale*; Boerhaave in the boundary-line of the grey and white substance; Mayer in the *medulla oblongata*, and Camper in the *pineal gland*, *nates*, *and testes*. They might just as well have placed it in the jawbone or eyebrows, as far as any scientific warrant can be given for one of these opinions. And if their modern successors have been less palpably absurd, they seem almost equally to have wanted any guiding principle.

Much more philosophical was the conception of Whytt. "As the schoolmen," he says, "supposed the Deity to exist in every *ubi*, but not in *any place*, which is to say in Latin that he exists *everywhere*, but in English *nowhere*; so they imagined the soul of man not to occupy space, but to exist in an indivisible point. Yet whoever considers the structure and phenomena of the animal frame, will soon be convinced that the soul is not confined to an indivisible point, but must be present at one and the same time, if not in all parts of the body, yet at least wherever the nerves have their origin; *i. e.*, it must be at least diffused along a great part of the brain and spinal marrow."[*]

Some years later the admirable Prochaska adopted a some-

[*] WHYTT: *Essay on the Vital and other Involuntary Motions*, 1751, p. 380.

what similar view. He conceived that the Brain (*cerebrum* and *cerebellum*) was devoted to the purely intellectual operations — to the "soul-sensations," as he calls them — and the rest of the spinal axis, including the under portions of the Brain, formed the *sensorium commune*, devoted to the "body-sensations." He defined the sensorium much as Whytt did: "it is coextensive with the origin of the nerves." Like Whytt and Unzer, he rightly perceived that the sensorium must extend to the spinal chord, because decapitated animals manifest actions "which cannot take place without the consentience and intervention of the nerves; for the decapitated frog, if pricked, not only withdraws the punctured limb, but creeps and leaps, which cannot be done without the consensus of the sensorial and motor nerves, the seat of which consensus must necessarily be in the spinal chord."*

In this, as in so many other questions, Prochaska seems to me to have been very near the truth. He falls short in the want of a clear conception of the relation between property and tissue. Had he made the identity of ganglionic substance the ground for assuming an identity of property in all ganglia, his own admirable conception of the Reflex Actions would not have been displaced by the modern, and, as I think, erroneous, Reflex Theory, but would have furnished convincing evidence of the truth of his views respecting the sensorium.

According to the view adopted in these pages, the *sensorium commune*, or general seat of Sensibility, is the sum total of all the nerve-centres; while each centre is itself a small sensorium. But although all nerve-centres agree in having one *common tissue*, and one *common property*, they differ more or less among themselves in their organic connections with other parts, and must therefore differ in their *functions*. It is the neglect of this distinction which has for so long masked the truth.

A careful inspection of the various ganglia suffices to show, that while the *arrangement* of their tissues is somewhat various, the tissues themselves remain identical. In the Brain, for example, the white matter is inside, and the grey matter outside; whereas in the Spinal Chord the reverse takes place; and

* Unzer and Prochaska: *On the Nervous System* (translated by Dr. Laycock), p. 430.

in some other Ganglia the white and grey are intermingled. But such variations will not alter the fundamental properties. It may be anticipated, indeed, that men sharing the ancient prejudice respecting the Brain as the exclusive seat of sensation, will point to the different morphological structure of the Brain as a proof that its properties must be different from those of the Spinal Chord. But I think the evidence is irresistible which shows, First, that the Sensibility of the Brain depends on *histological*, not on *morphological* structure — in other words, on the tissue itself, and not on any arrangement of that tissue; and Secondly, that the Spinal Chord *is* a seat of sensation. The first point only can be touched on for the present.

It will scarcely be denied that Insects, Crustaceans, and Molluscs are endowed with Sensibility. Those who deny them every vestige of Intelligence will nevertheless admit that they can *feel*. Unless we adopt the hypothesis of Descartes, that all animals are mere machines,[*] we must admit that, in spite of the varieties in their nervous systems, they have one thing in common

Fig. 43.

Nervous System of the Aplysia. — (After Dalton.)

— Sensibility.

But now, what does comparative anatomy teach us? It teaches that, corresponding with this *property*, which all animals have in common, there is a *tissue* they have in common; but with this fundamental *histological* resemblance, there is a great *morphological* diversity. Nerve-tissue is everywhere similar; but the arrangements of that tissue are very various. In the simplest form of the Nervous System yet discovered — namely, that of the *Ascidian* (an animal shaped like a flask with two short necks, remaining for ever fixed on one spot) — it consists of one ganglion and a few nerve-threads. Higher in the scale we meet with a mollusc such as the *Aplysia* (sea-hare), having five ganglionic masses (fig. 43).

[*] I shall hereafter endeavour to show that although the animal organism is in many respects a mechanism, it is always a *sensitive* mechanism.

A still higher development, and one approaching the vertebrate form, is seen in fig. 44, where the ganglia are arranged symmetrically along the axis of the body. These *forms* are, it is obvious, very unlike those of man or vertebrate animals; yet if we examine the *tissue* of these ganglia, we shall find it to be as much like the ganglionic tissue of men, as the muscles of these animals are like the muscles of men. From this resemblance in structure we conclude that there is a corresponding resemblance in property; and finding that insects and molluscs manifest signs of Sensibility, we have no difficulty in assigning Sensibility to this very structure.

The ganglia placed in the head of an insect are, morphologically, utterly unlike the Brain of a vertebrate animal; nevertheless having similar *organic relations* — that is to say, being in connection with the higher organs of Sense — we have no hesitation in speaking of the brain of a Bee. What amount of intelligence the bee may possess we do not know; but we see that it has Sensibility and Volition; and anatomists generally regard the ganglia connected with the organs of Sense as the seat of this Sensibility and Volition. For my present purpose it is enough to take note of this admission. If the cephalic ganglia of an insect can be credited with Sensibility and Volition, in spite of their morphological unlikeness to the Brain, and in virtue of their possessing a similar tissue, and similar organic connections; surely the ganglia of the Spinal Chord may be credited with Sensibility and Volition, in spite of their morphological unlikeness to the Brain, seeing now very closely they resemble the Brain in tissue?

Let no one suppose that the mere position of the Brain and cephalic ganglia, endows them with this property of Sensibility.

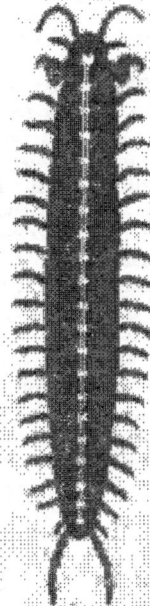

Fig. 44.

NERVOUS SYSTEM OF CENTIPEDE.
(After Dalton.)

Properties do not originate in anatomical positions. Unless the Sensibility were present, no connection with the organs of Sense would avail. In experiments on the Sensorial Centres of Insects (not yet published), I found that the ganglia styled "Brain" are in no respect different from the other ganglia in structure or in property; the only differences observable arise from the organs of Sense, or Motion, with which they are connected: *i. e.* their *functions* differ. And we shall hereafter see that, in man and vertebrate animals, the differences in the functions of the various organs of the nervous system are all forms of Sensibility, determined by their different connections with other parts of the body.

The view adopted by modern physiologists is very different; but the facts remain the same, whichever interpretation be adopted; and I only urge mine because it is based on certain simple and indisputable principles, and makes the present chaotic condition of our knowledge a little less chaotic. The current view is this: Sensibility belongs only to the centres within the skull; all other centres have only the property of *reflecting* impressions. By this reflection of impressions is meant, that when an impression is made on a sensory nerve, and by it carried to the spinal chord, the impression there becomes *reflected* into a motion — the motor-nerve carries the impulse to a muscle; and thus an action results, unprompted, or unaccompanied by any sensation whatever.

In direct opposition to this, I maintain that unless an impression on the sensory nerve excites a sensation in the centre, *no* motion whatever takes place. But the proof of this must come later on.

VII. Sensibility, Sensation, and Consciousness. — We have now reached the cardinal question in nerve physiology, the clear answer to which must necessarily determine our answer to many other questions.

It is somewhat remarkable that while many physiologists might be disposed to concede that all nervous centres were endowed with Sensibility, they would almost unanimously reject the inevitable consequence, that all nervous centres, in action, give rise to *Sensation*, and thus furnish elements to the general *Consciousness*. They have no difficulty in admitting that Contraction is the active state of Contractility in a muscle; but that Sensation should be the active state of Sensibility in a nerve-centre, does not seem to them so clear. Guided in their use of language by the deep-rooted prejudice respecting the Brain, they establish a wide distinction between "sensitive impressions" and "sensations," and hence they find no difficulty in speaking of "unfelt sensations," and of "unconscious sensibility." It is not with a view to accuracy in language only that I suggest the desirableness of getting rid of such terms; no impression can be sensitive without sensation. Let us see if greater accuracy of language will not help us in our inquiry. It is maintained on all hands that sensation is impossible without consciousness. Let this be granted. But when Consciousness itself comes to be spoken of, we find that the Brain is regarded as its exclusive seat; and the conclusion of course is that no sensation can be produced by an impression, unless that impression reach the Brain. If an animal without its Brain is shown to exhibit every sign of sensation, exhibited when the Brain was present, the physiologists argue that we must not suppose the brainless animal really *has* sensations; far from it: it has only *sensitive impressions* which produce *reflex actions*, without any Consciousness on the part of the animal. To have sensations and to be conscious of sensations, is one and the same thing. To *have* a sensation and to *know* that we have it, are two things, not one thing. Knowledge cannot exist without consciousness; but consciousness may, and often does, exist without knowledge.

But what is meant by Consciousness? Unhappily there are scarcely two writers who precisely agree in their use of this term.* Some use it as the synonym of the soul; others as a distinct faculty. It is sometimes employed to designate sensation, and at others only those sensations which usurp the attention. All we can attempt in this place is to fix the precise meaning of our terms, and stick to that; and as Consciousness

* Mr. Bain fills no less than six large pages with an enumeration of the various meanings given to it by English writers. See "The Emotions and the Will," p. 599.

more generally implies sensation than anything else, we will
elect that meaning, and see if by it we cannot clear up manifold
contradictions.

The fact that we have a sensitive organism is indisputable;
not less so the fact that this organism is incessantly excited by
external and internal stimuli. Every such excitation of the sensitive organism must be a sensation. These sensations will necessarily be very various, as the organs excited, and the exciting
causes are various; but they must all be sensations, they are all
active states of the general property of sensibility. *Ergo*, they
must all be elements of Consciousness.

The established doctrine affirms, or implies, that only those
excitations of sensibility which are sufficiently vivid to predominate among the myriads fleeting over our organism, and thereby
to attract attention, are properly called sensations. Of these we
are said to be conscious. The rest are considered as non-ex-
istent — unconscious impressions, which may lead to actions,
but are not sensations.

It is of course permissible to define terms as you please.
Writers may call that, and that only, a sensation which separately solicits the attention; they may declare that unless it
is "perceived," no sensation can exist. So long as this language
is rigorously preserved, it may be unobjectionable. But it cannot long be preserved. Insensibly writers are led by it into the
glaring contradictions of unfelt feelings and unconscious consciousness.* For example, the chest expands and contracts in
respiration; and, if we attend to it, a peculiar sensation is perceived accompanying the process; but if attention be elsewhere
directed, the sensation is not perceived. Now we know that in
both cases a sensory stimulus, playing on the respiratory centre,
was reflected as a motor stimulus on the muscles, and we are
therefore forced to adopt one of two alternatives:

* "The subject has been mystified by Arnold and others, by discussions
about sensations with, and without, consciousness, as if the latter phrase were
not a contradiction in terms; and even Professor Alison writes in the following manner — 'In order that these sensations may be felt;' as if the phrase
were not one of perfect tautology." — MARSHALL HALL: *New Memoir on the
Nervous System* , p. 85.

Either, the same sensation was evoked in both cases, although
　　perceived only in the first;

Or, Attention is itself the creator of the sensation. This
　　latter alternative is too purely metaphysical for the
　　physiologist, who in vain endeavours to conceive the
　　Attention *endowing* a sensory nerve with such a qua-
　　lity.*

On this point let us hear Müller: "Sensation itself must be
distinguished from attention (the direction of the mind to sensations), and from the faculty of forming ideas from sensations.
Attention appears to be a function of the cerebral hemispheres;
by their removal the animal is rendered stupid, but sensation remains. Among a certain number of simultaneous sensations we
are able to direct our attention to a single one so as to perceive it
not only more distinctly than the rest, but definedly and in its
whole intensity."** We may also quote the remarks of Gerdy on
the popular confusion of terms. "If," he says, "it is necessary
that there should be a perception for the existence of a sensation,
it will follow that the words *sense* and *sensitive* have a double
meaning, the one *patent* — to wit, that the organs indicated are
sentient; the other *occult* — to wit, that the organs are not sentient in themselves, but only in conjunction with perception.
Whence it results that the senses are not sentient, because they
do not perceive; and the Brain alone has this privilege, because
it perceives although it is itself insensible."***

Every one will admit that *attention does not create the sensation.* All it can do is to *isolate* one sensation from the *crowd of
simultaneous sensations;* nay, one may ask whether attention itself be anything more than that very isolation of one sensation
from the crowd? Sir Henry Holland suggests that attention is
only the direction of the consciousness; † but leaving this matter to the psychologists, let us content ourselves with discriminating the elements of sensation from those of perception. Sir

* The eminent physiologist LUDWIG unequivocally declares that we only
receive a sensation so long as we attend to it. — *Lehrbuch der Physiologie,*
1858, I. 593; and many others might be cited to the same effect.
** MÜLLER: *Physiol.;* by BALY, I. 829.
*** GERDY: *Physiologie philosophique des Sensations,* p. 20.
† HOLLAND: *Chapters on Mental Physiology.*

William Hamilton, whose multifarious learning embraced even
the recondite questions of physiology, has announced the law:
That a nervous point yields a sensation felt as locally distinct in
proportion as it is isolated in its action from every other point.[*]
This law of local distinction must be extended to every distinction of sensations: only when one impression is isolated from the
several simultaneous impressions, can it so far arrest attention as
to be perceived.   Let an example be cited:

During the performance of an orchestra we may single
out a particular instrument, or group of instruments, following them with attention.   It is obvious that in doing so we
never endow these instruments with any real increase of intensity, or with any new power: the amount of sensation
they awaken in us is not exalted by our attention; nevertheless, because we have isolated that sensation from the
harmonious concord of sounds, amid which these instruments
move, we perceive sounds which before were unperceived, and
which by less experienced ears always would remain unperceived,
merged in orchestral thunder.   In common language we are said
not to hear the particular instruments, when we cannot separately
follow them.   Yet nothing is more certain than that we do hear
them.   We are affected by them.   Suddenly silence those instruments in the very climax of a crescendo, and the storm of
the others will not prevent our distinctly perceiving *some* difference.

We shall do well to hold fast by the maxim that to *have a sensation*, and to be *conscious* of it, are one and the same thing; but
to *have a sensation*, and to *attend* to it, are two different things.
Attention is the direction of the consciousness — not the consciousness itself.   We shall do well also to hold fast by the distinction very properly established between Sensation and Perception.   That this distinction is constantly overlooked, is the
cause of much disagreement, and it is the confusion of the two
terms which lies at the root of the current doctrine on the Sensorium.

Let us open Todd and Bowman's work, and read the following
passage, in which these eminent physiologists express with great

* HAMILTON: *Dissert. to Reid's Works*, p. 862.

. explicitness the view I am opposing: "A state of the sensitive organs and a corresponding perception by the mind, must concur to produce sensation; either condition may exist alone, but then the phenomenon is not a true sensation in the acceptation here given to the word. Thus light falling on the eye in sleep *excites the whole visual sensitive apparatus* while the organ of perception is inactive."*

Without denying to these writers the privilege of defining their terms as they please, I must ask what advantage there can be in blending together the two words Sensation and Perception, inasmuch as we must afterwards invent a term to express the excitement of the sensitive apparatus? This excitement is specific, and its sensational character is visible in the effects produced by it — for the sleeping man, thus excited, *perceives* no object, but he *feels* the sensation, and moves away his head from the light in consequence.

It will be more exact, and more convenient, to restrict the term Sensation to the simple reaction of the Sensitive Organism.

There is, I am aware, an unfortunate ambiguity in our popular language, which renders it plausible to say that unless a sensation is perceived, it is the same as if it did not exist. Yet closer scrutiny detects that we certainly must have many sensations which are not perceived at all. Thus if two sharp instruments be made to press gently on each arm, we shall have two distinct sensations, both perceptible. Whether these two sensations are simultaneous, or successive, matters not, the two impressions on the sensitive nerves excite two sensations in their centres. But now, while the left arm retains its sensibility, if the instrument be pressed so forcibly on the right arm as to cause pain, we become totally unaware of the sensation in the left arm — we can no longer perceive the sensation caused by the instrument, which nevertheless is pressing as before. Is the sensibility in the left arm destroyed? Not at all. Does the sensation cease to exist during the period when we cease to be aware of it? No: the impression has continued; the relation of the sensitive nerve to its centre has been uninterrupted, and the sensation must conse-

* Todd and Bowman: *Physiological Anatomy*, 1. 402.

quently have continued. It will be perceived, as soon as the pain in the other arm abates.

While I am writing these lines the trees are rustling in the summer wind, the birds are twittering among the leaves, and the muffled sounds of carriages rolling over the Dresden streets reach my ear; but because the mind is occupied with trains of thought these sounds are not perceived, until one of them becomes importunate, or my relaxed attention turns towards them. Nevertheless, when unperceived, the sounds reached my ear, and excited sensory impressions: if those sensory impressions are not to be called sensations, because they were not perceived, they must have *some* name given to them, and a name which will indicate that they are affections of the sensitive organism. They were not lost; they were not altered in character because their subsequent effects were not manifest in Thought; they were not without their influence in adding to the sum of general Consciousness. It is because they were states of Sensibility that they must be called sensations.

To elucidate this we must first consider the Law of Sensibility: *No sensation terminates in itself; it must either discharge its excitation in some secondary sensation, or in some motor-impulse. Generally it does so in both together.*

A self-terminating sensation is as inconceivable as a self-terminating motion. The wave of force is propelled onwards, and for ever onwards, now in this direction, and now in that. An impression made on the skin is transmitted by the sensory nerve to the ganglion, and this ganglion, being excited, excites the motor nerve in connection with it, producing a muscular contraction. If this ganglion and pair of nerves were all the nervous system, or were isolated from the others, nothing more would ensue; the sensory stimulus would have discharged itself in a muscular contraction, and what is called a Reflex Action would have been produced. The stimulus of light, for instance, falling on the eye, causes the muscles of the iris to contract. But inasmuch as every ganglion is connected with other ganglia and inasmuch as we have previously seen that the nerve-fibres which connect the two, have their Neurility excited when one of these ganglia is excited, the sensation awakened in the first ganglion not only discharges itself in a muscular contraction, or Reflex Action, but also in another sensation, — it plays on a muscle, and it plays on a centre. This *secondary* sensation, I have called Reflex Feeling, for the sake of marking its resemblance, as a physiological process, to Reflex Action. This secondary, or reflex, feeling may in turn discharge itself in an action, or in another feeling.

To take a rough illustration: A fly settles on your hand while you are writing. The tickling sensation may either cause you to withdraw your hand, by reflex-action, without attracting any attention to it, without exciting any reflex-feeling; or it may excite your attention, without causing you to withdraw your hand. Or, finally, it may cause you both to withdraw your hand, and to attend to it. In the first of these cases you would be said not to have felt the fly; your attention was elsewhere. But if you had not felt it, if the sensation had not been excited, no withdrawal of the hand would have followed.

We shall hereafter have to consider this point more thoroughly; enough for the present if we recognise that a sensation, once excited, *must* discharge itself in a reflex-action, or in a reflex-feeling, and *may* discharge itself in both.

In those parts of the organism which are so arranged that the easiest, readiest path for the issue of a sensation is that of muscular contraction, we shall find that every stimulus produces Reflex-Action — in other words, an action not indeed unaccompanied by sensation, but unaccompanied by *secondary* sensations, or Reflex-Feeling. The rhythmic motion of the heart, and the movements of the intestines, are examples. They do not go on without producing sensation; on the contrary, the feeling excited by them constitutes an integral part of the general Consciousness; but habitually they excite no *recognisable trains of secondary sensation;* and in popular language we are said not to feel them. Winking and Breathing are in like manner reflex-actions; but they are both liable to force double issues, and to excite reflex-feelings as well as reflex-actions, — we are then said to *feel* that we are winking or breathing. Contrasted with these, there are parts of the nervous mechanism in which the easiest path for a sensation is that of another sensation; one feeling excites, by reflex, another feeling, one idea

calls up another idea; and this either with, or without, exciting
a reflex-action. If a tone awakens your recollection of one bar
of a particular melody, you will find it is only by an effort that
you can prevent the whole of that melody from passing over your
mind; and this melody may either excite reflex vocal expression,
or be continued without such reflex-action.

Habits, Fixed Ideas, and what are called Automatic Actions,
all depend on the tendency which a sensation has to discharge
itself through the readiest channel. In learning to speak a new
language, to play on a musical instrument, or to perform any
unaccustomed movements, great difficulty is felt, because the
channels through which each sensation has to pass have not become established; but no sooner has frequent repetition cut a
pathway, than this difficulty vanishes; the actions become so
automatic that they can be performed while the mind is otherwise engaged; and sometimes, if once commenced, they must
continue. We have all our tricks of phrase or gesture, which
no effort can prevent. We utter, as meaningless expletives,
phrases, which originally cost us trouble to learn. It is in vain
that people laugh at us for the iteration of "you know," "well
then," and similar phrases, which are often ludicrously inappro-
priate; they have become automatic — the paths of discharge
have been established, and along these paths the sensation must
discharge itself. The same thing is observable in the region of
ideas. Old associations, old beliefs, are not to be displaced.
A man may be thoroughly convinced to-day by the logic of his
opponent, and yet to-morrow he will be heard uttering his old
convictions, as if no one had ever doubted them. His mind cannot move except in the old paths. It may be noted as the peculiar characteristic of vigorous intellects, that their thoughts are
ever finding new pathways instead of moving amid old associations. The vigorous thinker is one who thinks for himself; the
vigorous writer is one who expresses what he means, and does
not suffer one phrase automatically to determine another. If he
has a manner, or mannerism, it is his own. Inferior minds think
the thoughts of others, and write the phrases of others. Hence,
as Goethe says, in this world there are so few voices and so many
echoes.

Returning from this digression, we may now understand that although a sensation must discharge itself, and may do so in various directions, now exciting muscular contractions, and now trains of thought, we are not to suppose the sensation itself is dependent on these effects; or to suppose, as the dominant doctrine does, that, unless a train of thought be excited, no sensation at all has been excited. Sensation is simply the active state of Sensibility, which is the property of ganglionic tissue.

The mill-wheel, at first so obtrusive in its sound, ceases at length to excite any attention. The impressions on our auditory nerves continue; but although we hear them, we cease to think about them: the same reflex-feelings are no longer excited. It is held, indeed, that we cease to hear them, in ceasing to be "conscious" that we hear them; but this is manifestly erroneous. Let the wheel suddenly stop, and there is an immediate corresponding sensational change in us; so much so, that if it occurs during sleep, we awake. Let the wheel move with slower movement, and we shall at once be aware of it. Let it creak, and we hear it. Now, it is clear that unless we are all the while sensible of the sounds of the wheel, no alterations in the *degrees* of sound will affect us. If the sensation of sound has ceased, the *cessation* of that sound cannot awaken us. The truth seems to be that at first the sound of the wheel was *obtrusive* — excited reflex-feelings — gave determinate directions to our thoughts. It afterwards ceased to excite these feelings, and the sensations became *merged* in the general sum of sensations which make up our total Consciousness. "The habit of hearing the same sounds," says Jouffroy, "renders us sometimes highly sensitive to them, as in the case of savages; sometimes again almost insensible to them, as exemplified in the apathy of the Parisian or Londoner for the noise of carriages. If the effect were physical — if it depended on the body and not on the mind — there would be a contradiction, for the habit of hearing the same sound either blunts the organ or sharpens it; it could not at once have two, and two contrary, effects — it could have only one. The fact is, it neither blunts nor sharpens; the organ remains the same — the same sensations are determined; but when these sensations interest the mind, it applies itself to them, and be-

comes accustomed to their discrimination: when they do not
interest it, it becomes accustomed to neglect, and does not discriminate them." *

One cannot help the equivoques of language. It will always
seem absurd to say we can have sensations and not be conscious
of them, because the word consciousness has become restricted
to those sensations to which the attention is directed. The explanation given by Whytt is worth attending to: "When I say
we are not conscious of certain impressions made on the mind
by the action of material causes on the organs of the body, I mean
no more than that we have no such consciousness or perception
of them, as either convinces us of their existence when present,
or enables us, by the help of memory, to recall them when
past."** Consciousness is here considered as identical with Perception; it is generally considered identical with Sensation.
And the question recurs: Can there be sensation without perception?

Nothing is more certain than that we have many sensations
which are not perceived at all, of which we are said to be wholly
"unconscious." They are either so faint in themselves, or so
familiar, they are either so submerged in stronger sensations,
or so incapable of exciting trains of Reflex-Feeling in the preoccupied mind, that we are neither "conscious" of them when
present, nor capable of remembering them afterwards. For
example: it may happen that we fall asleep during a sermon
(such cases have occurred), or while a book is being read aloud.
The sound of the speaker's voice is heard, but the words gradually cease to be perceived. Page after page is read aloud,
exciting no perception at all in our minds; but has there been
no sensation excited? We have not *heard*, but have we not been
affected by the sounds? To prove that we have, is easy. Let
the reader suddenly cease, and if our sleep be not too profound,
we at once awake. Now, unless the sound of his voice affected
us, it is clear that the cessation of that sound could not have
affected us. Or let us suppose our sleep to be unbroken by the
cessation of the sound; even this will not prove that we have

---

* Quoted in HAMILTON: *Lectures on Metaphysics*, i. 326.
** WHYTT: *Of the Vital and Involuntary Motions*, p. 267.

been unaffected by the sounds, it will merely prove that those sounds, or their cessation, did not awaken a reflex-feeling. For let the reader, in no louder tone, ask, "Are you asleep?" and we start up, with round eyes, declaring, "Not at all." Nay, should even this question fail to awaken us, the speaker need only utter some phrase likely to excite reflex-feeling — such as "There's the postman," or "I smell fire," and we start up.

I remember once trying the experiment on a wearied waiter, who had fallen asleep in one of the unoccupied boxes of a tavern. His arm rested on the table, and his head rested on his arm: he snored the snore of the weary, in spite of the noisy laughter and talk of the guests. I called "Johnson," in a loud tone. It never moved him. I then called "Wilson," but he snored on. No sooner did I call "waiter," than he raised his head with a sleepy "yessir." Now, to suppose, in this case, that he had *no* sensation when the words "Johnson" and "Wilson" reached his ears, but had a sensation when the word "waiter" reached his ears, is to suppose that two similar causes will not produce a similar effect. The dissyllable "Johnson" would excite as potent a reaction of his Sensibility as the dissyllable "waiter:" but the secondary sensations — the reflex-feelings — were different, because the word "Johnson" was not associated in his mind with any definite actions, whereas the word "waiter" was so associated as to become an automatic impulse. *

Two sisters are asleep in the same bed, and a child cries in the next room. The sounds of these cries will give a similar stimulus to the auditory nerve of each sister, and excite a similiar *primary* sensation in each. Nevertheless, the one sister sleeps on undisturbed, and is said not to hear the cry. The other springs out of bed, and attends to the child, because she being accustomed to attend on the child and soothe it when crying, the primary sensation has excited secondary sensations, or reflex-feelings, which lead to accustomed actions. Could we look into the mind of the sleeping sister, we should doubtless find that the sensation excited by the child's cry had merged itself in

* Dr. Carpenter tells a similar story of Admiral Codrington, who, when a midshipman, could always be awakened from the profoundest slumber if the word "signal" were uttered; whereas no other word disturbed him.

the general stream of Consciousness, and perhaps modified her dreams. Let her become a mother, or take on the tender duties of a mother, and her vigilance will equal that of her sister; because the cry will *then* excite a definite reflex-feeling, and a definite course of action. But this very sister, who is so sensitive to the cry of a child, will be undisturbed by a much louder noise; a dog may bark, or a heavy waggon thunder along the street, without causing her to turn in bed. *

Although during sleep the nervous centres have by no means their full activity, they are always capable of responding to a stimulus, and Sensation will always be produced. When the servant taps at your bedroom door in the morning, you are said not to hear the tap, if asleep; you do not perceive it; but the sound reaches and rouses you nevertheless, since when the second tap comes, although no louder, you distinctly recognise it. In etherised patients, Sensation is constantly observed returning before any consciousness of what is going on returns. "I was called," says Mr. Potter, "to give chloroform to a lady for the extraction of ten teeth. The first five were extracted without the slightest movement, but as the operation proceeded, sensation returned, and I was obliged to use considerable force to keep her in the chair during the extraction of the last tooth. She came to herself very shortly after, and was delighted to find she had got over all her troubles without having felt it the least in the world." **

There is, I repeat, an unfortunate equivoque in language which makes it sound absurd to speak of unperceived sensations. Men have for so long confounded Sensation with Perception, because the two are so constantly blended, that it is startling to hear of one occurring without the other. But even the physiologists, whose views are here combated, fall into the same equivoque of language, and speak of "Unconscious Sensibility." In spite of all such verbal difficulties, we must steadily bear in mind that a sensation, being the active state of any one ganglion, is not dependent for its existence on the activity of any other

* Compare an interesting personal example given by JOUFFROY, quoted in Sir W. HAMILTON's *Lectures*, I. 331.
** *Lancet*, 10th July 1858.

ganglia which it may, by reflex-movement excite Every excitement of a nerve-centre produces a sensation; the sum total of such excitements forms the general Consciousness, or sense of existence.

We do not see the stars at noonday, yet they shine. We do not see the sunbeams playing among the leaves on a cloudy day, yet it is by these beams that the leaves and all other objects are visible. There is a general illumination from the sun and stars, but of this we are seldom aware, because our attention falls upon the illumined objects, brighter or darker than this general tone. There is a sort of analogy to this in the general Consciousness, which is composed of the sum of sensations excited by the incessant simultaneous action of internal and external stimuli. This forms, as it were, the daylight of our existence. We do not habitually attend to it, because attention falls on those particular sensations of pleasure or of pain, of greater or of less intensity, which usurp a prominence among the objects of the sensitive panorama. But just as we need the daylight to see the brilliant and the sombre forms of things, we need this living Consciousness to feel the pleasures and the pains of life. It is therefore as erroneous to imagine that we have no other sensations than those on which the attention falls — those which we distinctly recognise — as to imagine that we see no other light than what is reflected from the shops and equipages, the colours and splendours which arrest the eye.

The amount of light received from the stars may be small, but it is present. The greater glory of the sunlight may render this starlight inappreciable, but it does not render it inoperative. In like manner the amount of sensation received from some of the smaller ganglia may be inappreciable in the presence of more massive influences from other centres; but though inappreciable it cannot be inoperative — it must form an integer in the sum.

The reader's daily experience will assure him that over and above all the particular sensations capable of being separately recognised, there is a general stream of Sensation which constitutes his feeling of existence — the Consciousness of himself as a sensitive being. The ebullient energy which one day exalts life,

and the mournful depression which the next day renders life a
burden almost intolerable, are feelings not referable to any of
the particular sensations; but arise from the massive yet obscure
sensibilities of the viscera, which form so important a part of
the general stream of Sensation. Some of these may emerge
into distinct recognition. We may feel the heart beat, the intestines move, the glands secrete; anything *unusual* in their
action will force itself on our attention.

"What we have been long used to," says Whytt, "we become
scarcely sensible of; while things which are new, though much
more trifling, and of weaker impression, affect us remarkably.
Thus he who is wont to spend his time in the country is surpris-
ingly affected, upon first coming into a populous city, with the
noise and bustle which prevail there: of this, however, he becomes daily less sensible, till at length he regards it no more
than they who have been used to it all their lifetime. The same
seems to be the case also with what passes within our bodies. Few
persons in health feel the beating of their heart, though it strikes
against their ribs with considerable force every second; whereas
the motion of a fly upon one's face or hands occasions a very sensible and uneasy titillation. The pulsation of the great *aorta*
itself is wholly unobserved by us; yet the unusual beating of a
small artery in any of the fingers becomes very remarkable."

A large amount of sensation is derived from the muscular
sense, yet we are not aware of the nice adjustments of the
muscles, regulated by this sensibility, when we sit or walk. No
sooner are we placed in an exceptional position, as in walking
on a narrow ledge, than we become distinctly aware of the effort
required to preserve equilibrium. It is not the novelty of the
position which has increased our sensibility; that has only
caused us to attend to our sensations. In like manner, the
various streams of sensation which make up our general sense
of existence, separately escape notice until one of them becomes
obstructed, or increases in impetuosity. When we are seated
at a window, and look out at the trees and sky, we are so occupied with the aspects and the voices of external Nature, that
no attention whatever is given to the fact of our own existence;
yet all this while there has been a massive and diffusive sensation

arising from the organic processes; and of this we become distinctly aware if we close our eyes, shut off all sounds, and abstract the sensations of touch and temperature — it is then perceived as a vast and powerful stream of sensation, belonging to none of the special Senses, but to the System as a whole. It is on this general stream that depend those well-known but indescribable states of Consciousness, named "feeling well" and "feeling ill" — the *bien être* and *malaise* of every day. Of two men looking from the same window, on the same landscape, one will be moved to unutterable sadness, yearning for the peace of death; the other will feel his soul suffused with serenity and content: the one has a gloomy background of Consciousness, into which the sensations excited by the landscape are merged; the other has a happy background of Consciousness, on which the sensations play like ripples on a sunny lake. The tone of each man's feeling is determined by the state of his general consciousness. Except in matters of pure demonstration, we are all determined towards certain conclusions as much by this general consciousness as by logic. Our philosophy, when not borrowed, is little more than the expression of our personality.

Consciousness, in the general sense, is the sum total of all our sensibilities, the confluence of many streams of sensation. Consciousness, in the particular sense, is only another term for Sensibility: we have as many different forms of consciousness as we have different kinds of sensation. While some of these confluent streams are so slight that they are no more appreciable than are the stars at noonday, others are so equable and constant, that they attract no attention unless their currents are disturbed. Thus healthy men are scarcely able to distinguish the sensations excited by the circulation of the blood, or the movement of the intestines; yet a slight alteration in these sensations will be felt at once.

We may here conclude the discussion of this question by affirming that the evidence proves the inadequacy of the current hypothesis, which says that unless a sensation is perceived it does not exist — it is a mere *impression*. The hypothesis here combated says, explicitly or implicitly, that a nerve-centre may receive a stimulus, but this stimulus will not awaken a sensation,

unless it be transmitted from that centre to some *other* centre.
Though why one centre should have the property of Sensibility
which another centre, identical in substance, has not, no physiologist has attempted to explain.

I request the reader particularly to observe that it is no merely
verbal difference which is established, when what is usually
called an *impression* is here called a *sensation*, and when a *sensation* is distinguished from a *perception*. More than once has this
objection been urged, the objector thinking that my dissent
from established opinions amounted to no more than calling an
impression by another name. My dissent reaches to the very
foundations. A verbal difference, carrying with it no important
consequences, would not be worth so much labour as has been
bestowed on elucidating this point. Those who say that an impression which is not perceived has no element of sensation in it,
say that when the preoccupied mind does not hear the roll of
carriages in the street, the effect of the vibrations of the air
upon the auditory centre has been no more than the effect on the
window-pane: a mere physical impulse has been given. Whereas
I aver that just as the window-pane reacts according to the properties of glass, so does the auditory centre react according to
the properties of nerve-centres — and something more than an
impression is the result: the impression is *sensitive*.

It is surely much more than a verbal difference when one
school asserts that some animals have Minds, and other animals
only Instincts, and another school asserts that all animals have
Minds, but the minds of some are strikingly inferior in range,
complexity, and energy, to those of others. It is surely more
than a verbal difference when a philosophic naturalist, detecting
the uniformities which underlie the diversities noticeable in the
actions of animals, declares that they are all guided by sensations, and these are all due to a nervous system — in opposition
to those who call the actions of some animals mental, and the
same actions in other animals mechanical. And such is the
difference between the view I advocate, and the view I combat.
My view may be erroneous; at any rate it is not limited merely
to a change of terms. If it be said, that since I admit a dif-

ference between sensation and perception — that is, between one sensation and another — this amounts pretty much to the ordinary distinction between an impression and a sensation; the answer is very simple: a naturalist admits the difference between two animals, admits that a monkey is very unlike an oyster, and that the two should never be confounded; but while they differ, they also agree: he classes them according to their differences, but their fundamental agreements make him range both under the general conception of an Animal. Various as animals are, he knows that underlying all diversities there are certain uniformities; all animals belong to the grand division of *Animalia*, and obey the same biological laws. Now it is precisely this reform that I desire to see introduced into our physiology of the Nervous System — that we should recognise the uniformities underlying the diversities, and recognise that all nerve-centres, *as* such, have properties in common, laws in common. The sensations derived through the organic processes are very unlike those derived through the five Senses; and Pain is unlike both; yet they are all sensations. Hunger is unlike Thirst; Thirst is unlike Fatigue; Light is unlike Hearing. But these are all elements of the general Consciousness: all active states of nerve-centres. Instead of admitting this simple principle, physiologists, implicitly or explicitly, assert that one nerve-centre or group of centres has a property of Sensibility not possessed at all by similar centres. Even those who seem to have felt some scruple in denying sensibility to all the centres, have been forced, by their adherence to the notion of a sensation being impossible without the Brain, to establish two distinct classes — namely, the Conscious Sensibility, and the Unconscious Sensibility; in other terms, Animal Sensibility and Organic Sensibility. The latest upholder of this view thus expresses himself:

"All the secretions take place under the influence of a reflex action, and sometimes the sensation, which is the point of departure of this action, is a conscious sensation, at other times unconscious. Thus the salivary secretion, which takes place when vinegar is introduced into the mouth, is a secretion which succeeds a conscious sensation (*une sensation avec conscience*)

4 *

The secretions of gastric juice, pancreatic juice or bile, which
take place when food passes along the digestive tube, on the
contrary, succeed to sensations without consciousness." *

Now, physiologically, the process in each of these cases is
identical: a stimulus is given to the Neurility of a nerve, which
excites the Sensibility of a centre, and that, in turn, stimulating
the Neurility of the nerve distributed to the gland, produces
thereby a Secretion. There is a difference between the organ
of Taste, stimulated by the vinegar, and the stomach or liver,
stimulated by the food; there is a difference also in the secretions: but in each case the stimulus has first awakened Sensation, and then Secretion. If the sensation of the one is to be
called conscious, and the other unconscious, this use of language, though justifiable, will be excessively misleading. It
would be far better to say that the sensation produced by the
vinegar, being derived from a special sense (Taste), could be
distinctly recognised as special; whereas the sensations excited
by the food, being derived from no special sense, but from the
Systemic Sensibility,** must necessarily be unlike the taste of
vinegar, and not being a special sensation, is less readily recognisable.

The conclusion, then, which we have reached is briefly this:
In muscular tissue there is an inherent *property* named Contractility; this serves various *functions* in various muscles. All
the movements of our different organs depend on this property;
and the complex mechanism which performs the many movements, say of the hand, is a complex of simple muscular contractions. In like manner ganglionic tissue has an inherent property, Sensibility, which serves various functions in various
organs: however complex any one of these functions, we should
find, could we analyse it, that it was a complex of simple sensations. There is an incessant action and interaction of the various
parts of the sensitive mechanism: sensations cross and recross,
exciting and modifying each other; and the sum total is a feeling
of existence. In the lower animals, with a simple nervous system,

---

* CLAUDE BERNARD: *Système Nerveux*, I. 357.
** This distinction between special and systemic sensations will be elucidated hereafter.

the sensitive phenomena are simple: as the organisation increases in complexity, the sensitive phenomena necessarily become more complex; the elements of general Consciousness become more numerous.

VIII. VARIOUS FORMS OF CONSCIOUSNESS. — A basis has been laid, in the foregoing paragraphs, for a true zoological classification of mental phenomena. The unity of the nervous system throughout the Animal Kingdom has been generally recognised; but, strangely enough, the unity of Consciousness has not been deduced from it. In ascending the scale we pass from animals destitute of real *movements*, and manifesting only *contractions*; as we note in the higher animals the ever-increasing variety and complexity of movement, we find that no new property has been acquired; but that the same primordial tissue, with its Contractility, suffices for all the new complex phenomena. Yet we speak, and justly, of simple contractions, of voluntary and involuntary movements, of flexion and extension, and so on. I think we should do the same with Sensibility, or Consciousness, which may be conveniently grouped under three heads: 1. *Systemic-Consciousness*; 2. *Sense-Consciousness*; 3. *Thought-Consciousness*. A few words will explain these more fully.

Systemic-Consciousness includes all those sensations which arise in the system at large, chiefly in the organic processes, and form the more massive and diffusive elements of the sense of existence. This must belong to the simplest animals, unless we adopt the hypothesis of Descartes, that all animals are living machines, whose actions are wholly without consciousness. Many who reject this hypothesis feel great difficulty in crediting *all* animals with consciousness or sensation; because few writers can rid themselves of the embarrassing equivoque of our ordinary language. The equivoque here leads them to suppose some element of Thought is included in Consciousness, and even in Sensation. But although every animal must *feel*, it does not follow that it should *think*. Every animal must *contract*, but it does not follow that it should *move*. Thinking results from a more complex organisation than is given to every animal; but Consciousness is the attribute of every animal organism. Simple as the forms of Consciousness may be in the lower animals, it

must be nevertheless essentially akin to the more complex forms
in the higher animals. Unless we admit this, it will be impossible
to say where sensation first begins. If the Mollusc is without
sensation, the Crustacean is without it. If the crab is a machine,
so is the bee; if the bee, then the beaver, the elephant, the dog,
the monkey. It is true that when we pass from the monkey to
the man, a wide interval is obvious: the greater fulness and
splendour of conscious life which man possesses above all other
created beings may account for the disinclination of philosophers
to admit that animals can share even a modest claim to similar
prerogatives. But the time for such exclusiveness is passed:
science has shown that amid the infinite varieties of animal life,
certain constant uniformities exist; and that in the magnificent
drama of creation, the humble scene-shifter is of the same nature
as the more highly-endowed tragedian, who plays the noblest
parts. Unless we are to throw science to the winds, we must
admit that *all* animals are conscious (have sensations), though all
have not every form of consciousness. There are those that have
systemic sensations, but no senses, such as sight, hearing, smell.
There are others that have systemic sensations, and sense-sensations, but little or nothing of what we mean by Thought. All
depends on the complexity of the organism.

The Systemic sensations in man are massive in effect, and
constant; and because they are constant and familiar, seldom
rise into distinct recognition. This has led to their being denied
the character of sensations. It is said, for example, that we have
no sensations in the alimentary canal, unless pain be produced
there. And the following proof is offered: If we swallow iced-
water, there is a sensation of cold excited in the mouth, throat,
and gullet; but this sensation disappears as the water reaches
the stomach: if any vestige of sensation remain, it will be only at
the upper part of the stomach. This is, however, no proof at all.
The sensation of cold is a *special* sensation, of which, as we shall
see hereafter, only certain organs are susceptible — the same
nerve which is susceptible of cold when the cold substance
reaches it through the skin, is *not* susceptible of cold when the
trunk of the nerve is directly touched; and there is nothing remarkable in the stomach not having this special form of sen-

sibility.   But if the iced-water, on reaching the stomach, ceases
to produce a sensation of cold, it does not cease to affect the sensitive nerves; it therefore produces some other sensation — one
of comfort or discomfort, perhaps.   We are assuredly conscious
of some difference in our general feeling — a diffusive sensation
radiates from the stomach.   It may escape recognition, like a
rivulet mingling with a river, and adding to its general momen-
tum; but though *unrecognised*, it is not *unfelt*.

If instead of iced-water we swallow brandy-and-water, the
sensations of taste excited by the brandy, being special sensations, will cease in the stomach.   In the mouth, the brandy and
the water excited sensations of taste, and of cold; in the gullet,
of cold without taste; in the stomach, of neither cold nor taste,
but something else — a diffusive sensation quite familiar to all
readers, but not easily to be described.

Hereafter we shall have to consider more in detail the various
Systemic-sensations; enough for the present if we have indicated
the class.   The second class forms

The Sense-Consciousness, and includes all those sensations
which are derived from the organs of the five Senses.   As a rule,
it is only these, and Pain, which are admitted to be sensations at
all, by those who fail to perceive the distinction between Sensibility and particular forms of Sensibility.

Thought-Consciousness is the third and last class, and includes
all those phenomena of Thought and Emotion with which the
psychologist concerns himself; all that the physiologist can do
with them is to indicate the relation in which they stand to the
lower forms of consciousness; and the special organs of the
nervous system which serve them.   I have adopted the rather
clumsy term Thought-consciousness, in order to mark out distinctly the fundamental union of this with the other forms of
Sensibility, and at the same time to mark the *speciality* of its
phenomena.   What Thought is we do not know, perhaps we
never shall.   We do not know what Life is.   But the realm of
mystery may be reduced to one of "orderly mystery;" we may
learn what are the laws of Life, and what are the laws of
Thought.   The first is the province of the physiologist, the

second is the province of the psychologist. Let us keep to
our own:

"Musicians think our souls are harmonies;
Physicians hold that they complexions be;
Epicures make them swarms of atomies
Which do by chance into our bodies flee.

One thinks the soul is air; another fire;
Another blood diffused about the heart:
Another saith the elements conspire,
And to her essence each doth yield a part.

Some think one gen'ral soul fills every brain,
As the bright sun sheds light in every star;
And others think the name of soul is vain,
And that we only well-mixed bodies are.

Thus these great clerks their little wisdom show,
While with their doctrines they at hazard play." *

We will take the warning. Our task is difficult enough without extra complications. We have still to point out what light
Physiology can at present furnish, in the attempt to determine
the various organs for the various mental functions — in other
words, what is the relation between the MIND and the BRAIN.

* SIR JOHN DAVIES: *On the Immortality of the Soul.*

NOTE TO CHAPTER VIII

THE experiments of Claude Bernard and Kölliker have proved that the *woorara* poison affects the muscle-nerves, and leaves the skin-nerves unaffected, paralysing the limbs, but not destroying sensibility. At the reading of my paper on the Sensory and Motor Nerves at the "British Association," this fact was referred to as proof that a distinction existed between the properties of the two nerves. I had already satisfied myself that such a conclusion was erroneous; but it may be desirable here to refute the conclusion by one decisive argument. We are completely in the dark as to the *conditions* which determine the effect of a poison on the nerves; but that the resistance of the skin-nerves to an influence to which the muscle-nerves succumb, is no proof of a difference in the properties of the nerves, is demonstrated by the fact that only *some* of the motor-nerves are affected by the poison — and of these nerves, only their terminations in the muscles are affected, not the fibres of their trunks; whereas *other* nerves distributed to muscles resist the poison, no less decisively than the skin-nerves. An animal poisoned by woorara has its limbs paralysed; but its tail is as vigorous as ever. The nerves which move the muscles of the limbs are not different in properties from those which move the muscles of the tail; yet the one class succumbs, the other resists; evidently because there is some set of conditions which favours the action of the poison in the one case, and prevents it in the other. The nerves which move the heart and intestines are likewise unaffected by the poison. Moreover, the fact that the nerve-fibre is unaffected everywhere except at its termination, proves that there must be some other cause at work than the property of the nerve-fibre itself. A similar peculiarity is noticeable of the muscles, there being poisons which destroy the contractility of the muscles of the heart, and have no appreciable effect on the muscles of the trunk; yet no one ventures to assert that the muscles of the heart are essentially different from all other muscles.

।

CHAPTER IX.

THE MIND AND THE BRAIN.

SECTION I. — THE CEREBRUM.

Recapitulation — Prejudice respecting the Brain as the sole organ of the
Mind — Three sources of our knowledge: Experiment, Disease, Compara-
tive Anatomy — Description of the Brain — Evidence of Comparative
Anatomy against the idea of the Brain as the sole seat of sensation and will
— Nervous systems of Mollusc and Beetle compared — Weight of the Brain
— The convolutions; are they the seat of intelligence? — Functions of the
Cerebrum — Effect of pressure on the Brain: curious case — The researches
of Flourens — State of Animals when the Cerebrum is removed — Persistence of sensation and volition after removal of the Cerebrum — Experiments of Flourens, Bouillaud, Longet, and Dalton — Relation of the Cerebrum to the nerves — Forms of Sensibility peculiar to the Cerebrum —
Intellect and Emotion — How can identical convolutions have different
functions? — Phrenology — Explanation of the difficulty — Relation of the
Intellect to the Senses, and of the Emotions to the Viscera — Other functions of the Cerebrum.

In the preceding chapter I have endeavoured to establish the
following propositions, as the basis of a new doctrine of nervous
action: —

1°. All nerves have one common property — Neurility — by
means of which they excite contraction in a muscle, secretion in
a gland, and sensation in a nerve-centre.

2°. The property of nerves depends on their structure. The
functions, or uses, of nerves are determined by their anatomical
distribution — *i. e.*, their connection with other parts of the
organism.

3°. All nerve-centres have one common property — Sensibility — which is excited by, and in turn excites, the Neurility
of nerves; and thus produces either reflex-movements, or reflex-
feelings, according as the stimulus to the centre is reflected on
muscles, or on other centres.

4°. The property of nerve-centres depends on their structure. The functions, or uses, of each centre are determined by its anatomical connections; the optic-centre being in connection with a very different apparatus from that of the auditory-centre, and so of the rest.

5°. Every stimulus which affects a centre awakens its Sensibility; but the *kind* and *degree* of sensation thus awakened are necessarily determined by the kind and degree of the exciting cause, and the structure of the organs on which that cause first acts: the sensation of sound is very different from the sensation of light; a visceral sensation is unlike a muscular sensation; pressure is different from pain, and both are different from the sensation of temperature. *

Although in the establishment of these propositions I have attempted something like a systematisation of our knowledge on this great subject, led thereto by the necessity of clearing the ground of certain prejudices and misconceptions, and by the desire of drawing the student's attention to problems which may profitably employ his energy; the reader will not expect that in the following pages we can do more than ascertain the general relations of the Mind and the Brain. Before we enter on this interesting, but extremely complicated, inquiry, we must resolve, in a loving, seeking, earnest spirit, to keep our minds open to the reception of Fact; and calmly to acquiesce in it, when presented, instead of opposing it by preconceptions of our own. It is idle to interrogate Nature in the spirit so often animating the disputes of men, when each antagonist is less desirous of hearing the arguments of the other, than of thrusting forward his own. If we ask Nature a question, we must listen patiently to her reply; should that reply perplex us, we must ask again, putting the question in another form; and should again, and again, the same

* The reader is requested to consider what is said at page 50. The word Sensibility includes very various sensations, as the word Animal includes very various organisms. When I say that every nerve-centre has Sensibility, I no more mean that every sensation will resemble the sensations of pain, or of sight, or of taste, than that every animal must resemble a fish, a reptile, or a mammal.

reply be elicited, we must accept it, be it never so destructive of
our theories and anticipations. We must not dictate an answer
to the Oracle we consult.

A deeply-rooted preconception respecting the Brain has for
many years prevented men from duly acknowledging facts which,
otherwise, would have been clear enough. Biassed thus, they
have never thought of admitting the evidence of these facts to be
destructive of their conception of the Brain; but have had recourse to various theories, sometimes ingenious, often absurd, to
explain how these facts were really *not* what they seemed to be.
The conception alluded to is thus expressed (I take the first book
of authority at hand) by Todd and Bowman: "The brain, or
some part of it, is the sensorium commune; or, in other words,
mental nervous actions (*acts of volition and sensation*) *cannot take
place without a brain*." *

This is the doctrine of the schools. Now it should be observed
that all physiologists are aware of the fact that animals without
a brain (and animals which never had a brain) manifest some of
the *same* actions which are attributed to sensation and volition,
when the brain is present; yet these actions are said *not* to have
that character when the brain is absent, "*because* the brain is the
exclusive organ of sensation and volition." I confess that the
simpler dictate of logic is to me the easier conception; and that
I can more readily admit the facts to prove the brain *not* to be the
exclusive seat of sensation and volition, than admit that actions,
precisely similar, are in one case sensitive, in the other mechanical; and this inclination gains strength, when close examination
reveals that the reason why the actions of brainless animals are
said to be mechanical (reflex, and without sensation), is solely
because theory declares the Brain to be the only sensorium. If
you pinch a dog's tail, he cries out. His cry is supposed to indicate a sensation of pain. But the physiologist who would reprove
you for having hurt his yelping puppy, would quietly assure you
that this puppy's cries were no evidence of pain or sensation after
its brain had been removed: "Merely reflex, my dear sir!" and

* TODD and BOWMAN *Physiol. Anat.*, I. 522.

he would smile at your supposition that an animal without a brain could feel any sensation.* Nay, even when the brainless animal performs complicated actions to rid itself of some irritating object, and exhibits a *choice* of means for this purpose, men find it easier to consider these as "instinctive" (whatever *that* may be), "reflex," or the "effect of habit," than simply to acklowledge that the Brain is not the sole sensorium.

Science is the endeavour to make the order of our ideas correspond with the order of phenomena — to make our conceptions of things accord with the order of the things themselves; not to make out a scheme *for* Nature, which shall correspond with our ideas. Let us try, therefore, to ascertain what is the order of nervous phenomena.

There are three great sources of knowledge on this subject, all of which, however, are very imperfect: these are Experiment, Pathology, and Anatomy, especially Comparative Anatomy. It has been a fertile theme for declaimers, who knew nothing of the subject they were declaiming on, to brand with odium or ridicule the attempt of anatomists to discover anything respecting mental actions. "What! with your scalpel, fit only to deal with Death, do you hope to penetrate the mysteries of Thought? When you have taken the mechanism to pieces, do you expect the watch to reveal its action; or do you fancy the Soul is less mysterious than a watch?" Feeble nonsense of this kind has imposed on men, because they have been unacquainted with the real methods of science. That we shall ever penetrate the mystery of the Soul, is improbable; equally improbable that we shall ever penetrate the mystery of Life; yet it is certain that the methods of science have enabled us to discover some of the laws of Life, and to

* Indeed, some physiologists have incurred ridicule for having been misled by the cries and struggles of a brainless animal into the belief that the animal manifested sensibility. (See, for example, SCHRÖDER VAN DER KOLK : *Bau und Functionen der Medulla Spinalis*, p. 26, on the "Error shared by so many that the cries of an animal are a proof of Sensibility." The argument relied on by writers who attribute such manifestations to reflex-action, unaccompanied by sensation, rests on the fact that patients with spinal disease are often unconscious of the movements in their limbs produced by external stimulus; we shall hereafter see that this fact in no way contradicts our views, in no way warrants the reflex theory.

assign to the various organs the part each plays; and this in
spite of the fact that "the scalpel is fit only to deal with death."
I would ask these declaimers whether they think that the action
of the watch will be better understood by taking the mechanism
to pieces, and studying each part, and its relations to the rest; or
by assuming certain speculative postulates respecting it, and
making a system out of deductions from those postulates? The
Anatomist attempts to discover the mechanism; the physiologist
attempts to detect the influence which each part exercises. Were
our knowledge of the structure and properties complete, we
should soon know all that could be known respecting the vital
mechanism.

Unhappily our knowledge is very far from complete; and
hence it is that Experiment, though valuable, nay, indispensable,
is often very misleading. We shall see evidence of this in the
course of our inquiry. But there is one direction in which Experiment may always be relied on — the direction of *exclusion*. An
experiment may fail to tell us which is the organ of a particular
function; but it will never fail to tell us which is *not* the organ of
the particular function, if we see the function persisting after the
organ has been removed; and to know what parts are *not* necessary, is to arrive, by exclusion, at those which *are*.

Observation of the effects of disease, accident, or deformity
has a similar value to that of Experiment; but extreme caution
is necessary in interpreting these cases. Anatomy is, of course,
indispensable; and comparative anatomy becomes a sort of final
standard, because it displays the nervous mechanism in all
degrees of complexity, from the simplest to the highest, and thus
reveals what parts are essential. Here also great caution is
requisite, since we never can be quite certain in our interpretation
of the actions of animals.

The Brain, or Encephalon, includes several masses of grey
and white matter. Anatomists are not agreed as to the exact
limits of the brain, some including portions which others exclude;
but all limitations are arbitrary, since the cerebro-spinal axis is
really, a continuous whole — a series of ganglia connected
together by nerve-fibres. The easiest way of arriving at an

intelligible conception of this whole, is to begin by considering the somewhat similar axis in the insect, Fig. 45.

Fig. 45.

These numerous ganglia are separate; imagine them closely fused together, and enclosed by columns of fibres, and you have the Spinal Chord and Medulla Oblongata; then imagine other ganglia, and, superposed on these, the large ganglionic masses of Cerebellum and Cerebrum. The two latter are represented in Fig. 46. This is their external appearance, in profile. The con-

Fig. 46.

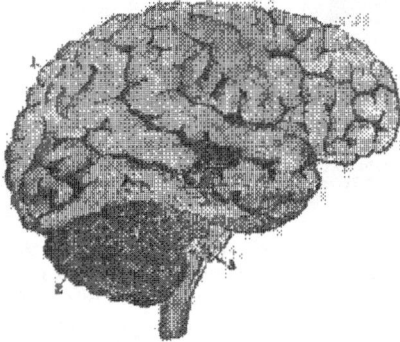

THE HUMAN BRAIN IN PROFILE.
1, Cerebrum; 2, Cerebellum; 3, Medulla Oblongata.

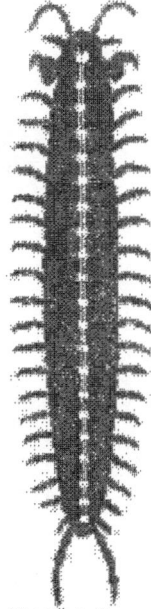

NERVOUS SYSTEM
OF CENTIPEDE.
(After Dalton.)

volutions of grey vesicular matter are outside the white fibrous matter, instead of inside, as in the Medulla Oblongata and Spinal Chord. Fig. 47 gives the aspect of the brain when divided longitudinally.

In the diagram on page 65 we find the general arrangement and connection of the parts lucidly presented, the black masses representing the grey vesicular matter, and the white representing the white fibrous matter.

The Cerebrum, with which we must first occupy ourselves, is composed of two halves, called cerebral hemispheres, united at their base by the *corpus callosum* (Fig. 47, 2). It is in these

Fig. 47.

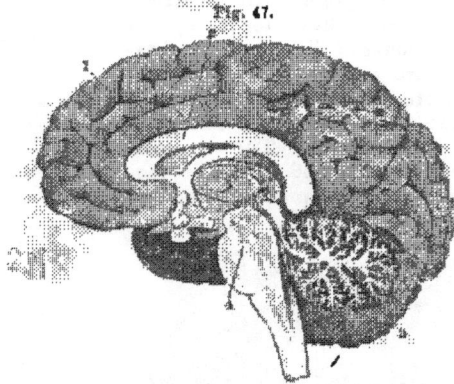

HALF OF THE HUMAN BRAIN IN PROFILE.
1, Convolutions of Cerebrum; 2, the Corpus Callosum, or White Band, which unites the two Hemispheres; 3, Arbor vitæ, or tree-like disposition of grey and white matter in Cerebellum; 4, Pons Varolii and Medulla Oblongata.

hemispheres, or, more strictly speaking, in the grey matter of the convolutions, that most physiologists have agreed to place the seat of Thought, Emotion, Volition, Sensation — in one word, Consciousness — to the exclusion of every other ganglionic mass. Here, and nowhere else, they aver, impressions become sensations. Some physiologists, indeed, are less exclusive, and extend to the ganglia at the base of Cerebrum — *i. e.*, to the *corpora striata*, *optic thalami*, and *corpora quadrigemina* (Fig. 48 — 3, 4, and 5), and to the Medulla Oblongata the privilege of sensation. The reader knows that neither of these opinions can be adopted in our pages: we hold that if the Cerebrum is the organ of what is usually named Thought, it is not the sole seat of Sensation, or Volition.

Comparative Anatomy is freely invoked when it can sustain the argument in favour of the Brain, or the Cerebrum, being the sole seat of Intelligence; but it is quietly disregarded when it flatly contradicts the idea of the Brain being the exclusive seat of Consciousness, or Sensation. We cannot allow two weights and two measures. If the evidence furnished by animals is good in one case, it is good in another. Now, what says evidence?

A survey of the vertebrate classes discloses a remarkable correspondence between the size and development of the Cerebrum, and the energy and variety of mental manifestations. As we pass from fishes and reptiles to birds, and from birds to mammals, and in mammals from the less intelligent

Fig. 48.

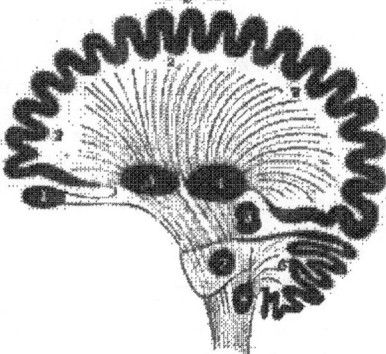

DIAGRAM OF VERTICAL SECTION OF THE BRAIN.

1, Olfactory Ganglion; 2, the Cerebral Hemisphere; 3, Corpus Striatum; 4, Optic Thalamus; 5, Tubercula quadrigemina; 6, Cerebellum; 7, Ganglion of the Pons Varolii; 8, Olivary body, or Ganglion in the Medulla Oblongata. The lines show the direction of the fibres.

(After Dalton.)

to the more intelligent, we notice a decided increase in cerebral development. It is a legitimate inference that the one is in some correspondence with the other, and that Intelligence is one of the functions of the Cerebrum.

Let this be admitted without reservation, although the well-informed anatomist may have many difficulties to propound. I now ask, what we are to make of the fact, that multitudes of animals have *no* cerebrum at all; and that even among fishes there is at least *one* known to be without a vestige of it (and zoologists may yet discover many more); so that, unless we pronounce the Amphioxus, and all the invertebrata, to be mere machines, without sensation, or consciousness, of any kind, we are forced to admit consciousness in the absence of the very organ which is said to be its exclusive seat. There are two answers open. First, it may be said, as it commonly is, that these animals have no Intelligence, only Instinct. This may be true; but to make it of the slightest use, we must be taught what Instinct is; and that teaching is yet to seek. Instinct, like Chance, is one of the words under which men conceal their ignorance from themselves. That the actions of a Bee, or a Crab, which manifest sensation, memory, invention of new methods under new circumstances, not to mention anger, desire, and some unexplained mode of communicating with each other — that these are the actions of "blind instinct," might not be inconceivable, if we knew what instinct really was; but we shall find it difficult to conceive how precisely similar phenomena are attributed to intelligence, when displayed by the Dog or the Monkey. It is probable that the Bee and Crab have no power of forming abstract propositions. It is probable that they are unable to carry on *trains of thought*, *remote from the sensations which are immediately affecting them.* And if we limit the term intelligence to those processes by which one idea calls up another, without the intervention of an external stimulus — to *trains* of ideas, in lieu of single ideas excited by Reflex-Feeling — there may be little objection to saying that Bees have not intelligence.

As our desire must be to come to a distinct understanding on this important point, and not to quarrel over phrases, let us, for a moment, grant that no invertebrate animal has intelligence, in any sense in which it may have pleased men to employ the term. Let instinct explain everything, without itself needing explanation. It will not remove an iota of the objection against the assumption that the Cerebrum is the exclusive seat of sensation and volition. The Bee may have no vestige of intelligence, but you cannot deny that it has sensibility and volition. The brainless Amphioxus may be a very stupid fish, indeed; but you will hardly assert that he wants the consciousness, the sensibility, of other fishes. If you grant me this, dispute is at an end. You merely say that the Cerebrum has certain special functions, among which Intelligence is one; you do not thereby exclude from other ganglia other forms of Sensibility.

So much or the first of the two answers which might be made

to our original difficulty. The second answer will run thus: "It is true that the Bee manifests a certain degree of consciousness, perhaps even of intelligence; but it does so because the ganglia encircling the œsophagus, although not the same as the brain, *represent* the brain in the insect. The two organs are *analogous*, not *homologous*; just as the wings of the bee are analogous to the wings of the bird, but are not the same organs."

It will scarcely be denied that I have placed the strongest argument which the case admits into the mouth of my antagonist. To answer it we have only to consider steadily the relation which function bears to property and structure. Function, as we formerly saw, is the *use* to which certain organs are applied, in virtue of the properties inherent in the structure of those organs. The wings of the bee and the bird are organs moved by muscles, under the stimulus of nerves, so as to beat with a light, expanded surface on the air, and thus make a lever to raise and sustain the body. There are several fundamental resemblances in the two wings; and as these imply similarity in properties, there need only be similarity in the anatomical distribution, to produce a similarity in the uses of the wings. The point to which I wish attention directed is that analogy of structure and connection which determines the analogy of function. Without the moving muscles, the wing would be no organ of flight; without the Contractility of the muscle-fibre, the muscles could not move; without the stimulus and co-ordination of the nervous system, the muscle-fibres could not contract harmoniously, so as to produce this flying movement. It is because the two wings resemble each other in such particulars, that, in spite of their many differences, the wing of the bee and the wing of the bird are both organs of flight.

In the same way the brain of a bee is analogous to the brain of a bird; there are many and important differences, but there are fundamental resemblances of structure and connection, of property and function. It is because they are both formed of ganglionic substance that they have both the property of Sensibility. It is because they are both connected with the organs of special Sense, and are the chief centres with which directly, or indirectly

5*

all the nerves are connected, that they both have the supreme function of what has been aptly termed *Cerebration.*

This is the teaching of Comparative Anatomy, and its lesson is valuable. If it shows us how the cephalic ganglia of an insect may represent the Brain of a vertebrate animal, and thus seem to justify the doctrine of the brain being the exclusive seat of consciousness; it also, and by the same evidence, shows that Sensibility must belong to *all* ganglia, as ganglia, and not to any special group. It shows that the Brain of a vertebrate animal does not derive its functions from any arrangement of its tissues, nor from the possession of cerebral hemispheres, nor from any other morphological character: since these functions are performed (the chief of them at least) by ganglia having no other resemblance to the Brain than fundamental similarity of tissue, and similarity of organic connection. The Brain derives its Sensibility from its ganglionic structure, *in which it resembles all other ganglia.* It derives its functions from the various organs to which this Sensibility is made subservient by anatomical connection.

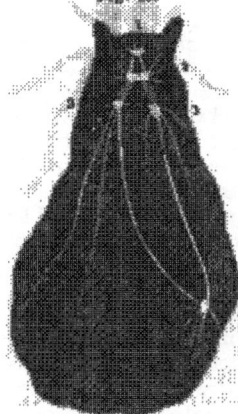

Fig. 49.

NERVOUS SYSTEM OF APLYSIA. (After Dalton.)

This point may be illustrated in a comparison of the organisation of a mollusc and an insect. Fig. 49 shows the nervous system of a Sea-Hare (*Aplysia*) in its organic relations. The ganglia of this mollusc are large enough to serve many functions, if they were connected with various organs. But the body of the Sea-Hare is not divided into segments, each segment having different organs: it is one large contractile mass, having no legs to walk with, no wings to fly with, no claws to grasp with; it crawls slowly along by means of its large fleshy under-surface, called "the foot." Having so few means of acting on the external

world, there can be little *combination* of actions, little of the
multifarious instinct shown by the garden-beetle, (Fig. 50.)

Here we see **an** organism made up of a number of *different*
organs, each organ having different uses; consequently **its**
nervous system has more various functions. Could we measure
the nerve-force developed by the shape-
less Sea-Hare, and the tiny but complex Beetle, we should doubtless find
that in *amount* the superiority of the
former was manifest, although its *functional* character was lower.

I conceive, therefore, that Com-
parative Anatomy irresistibly disproves
the notion of the Brain, or any other
ganglionic mass, being the sole and exclusive seat of Sensibility or Consciousness; and we shall hereafter see still
stronger evidence in the observations of
experimentalists and pathologists. No
one will misunderstand these remarks
to mean that the Brain is not one great
centre of Sensation and Volition — the

Fig. 50.

NERVOUS SYSTEM OF GARDEN
BEETLE.
(After Milne-Edwards.)

chief and dominant organ of the whole psychical mechanism.
I have said before that it has the noblest functions, but it does
not exclude the other ganglia from their share in the general
Consciousness. In it all the sensations derived through the
Senses and Viscera are summed up, combined, modified, and in
some profoundly mysterious manner elaborated into ideas. It is
generalissimo of the whole army, controlling, directing, and in-
spiring the actions of all subordinate officers. But to suppose
that these subordinates have not also their independent functions,
is a mistake. The generals, colonels, captains, sergeants, cor-
porals, and common soldiers, are individual men, like their com-
mander-in-chief, with inferior power, and with different functions,
according to their respective positions. But if the commander-
in-chief be killed, the army has still its generals. If the generals
be killed, the regiments have still their colonels. Nay, even a
corporal's company may be kept together by an energetic cor-

poral. And this we shall see to be the case with animals when their brain has been removed; each separate part of the organism has its general, colonel, or corporal.

The Brain, as generalissimo, needs an enormous supply of blood. Haller estimates the quantity at one-fifth of the amount sent to the whole body. In mere mass, also, the brain predominates; but this is only true in the higher animals: in frogs, reptiles, aud fish, it is *less* than the Spinal Chord.

In man the *average* weight of the whole brain is fifty ounces. In woman the average is five ounces less. Taking 50 oz. 3¼ drachms as the weight of the whole encephalon, the following are the respective weights of the three principal masses:—

				oz.	drs.
Cerebrum,	.	.	.	43	15¼
Cerebellum,	.	.	.	6	4
Pons, and Med. Oblong.,	.			0	15½
				50	3¼*

In the Cerebrum and Cerebellum, or big and little brain (Fig. 46 — 1, 2), the grey cellular matter is outside, and the white fibrous matter is inside. The outside presents a series of irregular folds or *convolutions;* and it is in the convolutions of the Cerebrum that physiologists have imagined all Sensibility and Thought exclusively reside. The degree of intelligence possessed by a man, or animal, has been confidently attributed to the number and depth of these convolutions — *i. e.* to the amount of grey matter. This idea has become so popular that I shall probably excite surprise when I suggest that it is altogether without a scientific basis. In the first place, intellectual action, which is surely a *function,* is made on this hypothesis a *property* of the grey matter, irrespective of any anatomical connection; and this is very unscientific. In the second place, although the amount of grey matter may, other things being equal, determine the amount of force developed, yet, as we saw in the comparison of the Sea-Hare with the Beetle, it will not determine *functional* superiority. In the third place, accurate measurements show

* QUAIN's *Anatomy.* By SHARPEY and ELLIS, 6th edit., II. 434.

that there is no solid ground for the opinion to rest on. M. Baillarger instituded an elaborate series of measurements, from which it appeared that the increase of the grey matter was *not* accompanied by an increase of intelligence; whereas increase of the white matter was accompanied by increase of intelligence.[*] Further. M. Camille Dareste has shown that the number and depth of the convolutions bear *no constant* relation to the amount of intelligence in animals.[**] Once imagine that intelligence has its seat in the grey matter of the convolutions, and these facts become inexplicable. But conceive intellectual action as *functional*, and the difficulty vanishes. No development of the pectoral muscles will enable an ostrich to fly, because the ostrich has not wings adapted for flight. In like manner no development of the grey convolutions will enable an animal to manifest intellectual actions, unless these convolutions are in direct connection with the other necessary parts of the mechanism. We can understand how particular aptitudes—say for drawing or music—may exist in men of small brains; or be entirely deficient in men of large brains. The requisite adjustment of the nervous mechanism is present in the one case, and absent in the other. Now what is true of particular forms of intellectual action, must be true of all. I conclude, therefore, that a larger amount of grey matter will produce a larger amount of Sensibility; but the uses which this Sensibility will subserve in the animal economy, will depend on the anatomical connections—on the complexity of the nervous mechanism.

II. FUNCTIONS OF THE CEREBRUM. — These preliminaries may help us to some understanding of the cerebral functions, by directing attention to its organic connections, native or acquired. Unhappily, as every one knows, Anatomy will not of itself disclose function; but it will help us to *explain* function, when discovered. The mere inspection of a knife would never disclose to a child the various uses of the knife; but having seen the knife in use, he would learn that it was the blade, and

[*] BAILLARGER. *Gazette Médicale*, 19th April 1845.
[**] DARESTE: *Annales des Sciences*, 3ᵉ série, xvii. 50, and 4ᵉ série, i. 73.
Compare also LEURET, L 577 *et seq.*

not the handle, which had the property of cutting; and after a
little experience, he would ascertain that this property of
cutting depended on the fineness of the edge. From this he
would rapidly generalise, and conclude that all hard substances
having a fine edge might be employed to cut with; and that
steel, by reason of its hardness, was pre-eminently suited to
that purpose. It is the same with anatomy. When observation
has shown us the use of an organ, we can explain the action
of its separate parts.

Observation has, in various ways, remarked that the cerebral hemispheres are pre-eminently, if not exclusively, devoted
to the intellectual actions. Whenever we hear of an idiot, we
conclude that his cerebrum is very small, or malformed; whenever we see a man with an unusually small cerebrum, we conclude him to be an idiot.

There can be no doubt of the all-important participation
of the Cerebrum in mental manifestation, when we learn that,
if accident have produced a hole in the skull, we can, by a
slight pressure on the Cerebrum, throw the patient into a state
of stupor, seeing nothing, hearing nothing, thinking nothing.
Pressure on the Cerebellum produces no such results.

Sir Astley Cooper relates in his *Lectures on Surgery* the
following remarkable case: A sailor fell from the yard-arm on
the deck, and was taken up insensible. For some months he
remained in the hospital at Gibraltar perfectly insensible, yet
otherwise healthy. He was then conveyed to Deptford, where
Mr. Davy visited him, having been informed by the surgeon
of the curious case. "It is a man who has been insensible for
many months: he lies on his back with very few signs of life; he
breathes indeed, has a pulse, and some motion in his fingers;
but in all other respects he is deprived of all powers of mind,
volition, or sensation." Mr. Davy, on examining the patient,
found a slight depression on one part of the head. Being informed of the accident which had occasioned it, he had the man
removed to St. Thomas's Hospital under the care of Mr. Cline.
It was here Sir Astley Cooper saw him "lying on his back,
breathing without any great difficulty, his pulse regular, his
arms extended, and his fingers moving to and fro to the motion of

his heart, so that you could count his pulse by the motion of his fingers. *If he wanted food, he had the power of moving his lips and tongue; and this action of his mouth was the signal to his attendants for supplying this want.*"

I interrupt the narrative at this point to request the reader's attention to the passage in italics, which has apparently escaped the notice of the numerous writers who have referred to this case. The man's "consciousness" is said to have been obliterated; he had, we are told, lost all sensation and all volition; yet we see that the sensation of Hunger was not gone, nor the volition which indicated by signs that food was wanted. The current doctrine is incompetent to explain such facts; but according to the doctrine propounded in these pages, the facts are such as *a priori* might have been announced.

"Mr. Cline," continues Sir Astley, "on examining his head, found an obvious depression; and thirteen months and a few days after the accident, he was carried into the operating theatre and there trephined. The depressed portion of the bone was elevated from the skull. While he was lying on the table the motion of his fingers went on during the operation, but no sooner was the portion of bone raised than it ceased. The operation was performed at one o'clock in the afternoon; and at four o'clock, as I was walking through the wards, I went up to the man's bedside, and was surprised to see him sitting up in bed. He had raised himself on his pillow. I asked him if he felt any pain, and he immediately put his hand to his head. This showed that volition and sensation were returning. In four days from that time the man was able to get out of bed, and began to converse; and in a few days more he was able to tell us where he came from. He recollected the circumstance of his having been pressed and carried down to Plymouth or Falmouth; but from that moment up to the time the operation was performed, his mind had remained in a perfect state of oblivion. He had drunk, as it were, of the cup of Lethe; he had suffered a complete death as far as regarded his bodily and mental powers; but by removing a small portion of bone with the saw, he was at once restored to all the functions of his mind, and almost all the powers of his body."

This is in many respects an interesting case. The psychologist should note that the man's memory was incompetent to recall not only everything that had passed from the moment of the accident, but also the whole series of events and sensations which occurred from the time of his impressment till that of his accident, which occurred in the Mediterranean.

It would be easy to multiply cases which point in this direction, and warrant the suspicion that the Cerebrum is the seat of intellectual action. But they only warrant a suspicion, they do not establish a certitude. Other evidence is needed. It might be asked whether other parts of the encephalon may not have been implicated — whether, when the Cerebrum is pressed upon, some interference with the masses underneath has not been induced — and whether the loss of mental manifestation may not result from this interference. The heart is assuredly not the seat of intelligence; yet if we check the action of the heart, we suspend all mental manifestations. What proof have we that the Cerebrum does not also act in some such indirect manner? Here precise Experiment becomes necessary. Unhappily precise Experiment is here of such excessive difficulty, that we shall find experimenters often arriving at different results. The Cerebrum is not a mass definitely separated from the other masses, so that its removal can be effected without interfering with other parts. The very complexity of the connections established between it and other centres, renders every experiment dubious, except in that negative direction previously pointed out (p. 62).

The researches of Flourens made an epoch.* They were very striking: the conclusions he drew from them were announced in that systematic, definite, and absolute style, which is characteristic of French writers; and by reason of their being easily understood and easily remembered, they gained European acceptance, in spite of the reservations of Cuvier and Müller. They are really very captivating works. They seem to make the whole matter so clear and simple, that criticism and reservation are regarded as impertinent disturbers of a com-

* FLOURENS: *Recherches expérimentales sur les propriétés et les fonctions du Système Nerveux*, 1824; and *Expériences sur le Système Nerveux*, 1825.

fortable conviction. But the serious student learns to distrust all epigrams in science. Whenever a complex question is answered by a neat formula, pretending to embrace all the phenomena, and to clear up all obscurities, it is a wise caution which suspects there is something wrong. I am far from wishing to detract from the merit of Flourens. He made an epoch, and deserves honourable recognition. But I do not think his conclusions tenable in the face of evidence; his facts are not unfrequently in contradiction with what more careful experiment and observation disclose; and his conclusions are occasionally contradicted by the very facts he himself records, although theoretic preconceptions blinded him to their significance.

Flourens declares that when he removed the whole of the Cerebrum from Pigeons and Fowls, they lost *all* sensation, *all* perception, *all* instinct, and *all* volition. They lived perfectly well for months after the operation, if the food were placed in their mouths; but they never *sought* their food; they never *took* it, even when their beaks were plunged into it: they could swallow, and digest the grains; but they had no instinct to make them seek, no volition to make them pick up the grains. They *saw* nothing, although the iris remained irritable; they heard nothing; they could not smell. A state of stupor came on, resembling that of deep sleep. All voluntary action ceased. If they were thrown into the air, they flew; if irritated, they moved away; but if left to themselves, they remained motionless, with the head under the wing, as in sleep. Now, inasmuch as these effects always ensue when the Cerebrum is removed, and *never* when only the Cerebellum is removed, he concludes that all instincts, volitions, and sensations "belong exclusively to the cerebral lobes."

It should be stated that all experimenters agree in one cardinal point, namely, that removal of the cerebral hemispheres throws the animal into a stupor resembling that of deep sleep, Memory being almost, if not totally, destroyed. In this respect we may compare the case previously cited from Sir Astley Cooper (p. 72).

But all experimenters do not agree in other points named by Flourens; nor in the conclusions he has drawn. On the con-

trary, it is very certain, and we shall find evidence even in
Flourens himself, that all instincts and all sensations are *not*
destroyed by the removal of the cerebral lobes.

Let us hear Bouillaud on this subject.* He repeated the experiment of Flourens, removing the whole of the Cerebrum from
the Brain of a fowl; and he thus records his observations: "This
fowl passes the greater part of her time asleep, but she awakes
at intervals, and *spontaneously*. When she goes to sleep, she
turns her head on one side and buries it in the feathers of the
wing; when she awakes, she shakes herself, flaps her wings,
and opens her eyes. In this respect there is no difference observable between the mutilated and the perfect bird. She does
not seem to be moved at all by the noise made round about her,
but a very slight irritation of the skin suffices to awaken her
instantaneously. When the irritation ceases, she relapses into
sleep. When awake, she is often seen to cast stupid glances
here and there, *to change her place, and walk spontaneously*. If
put into a cage, *she tries to escape;* but she comes and goes without any purpose, or rational design. When either foot, wing,
or head is pinched, she withdraws it; when she is laid hold of,
she *struggles to escape, and screams;* but no sooner is she liber-
ated than she rests motionless. If severely irritated, she
screams loudly; but it is not only to express pain that she uses
her voice, for it is by no means rare to *hear her cackle and cluck
a little spontaneously;* that is to say, when no external irritation
affects her. Her stupidity is profound; she knows neither objects nor places, nor persons, and is completely divested of
memory in this respect: not only does she not know how to
seek or take food, she does not even know how to swallow it
when placed in her beak — it must be pushed to the throat.
Nevertheless her indocility, her movements, her agitation,
attest that she *feels* the presence of a strange body. Inasmuch
as external objects excite in her no idea, no desire, she pays no
attention to them; but she is not absolutely deprived of the
power of attention, for if much irritated her attention is
awakened. She knows not how to escape an enemy, nor how to

* BOUILLAUD: *Recherches Expérimentales sur les Fonctions du Cerveau en
général*, 1830, p. 5 et seq.

defend herself. All her actions, in a word, are blind, without reflection, without knowledge."

In this recital, the evidence both of *sensation* and *instinct* is incontestable, to any unprejudiced mind. Bouillaud, in commenting on his observations, remarks, that assuredly *all* sensation was not destroyed since the sensibilities of touch and pain were very manifest. Nor is it certain, he says, that the fowl heard nothing, saw nothing. It is true that she stumbled against objects, and knew not how to avoid them; but having lost all *memory*, that is intelligible. She opened her eyes on awaking, looked about, and showed a sensibility in the pupil to light; which, he thinks, is incompatible with the absence of all sensation of sight.

The experiments of Longet* seem decisive on this latter point. Having removed the whole of the Cerebrum from a pigeon, he observed that whenever he approached a light brusquely to its eyes, there was contraction of the pupil, and even winking; but, what was still more remarkable, "when I gave a rotatory motion to the candle, and at such a distance that there could be no sensation of heat, the pigeon made a similar movement with its head. These observations, renewed several times in the presence of persons who were at my lectures, left no doubt of the persistence of sensibility to light after removal of the cerebral lobes." We have only to think of the baby following with its eyes the light moved before it, to understand the kind of impression produced by the candle on the pigeon. Longet also declares that his experiments prove the existence of sensations of sound, after removal of the whole cerebrum.

Dr. Dalton, giving the results of numerous experiments he performed, says that removal of the Cerebrum plunges the animal in "a profound stupor, in which he is *almost* entirely inattentive to surrounding objects. . . . Occasionally the bird opens its eyes with a vacant stare, stretches his neck, perhaps shakes his bill once or twice, or smooths down the feathers upon his shoulders, and then relapses into his former apathetic condition. This state of immobility, however, is *not* accompanied by the loss of sight, of hearing, or of ordinary sensibility. *All these functions*

* LONGET: *Traité de Physiologie*, II. 240.

remain, as well as that of voluntary motion. If a pistol be discharged behind the back of the animal, he at once opens his eyes,
moves his head half round, and gives evident signs of having
heard the report; but he immediately becomes quiet again, and
pays no further attention to it. Sight is also retained, since the
bird will sometimes fix its eye on a particular object, and watch
it for several seconds together." *

While, therefore, Flourens concludes from his experiments
that the Cerebrum is the seat of *all* sensation and all volition; and
Bouillaud concludes that it is most probably the seat of *none*;
Dr. Dalton, more philosophical than either, concludes that the
functions of the Cerebrum are restricted to those usually classed
as intellectual. "The animal," he truly says, "is still capable,
after removal of the hemispheres, of receiving sensations from
external objects. But these sensations appear to make upon
him no lasting impression. He is incapable of connecting with
his perceptions any distinct succession of ideas. He hears, for
example, the report of a pistol, but he is not alarmed by it; for
the sound, although distinctly perceived, does not suggest any
idea of danger or injury. The memory is altogether destroyed,
and the recollection of sensations is not retained from one moment to another. The limbs and muscles are still under the
control of the will; but the will itself is inactive, because apparently it lacks its usual mental stimulus and direction." **

Translated into the language of these pages, the experiments show that sensations are excited in the centres to which
the respective sensory nerves belong; these centres, in turn, excite the sensibility of the great centre (Cerebrum) with which
they are connected: these reflex, or secondary, excitations call
forth others (trains of ideas), and one of these (say the idea of
danger) acts by reflex on the motor-organs. By removing the
great centre, you remove the possibility of its various reflexes;
you do not remove the sensibility of other centres.

Dr. Dalton reminds us how disturbance of the cerebral func-

* DALTON: *Human Physiology*, Philadelphia, 1859, p. 362. This lucid
exposition of the principles of Physiology is — like the similar work of
Dr. Draper — an honour to American science.
** DALTON, p. 362.

tions in human beings recalls these observations on animals.
"In cases of impending apoplexy, or of softening of the cerebral
substance, among the earliest and most common phenomena is a
loss or impairment of the memory. The patient forgets the
names of particular objects, or particular persons; or he is unable to calculate numbers with his usual facility. His mental
derangement is often shown in the undue estimate which he
forms of passing events. He is no longer able to appreciate the
true relation between different objects and different phenomena.
Thus he will show an exaggerated degree of solicitude about a
trivial occurrence, and will pay no attention to other matters of
importance. As the difficulty increases, he becomes careless of
the directions and advice of his attendants, and must be watched
and managed like a child or an imbecile. After a certain period
he no longer appreciates the lapse of time, and even loses the
distinction between day and night. Finally, when the injury to
the hemispheres is complete, the senses may still remain active
and impressible while the patient is completely deprived of intelligence and judgment."*

Having seen how far other experimenters are from confirm-
ing the conclusions of Flourens, let us glance at his record of observations, and we shall find there evidence that *all* sensation
and *all* volition cannot be localised in the Cerebrum.

Speaking of a fowl whose Cerebrum was removed the day before, he says, "she shakes her head and feathers, sometimes
even she cleans and sharpens them with her beak; sometimes she
changes the leg on which she sleeps, for, like other birds, she
sleeps habitually resting upon one leg. In all these cases she
seems like a man, asleep, who, without quite waking, changes
his place, and reposes in another, from the *fatigue* occasioned
by the previous posture; he selects one more *comfortable*, stretches
himself, yawns, shakes himself a little, and falls asleep again.
. . . On the third day the fowl is no longer so calm; she comes
and goes, but without motive and without an aim; and if she
encounters an obstacle on her path, she knows not how to avoid
it."** In his second work he remarks of a Duck operated on in
the same way: "As I mentioned last year *à propos* of fowls, the

* DALTON. p. 363.   ** FLOURENS, p. 89.

duck walks about oftener, and for a longer time together, when
it is fasting than when it is fed."*

Here he observes the unmistakable evidence of feelings of
Hunger, Fatigue, and Discomfort in animals which, according
to him, have lost all sensation. He also observes the operation
of instinct (cleaning the feathers), and of spontaneous activity
(walking about), in animals said to have lost all instinct and all
volition. We can only repeat the judgment of Johann von
Müller: "Flourens concluded from his experiments that the
cerebral hemispheres are alone the central organ of sensations.
But this is not a legitimate inference from his highly interesting
observations, which, as Cuvier remarked, prove directly the
contrary of this."

If we review the evidence furnished by experiment and observation, we shall perceive that although the cerebral hemispheres play an important part in the psychical mechanism, they
are not the exclusive centres of sensation, instinct, or volition,
since all these are manifested when the cerebrum is removed.
This is one step towards the demonstration of the truth, that
neither the whole brain, nor any portion of it, can be the exclusive organ of the mind. This is only a step, however, and
we must wait until the whole nervous system has come under review before the demonstration can be complete.

We have still to ascertain what are the functions of the
Cerebrum. The first point we notice is, that no nerve whatever
issues from it. It is the ganglionic centre with which all nerves
are indirectly connected, but from which no nerve takes its rise.
All its vast array of nerve-fibres forms but a connecting apparatus,
by means of which it is played upon by all other centres, and can
play upon them. We are justified, therefore, in concluding
that not one of the sensations excited by external stimuli can be
directly produced in the Cerebrum, but must reach it through
the ganglion of each stimulated nerve. It is on this ground, I
presume, that Prochaska, Müller, Schröder van der Kolk, and
others, have maintained that consciousness of sensations is no
function of the Cerebrum at all. I am not sure that I perfectly
seize their meaning; but every argument seems to be against the

* FLOURENS: Expériences, p. 30.

idea that the Cerebrum acts as the original seat of *sensations derived through the sensory nerves*. This position must be clearly understood. The Cerebrum I conceive to be a seat of Sensibility, because of its ganglionic nature. But the forms of Sensibility excited in it must necessarily differ from those excited in other ganglia, which have different organic connections. It has no nerves distributed to the skin, or to the organs of special sense; it cannot, therefore, have the peculiar kinds of sensation which are excited through the skin and organs of sense. Its Sensibility can only be excited through the agency of its own nerve-fibres; and these connect its several parts together, and connect it with the other centres, upon which it plays, and through which it is played upon. We have no difficulty in understanding that, because the organic apparatus with which the optic centre is connected, differs from that of the auditory centre, the forms of Sensibility excited in these centres will be different. Nor should we have any difficulty in understanding why a ray of light acting on the optic centre must excite a different form of Sensibility from that which would be excited by its acting on the Cerebrum *through* the optic centre, *i. e.* giving the *sensation* of light in the one case, and the *perception* of light in the other.

By this explanation I have endeavoured to make it clear how the *forms* of Sensibility excited in the cerebral hemispheres must necessarily be in many respects unlike those excited in the ganglia, which are *directly* stimulated by sensory nerves. The difference between a *perception* of sound and a *sensation* of sound is as great as the difference between the sensation of pain when a skin-nerve is divided, and the sensation of a flash of light when the optic nerve is divided.

The Sensibilities of the Cerebrum are usually grouped under two general heads — Intellect and Emotion. Hitherto it has been mysterious how an organ so homogeneous as the Cerebrum, wherein each convolution is but a repetition of the others, should nevertheless serve functions so various as those of the Intellect and the Emotions. Even those who reject the phrenological localisation of the separate faculties, admit that the front part of the Cerebrum seems specially devoted to the Intellect, and the middle and back parts to the Emotions and Instincts. But nei-

ther phrenologists, nor their antagonists, to my knowledge, have
had any scientific explanation to offer; and as the views advocated in these pages seem to me to present a possible elucidation
of the difficulty, I will first state the objection, and then endeavour to remove it.

The convolutions of the Cerebrum are everywhere similar and
continuous, like so many folds in a piece of velvet. They are not
separate; they are not different; they are identical. Why, then,
can we suppose they are the organs of very different functions?
We do not imagine that one lobe of the liver, or lobule of the
kidney, plays a different part from that of its fellows; why, then,
do we imagine that one convolution, or group of convolutions,
can be devoted to reasoning, and another to loving, one to the
perception of colours, and another to an instinct?

The phrenologists evade this difficulty by saying that "observation teaches them the facts *are* so." Without here disputing
this assertion, I must remark that it in no way removes the scientific difficulty; and as Phrenology professes to be the Physiology of the Brain, it is bound to connect its observations
with some scientific explanation of the nervous mechanism involved.

We need not evade the difficulty; for if Function be determined by anatomical connection, it is clear that, although the
Cerebrum may be one homogeneous structure, it will have
various functions if it be connected with various organs. Assuming that every convolution has the same general property of
Sensibility, our principles lead to the conclusion that the peculiar
kind of Sensibility excited in each will depend upon the nature
of the stimulus; and the nature of the stimulus will of course be
determined by the organic apparatus effecting it. A stimulus
through the optic centre must be different from a stimulus through
the gustatory centre; and both of these must be different from a
stimulus through the viscera. The stimulus received through
the centre of Perception, will necessarily differ from that received
through the centre of the Appetites; and thus, widely as an Idea
differs from an Emotion, they are both peculiar forms of Sensibility.

Although the general relations of the cerebral convolutions

are thus indicated, it would require an entirely new investigation
of the anatomy of the Brain to carry this into detail. For the
present our knowledge is too imperfect to admit even of an attempt at detail. I will, however, venture to suggest the point of
view which might direct inquiry. If we ask what are the chief
divisions into which all psychical phenomena group themselves,
we shall find that the popular classification into Thinking and
Feeling, or Mental and Moral, lucidly and broadly indicates the
primary groups. Let us, ideally, decompose these into six
centres, three for each division. In the first group we may place
Sensations, Perceptions, and Ideas — the various combinations
of which represent intellectual activity. In the second group we
may place Sensations, Instincts, or Appetites and Emotions — the various combinations of which represent moral activity.

Sensation thus forms the point of departure for each series.
But we have already seen that there are various *kinds* of sensation, and that these fall into two distinguishable groups —
namely, Sense-sensations and Systemic-sensations. The first are
derived through the organs of special Sense, *i. e.* Sight, Hearing,
Taste, Smell, and Touch. The second are derived from the
Viscera, Muscles — in a word, from the system at large. The
first may almost be considered as *impersonal*, because they bring
us into conscious relation with external objects — with the Not-
self. The second are, on the contrary, intensely personal, because they do not bring us into conscious relation with external
objects, but only with what is passing within our bodies. Reason
has often been considered impersonal, but no one ever considered
Emotion to be so. The intellectual operations always imply an
externality; even when we are speculating about our own feelings or mental operations, we always view them as if *apart* from
ourselves. The Emotions have a deeper root in personality.
Every man, unless he be a subtle psychologist, believes that the
redness is in the rose, the sweetness in the apple, and the loudness
in the thunder. But no man, not even the psychologist, believes
that the love or hate, the fear or reverence, the desire or disgust,
which moves him, belongs to the object which excites the
feeling.

6*

This externality of the Sense-sensations, and internality of the Systemic-sensations, creates a broad line of demarcation between the Perceptions which arise from the one, and the Appetites, or Instincts, which arise from the other; and these, in turn, issue in the very different forms of Sensibility known respectively as Thought and Emotion.

It has never been doubted that our perceptions and ideas have their origin in sensations. The old philosophic adage that nothing is in the intellect which was not previously in the sense, may be equivocal, from a restricted use of the word sense; but it points to the well-authenticated fact, that sensation lies at the basis of all intellectual operation. I feel myself justified, therefore, in considering *Ideation* as the form of cerebral sensibility which is determined by the cerebral connections with the ganglia of special Sense. In like manner, *Emotion* may be considered as the form of cerebral sensibility which is determined by connections with the ganglia of visceral sensation. It was formerly believed that the heart, the liver, and the spleen, were seats of the passions; popular language still preserves this notion; but Bichat was the last great anatomist who countenanced the doctrine. Since that doctrine has fallen into discredit there has been an undue neglect of the important fact which it endeavoured to explain, namely, the immediate influence exercised over the emotions by the condition of the viscera, and the influence exercised over the viscera by the state of the emotions. Both the ancient and the modern doctrine are reconciled in the view I have put forth, which makes the viscera the *main* source of emotions, just as the organs of sense are the main source of ideas.

Although the mental phenomena are thus grouped under two primary and six secondary divisions, to which anatomy may one day assign corresponding parts of the nervous apparatus, we must never lose sight of the fact, that there is perpetual action and interaction between the various centres. But this consideration leads us into the domain of Psychology, and we must therefore pause here. It is not for us to attempt to unravel the tangled mystery of mental operations. We have not been able to do more than indicate in a very general manner the relations existing between the Mind and the Brain; and having done so, we have now to ask, whether the cerebral hemispheres have any *other* functions? I think they have; but as physiologists have. not directed their attention in this direction, there are no experiments on record to throw light on it. Lallemand conceives that there must be some necessary dependence of the Spinal Chord on the Cerebrum in the higher animals, and it is to this he attributes the fact, certainly significant, that children born without a brain never live more than three or four days: they do not die of starvation, for they swallow food quite well. He also observes that the *movements* of these brainless children are much feebler than those of others at the same age.* One might, indeed, suspect the cause to lie deeper; the same cause which determined the malformation may determine the feeble vitality. But Lallemand's idea is strengthened by the observation of Flourens,** that removal of the cerebrum retards digestion; and by the familiar fact of the intimate sympathy between the Mind and all the organic functions.

It is perhaps on this ground that we may explain the disproportion between the mental activity and the size of brain in certain animals. The elephant has a brain three times heavier than that of man; and that of the whale is nearly twice as heavy as that of man. It is true that in the elephant and whale the cerebrum is not so much greater than the other parts, as is the case in man, in whom, as we saw, it is eight times the size of the other parts; nevertheless the preponderance of the cerebrum is considerable, and there is certainly no preponderance of mental power to correspond with it. When, however, we conceive the cerebrum as the chief nervous centre having dominion over all others — when we assign to it participation in other functions besides those of mental activity, the immense size of the body of the elephant and whale seems to justify an equivalent development of the cerebrum.

On this, however, we must be content with hypotheses. Science has no carefully-collated facts to justify us in anything

* Quoted by SOLLY, *On the Brain*, p. 455.
** FLOURENS: *Recherches*, p. 129.

beyond a general surmise that the cerebral hemispheres have more than an intellectual and volitional part to play: that they are directly connected with the functions of intelligence, no reasonable man will doubt; and having arrived at this conclusion, we will now pass on to the examination of the other centres, by anatomists grouped together under the general term Brain.

CHAPTER IX.

(Continued.)

THE MIND AND THE BRAIN.

SECTION II. — THE CEREBELLUM AND MEDULLA OBLONGATA.

Description of the Cerebellum — Gall's hypothesis — Experiments of Flourens to prove that the Cerebellum co-ordinates muscular movements; arguments against such an hypothesis — Flat contradictions — The experiments of Schiff — Evidence furnished by Comparative Anatomy; and by Disease — Absence of the Cerebellum not accompanied by absence of co-ordination: Combette's case — The Cerebellum as a seat of sensation and volition — Has the Cerebellum any share in intellectual operations? — Description of the Medulla oblongata — Is the Medulla distinct from the Spinal Chord? — The Medulla a seat of volition — Why it is considered a seat of sensation — Is there a "vital point?" — Experiments of Flourens contradicted by the experiments of Schiff and Brown-Séquard — Influence of the Medulla on the heart's action — Why a "shock" of grief or joy causes death — Pain the cause of death — Summary of the functions of the Brain.

AFTER the Cerebrum, or big brain, our attention must be claimed by the Cerebellum, or little brain, which, in man, lies underneath the greater mass, as seen in Fig. 51, 2. The two organs present some differences in structure, but they agree in principal points: they are both composed of grey matter externally, and internally of white matter. The convolutions of the Cerebellum are more compressed, and have the appearance of leaflets. Like the Cerebrum, it is totally insensible to pricks or

Fig. 51.

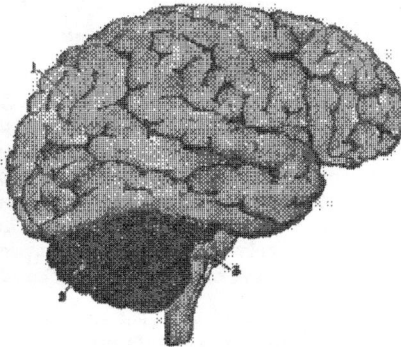

THE HUMAN BRAIN IN PROFILE.
1, Cerebrum; 2, Cerebellum; 3, Medulla Oblongata.

pinches. Its relation to the other centres is roughly indicated in the following diagram (Fig. 52).

Gall, to whom we owe so great a debt for the impulse he gave to the study of the nervous system, assigned the sexual instinct to the Cerebellum. This hypothesis, after having been extensively discussed, is now, I believe, rejected by all good physiologists; and we must declare with Longet that a calm survey of the evidence forces the conclusion that neither Anatomy nor Pathology, neither Experiment nor Comparative Anatomy, justifies our assigning the sexual instinct to the Cerebellum. *

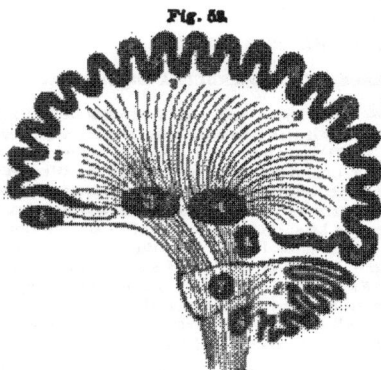

Fig. 52.

DIAGRAM OF VERTICAL SECTION OF THE BRAIN.

1, Olfactory Ganglion; 2 the Cerebral Hemisphere; 3, Corpus Striatum; 4, Optic Thalamus; 5, Tubercula quadrigemina; 6, Cerebellum; 7, Ganglion of the Pons Varolii; 8, Olivary body, or Ganglion in the Medulla Oblongata. The lines show the direction of the fibres.

(After Dalton.)

It is extremely probable that an antagonism to Phrenology, and a desire to find it in the wrong, has considerably sharpened the wits of physiologists, in the investigation of this point, making them at once more patient in research, and more circumspect in interpretation, than they are wont to be when no doctrine is at stake. If a little of this animus had moved them to scrutinise more closely the hypothesis first propounded by Flourens, it would never have obtained the too facile acquiescence of Europe;

* LONGET: Traité de Physiol. II.; LELUT: Rejet de la doctrine organologique; LEURET et GRATIOLET: Anat. Comp. du Système Nerveux, t. 427, 547. Dr. CARPENTER has also collected evidence on this point in his Human Physiology.

and our science would have been burdened with one error less. But there was nothing at stake in the hypothesis that the Cerebellum was the organ of muscular co-ordination — nothing but Truth; and, unhappily, the desire for Truth does not move the passions of men with the same energy as a desire to attack or defend a system.

If there is a position which our text-books represent as impreguable, it is that the co-ordination, or regulation, of muscular movements is the peculiar function of the Cerebellum. It seems looked on as a first truth. The experiments of Flourens and Bouillaud are considered as having established the point beyond dispute.* With what justice we will now inquire.

Flourens removed, by successive slices, the Cerebellum of a goose. With the first slices he noted hesitation and want of harmony in the movements of the bird; with the second slices the walk became a stagger; with the final slices all power of locomotion, all power of retaining the equilibrium of the body, disappeared. Throughout these operations the intellectual and sensitive faculties were undisturbed. "The Cerebellum, therefore," concludes Flourens, "is the seat of the co-ordination of muscular movement; but not the seat of intelligence, sensation, volition. The Cerebrum *feels* and *wills;* the Medulla oblongata and spinal chord *execute;* the Cerebellum *co-ordinates.*" This is one of those neat epigrams which captivate assent, and rest in the memory; and as regards the Cerebellum, it receives further assistance from the following statement made by Longet: "Take two pigeons — from the one remove the whole Cerebrum, from the other only a part of the Cerebellum; on the morrow, the first will be firm on its feet, the second will have the gait of a drunken man." **

The fact is indisputable; but does it carry the conclusion? It seems to me that there is a misconception of the bearing of experimental evidence, in the supposition that injury to an organ,

* FLOURENS: *Recherches*, &c. BOUILLAUD: *Recherches tendant à réfuter l'opinion de M. Gall sur les fonctions du Cervelet*, 1827. Although BOUILLAUD controverts FLOURENS on some points, showing that it is only over the muscles of the extremities that the co-ordinating power extends, yet he agrees with him on the main point.

** LONGET, II. 265.

followed by disturbance of a particular function, *proves* that the
function in question has its seat in that organ: nothing more than
a suspicion can be warranted by such evidence; and in the present case the suspicion is proved to be erroneous, by the fact that
the function can in some cases be exercised when the organ is absent. Experiment and Pathology, if sufficiently examined, distinctly pronounce against the hypothesis.

The idea of there being one particular seat of muscular co-
ordination appears to me illusory. Each centre co-ordinates the
muscles to which its nerves are distributed; and the co-ordination
of the whole depends on the integrity of the whole mechanism.
The Spinal Chord is the general centre from which spring the
nerves distributed to the limbs and trunk. If this chord be
divided, lengthwise, into two halves, each half will co-ordinate
the muscles of each side of the body; but the two sides will not
move harmoniously, because the integrity of the mechanism has
been disturbed; and as regards the movements of the limbs, the
two halves might be two animals. It is the same when the chord
is divided across; this cuts the body into two halves; but the
fore-legs are co-ordinated by the anterior half, the hind-legs by
the posterior half. But if the division has not been complete, if
we leave the grey matter to be on one side continuous, then
Stilling assures us, the continuity enables both sides to be co-
ordinated.[*]

The experiments of Flourens and Bouillaud certainly prove
that the Cerebellum exercises some marked influence on muscular movements, at least those implied in sustaining equilibrium.
But this is true only of birds and mammals. It is unequivocally
not true of lizards, frogs, tritons, &c. Flourens indeed says:
"I removed the Cerebellum of a frog; walking, leaping, even
standing, were suddenly abolished. I removed the Cerebellum,
bit by bit, from another frog; walking, leaping, and standing
were gradually abolished."[**] The facts were doubtless as he
describes them; but I venture to say that if he had allowed half
an hour to elapse, so as to allow the shock of the operation to

pass away, he would have seen the frogs leaping and swimming as vigorously as ever. Every one who has experience in these matters will remember that unless the frogs so operated on (or even after the entire removal of the brain) were carefully secured, they were soon hopping about the house — to the horror of maid-servants, and amusement of the experimenter.

Here then is a patent contradiction: The Cerebellum, which has such marked influence over the movements of birds, has none at all, that is appreciable, over the movements of frogs. Those who suffer phrases to do duty for ideas, may get over this contra-diction by saying that birds are "differently constituted" from frogs, and therefore the Cerebellum may have a function in the one which it has not in the other. But no biologist, who pre-tended to philosophy, would be satisfied with a phrase so vague; he would demand in what this said difference of constitution con-sisted. He would know that function is determined by anatomi-cal connection, and would inquire what were the anatomical differences in these cases.

I was groping my way through this obscurity, when the ex-periments of Schiff seemed to flash a sudden streak of light. He showed that the strands of nerve-fibres which pass into the Cere-bellum (called the *crura cerebelli*) are instrumental in fixing the vertebral column in the region of the neck; and that when an injury to the Cerebellum disturbs the harmony of movements, it is by acting on these neck-fixing parts. If the Cerebellum, he says, be cut through on one side, the movements become irre-gular; but if it be cut through on both sides, in a perfectly sym-metrical manner, the movements do not at all become irregu-lar.[*] No one need be told that the equilibrium of the body is maintained by the adjustment of the vertebral column. This must be notably the case with a long-necked bird; it is not, however, the case with the short-necked frog, or triton, which requires no such adjustment of its column to preserve equili-brium.[**]

---

[*] Schiff: *Lehrbuch der Physiol.*, I. 355.
[**] Since this was written, the German translation of Schröder van der Kolk's work has appeared, in which he declares it has always been incom-prehensible to him how men could believe the cerebellum to be the seat of co-

After this refutation, it is interesting and instructive to read the array of facts which can be brought from Comparative Anatomy to give countenance to the hypothesis: "On ascending the scale of mammiferous animals, we cannot but be struck with the rapid advance in the proportional size of the Cerebellum which we observe as we rise from the lowest (which are surpassed in this respect by many birds) towards man, in whom it attains a development which appears enormous even when contrasted with that of the Quadrumana. In proportion, in fact, as the extremities acquire the power of prehension, and together with this a power of application to a great variety of purposes — still more in proportion as the animal becomes capable of maintaining the erect posture, in which a constant muscular exertion, consisting of a number of most elaborately combined actions, is required — do we find the size of the Cerebellum and the complexity of its structure undergoing a rapid increase. Thus, even between the dog and the bear there is a marked difference; the latter being capable of maintaining for some time the erect posture, and often spontaneously assuming it; whilst to the former it is anything but natural." *

This evidence is valuable as indicating some connection between the Cerebellum and muscular movements, but it cannot weigh against the positive evidence just adduced. Nor can much countenance be gained from the evidence of Disease, although that also is frequently invoked. Irregularity of co-ordination is indeed sometimes found accompanying disease of the Cerebellum; but more frequently not; and it sometimes accompanies disease of the Cerebrum. Andral has collected ninety-three cases of diseased Cerebellum, and of these "there is *only one* which tends to favour the opinion of physiologists." Longet, who quotes this, remarks that inasmuch as the diseases were for the most part chronic, it is possible that the unaffected portions may have performed the co-ordinating function; and he considers the evidence of Experiment to be more conclusive. On the other

ordination, which he places in the spinal chord, and he adduces the movements of decapitated frogs as proof. — *Bau und Functionen der Med. Spin.,* 1859, p. 63.

* CARPENTER: *Human Physiology,* p. 531.

hand, Ludwig curtly declares that all experiments on birds are valueless for the physiology of man, since no one has ever observed these phenomena of imperfect co-ordination when the human Cerebellum has been injured. * I agree with Longet that experiment is more conclusive; but it concludes *against* the hypothesis. Pathology, however, records one very striking case, which of itself would suffice to settle the question, because it shows us the *absence* of a Cerebellum in a human subject. It was first published by Combette, in the *Revue Médicale*, 1831, and is constantly alluded to. Mr. Solly reports it thus, in his work on the Brain: —

"This was a case in which the Cerebellum was entirely wanting, nothing being found in its place but a *quantity of serous fluid* contained in the membranes: on each side a pedunculated body, not larger than a pea, was attached to the *corpora restiformia;* all the rest seemed replaced by a nervous sac. The pons Varolii, as well as the Cerebellum, were absent, and the individual in whom this remarkable lesion was observed had attained the age of eleven years.

"This case shows that *agenesia cerebelli*, or total want of the Cerebellum, does not necessarily render existence impossible, provided the other parts of the nervous centres be well conformed. The individual may even live for a considerable time. The child here was nearly twelve years of age, and we have reason for considering the disease as congenital; for had it been acquired — had this absence of the whole Cerebellum depended on an actual destruction of the nervous substance by an organic lesion, it is not probable the child would have survived so long.

"What were the phenomena observed during life? What effect did this complete atrophy produce on the intellect? What modification in the function of motion? The intellectual faculties were obtuse, though not to a remarkable degree; the answers slow and difficult; the whole countenance expressive of stupidity: in a word, the child, though not exactly idiotic, still showed a deviation of the mental powers. The motility was also modified; the power of motion was considerably weakened in the

* LUDWIG: *Lehrbuch der Physiol.*, i. 310.

lower limbs, which did not possess their natural force and vigour; hence the child was unable to support itself with any firmness; it fell down frequently; the legs crossed each other during walking, and the gait was irregular and unsteady. At length the child was compelled to confine itself altogether to bed, and after some time was unable to stir, even when lying in a horizontal position. Thus the modification of motility consisted in the gradual abolition of motion: to this were joined epileptiform convulsions, which continued for some time, and finally carried off the patient. The sensation of the integumental covering was not modified in any way whatever. There was no increase of sensibility in the commencement — no obtuseness or diminution of feeling, even when paralysis was most complete; the senses also remained intact. The child could see, hear, and taste, in a perfect manner. The functions of nutrition, circulation, and respiration were carried on without any notable disturbance."

This remarkable case has been quoted to prove the truth of the opinion advanced by Flourens; it is alluded to by Longet as one subversive of *all* the hypotheses that have been advanced. If we examine it by the light of the experimental canon previously laid down — namely, that "the disappearance of a function, on the removal of an organ, is no proof whatever that the function had its seat in that organ; but the *persistence* of a function, after the removal of an organ, is rigorous proof that the function had *not* its seat in that organ" — we shall clearly see that the opinion of Flourens is refuted by this case. The co-ordinating power was weak, indeed, at least in the lower extremities (nothing is said of the upper); but the whole motility was weak, and at last destroyed. Now the hypothesis which assigns co-ordination as the function of the Cerebellum, expressly denies that organ to be the seat of motility, — that being assigned to the Spinal Chord. It is co-ordination alone which the Cerebellum is said to effect; and when the whole of that organ is removed, all co-ordination, at least of the extremities, is said to disappear. But this was assuredly not the case in the instance just quoted; the whole of the Cerebellum was absent, and only a slight *part* of the co-ordinating power was affected. This persistence of the function in the absence of the organ is a demonstration of the error of

Flourens. Whatever were the causes which affected the motility of the child, who was half an idiot, they also necessarily affected her power of co-ordinating her movements. *

Two other cases are referred to by Brown-Séquard, wherein total destrustion of the Cerebellum by disease was unaccompanied by paralysis, or any other trouble in the functions of animal life. "I have ascertained," he says, further, "that it is by the irritation they produce on various parts of the basis of the brain that the diseases of the Cerebellum, or its extirpation in animals, cause the disorder of movements which has been considered as depending upon the absence of a guiding power. In fact, the least irritation of several parts of the brain, with only the point of a needle, may generate very nearly the same disorder of movements that follows the extirpation of the Cerebellum." **

Lockhart Clarke is also indisposed to accept the current hypothesis. "That the Cerebellum," he says, "is in some way concerned in the regulation and co-ordination of muscular movements, appears to follow from experiment and pathological investigation; but I think there are many reasons for believing that the mode of action usually assigned to it is unsatisfactory, and at variance with many established facts." ***

It is an interesting illustration of the powerful bias which may be given to the mind by a striking experiment, or a captivating formula, that a multitude of facts which contradicted Flourens have either been disregarded, or have been only admitted as suggestive of doubts. But the reader will, I hope, now see that the hypothesis of the Cerebellum being the organ of muscular co-ordination is not doubtful — it is utterly erroneous.

II. THE CEREBELLUM A SEAT OF SENSATION AND VOLITION. —

* Dr. ROBERT WILLIS, in the valuable notes to his translation of Wagner's Physiology, takes a similar view: "The poor child was almost an idiot; but as she spoke, and walked, and used her hands, it is obvious that the Cerebellum could have had nothing to do with the highly complicated movements requisite in all these acts" (p. 637).

** BROWN-SÉQUARD: Lectures in Lancet, 27th August 1858.

*** LOCKHART CLARKE: Philosophical Transactions, 1858, p. 591.

What, then, is the function of the Cerebellum? Unhappily no clear answer can be given to that question; and mainly because the answer has not been sought in the right way. All I can attempt at present is to show that the Cerebellum must be a seat of Sensation and Volition, because it is a great ganglionic centre, or group of centres, having the same tissues as those other cranial centres which every one admits to be endowed with Sensibility.

It has been held by very eminent investigators that the Cerebellum is *the* seat of Sensibility.* This is an exaggeration; but it suffices, even as an exaggeration, to show how many facts speak in favour of Sensibility in this organ. Mr. Solly has quoted the following passage from Foville, which bears upon the point: "The opinion advanced by some physiologists that the Cerebellum is the regulator of the voluntary movements, if we attentively consider the reasoning on which it rests, seems to me to strengthen the idea which places the central seat of sensibility in the Cerebellum. After having injured the structure of the Cerebellum extensively, we have observed that animals preserved their power of moving their limbs, but had lost that of co-ordinating the movements of these in a manner convenient to station, progression, flight, &c. But when we *will* to perform, and actually perform, certain movements, do we not distinctly feel that we execute them? The man who, with his eyes shut, moves his hand or his arm, does he not also distinctly feel that he moves these parts as if he followed them with his eyes? While the paralysed man who, with his eyes shut, is desired to move his paralysed limbs, may be very willing to do so, though incapable and perfectly aware of his incapability of obeying. If this be true, how can we expect that an animal deprived of the faculty of perceiving the sensation of the movements which it executes, should execute them in the *ensemble* with harmony, and in accordance with a proposed end? How can we expect it to walk deliberately and to keep its equilibrium, if it does not feel the ground upon which it stands, if it is ignorant

---

* Compare LONGET, *Traité*, II. 263, for authorities. He himself thinks that it participates in sensation but is positive, that it is not the exclusive one.

of the position in which its limbs are placed? I remember conversing with Sir Astley Cooper on this subject towards the end
of 1830. Sir Astley cited to me the case of a man completely
deprived of the faculty of sensation in one arm and hand, the
muscular power of which was, however, preserved. When this
man was desired to take hold of and to lift anything, he did so
quite well; but if, whilst holding the object, his attention was
taken away from the hand, irregular contractions of the limb
commenced, and very soon the object fell to the ground: as
soon as the patient ceased to follow the contractions of his fingers
with his eyes, nothing remained to inform him that he held the
object, when, of course, it escaped from his grasp. This, and
other cases of a similar description, seem conclusive as to the
fact of sensation being the true regulator of the muscular motions: it is by means of sensations that we are aware of the mode
or degree of action in our muscles, that we have the power of co-
ordinating their contractions in a suitable manner, and of
executing a succession of voluntary movements in harmony with
one another."

Indeed there will be few physiologists now to dispute the
position, that the facts which indicate the Cerebellum to have a
considerable share in muscular co-ordination, also prove that it
must have a share in Sensation, since without Sensation no co-
ordination is possible. What that share precisely is, we cannot
say. It is clear that the Senses are not dependent on the Cerebellum; for the girl in Combette's case was in perfect possession
of Sight, Hearing, and Taste. It is equally clear that Pain
has not its centre there. But nothing can be said decisively as
to the other sensations. *

Has the Cerebellum any share in the intellectual operations?
Flourens and Bouillaud declare not; but Longet properly remarks, that inasmuch as animals deprived of that organ survive
but a little time, and generally in a state of great agitation,
it is difficult to form an opinion as to the state of their intel-

* Dr. NOBLE, in his work, *The Human Mind in its Relations with the Brain
and Nervous System*, p. 49 seq., advances the hypothesis that the ganglionic
masses of the Cerebellum named *corpora dentata* are the seat of tactile sensibility.

ligence. Nor can much reliance be placed on pathological cases.
Very frequently no trouble whatever of the intellectual faculties
seems to accompany disease of the Cerebellum; but inasmuch
as disease of the Cerebrum is also frequently unaccompanied by
disturbance of the intelligence, no conclusion can be founded
on that. Disease sometimes notably disturbs the intelligence;
and in Combette's case the girl was nearly idiotic.

When, therefore, we consider the great similarities in structure and position between the Cerebrum and Cerebellum; and
when, further, we reflect that the Cerebellum in the various
stages of the animal scale is always found to be developed in
proportion to the intellectual development of the animal, being
beyond all comparison greatest in man, and smallest in fishes,
there is, it must be confessed, reason to suspect that the Cerebellum also *participates* in some degree in the production of
mental phenomena. At the same time we must admit that there
is no direct evidence on the point, either for or against it.

III. FUNCTIONS OF THE MEDULLA OBLONGATA. — Besides the
Cerebrum and Cerebellum, there are other smaller ganglionic
masses at the base, the most important of which are the *corpora
striata* and *optic thalami* (Fig. 52, s, 4, p. 88), and each of which
must play some important part in the nervous mechanism. But
what that part is, can in no case be stated with even an approach
to certainty. The hypotheses are numerous and contradictory;* but except the share which the *corpora quadrigemina*
have in vision, there seems to be no solid ground of fact yet ascertained. We will therefore pass over these ganglia, and direct
attention to the third important organ of the encephalon — the
Medulla Oblongata.

Although included among the parts of the Brain, or encephalon, because it is included within the cavity of the skull,
and because its columns pass into both Cerebellum and Cerebrum, the *Medulla Oblongata* is really and truly the upper part
of the Spinal Chord, and bears more resemblance to the Spinal

* The latest I have met with is that of Dr. NOBLE, who regards the optic
thalami and corpora striata as the seat of emotional sensibility. — *The Human
Mind*, p. 60.

Chord than to any portion of the Brain. This, which is obvious on a superficial examination, becomes still clearer on a microscopic investigation; and although the point is of little importance as a matter of naming, it will presently be seen to have considerable importance when we come to the interpretation of functions. In Figs. 53 and 54 we see the Medulla in its connections with the Brain and Chord.

Fig. 53.

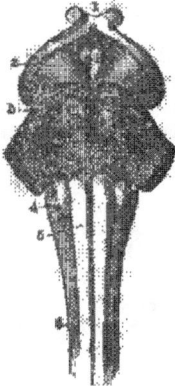

FRONT OR UNDER VIEW OF THE
MEDULLA OBLONGATA.

1, The Optic Nerves; 2, *Crura Cerebri*, or strands of white matter running into the hemispheres; 3, *Pons Varolii*; 4, Olivary Bodies; 5, Anterior Pyramids; 6, Spinal Chord.

Fig. 54.

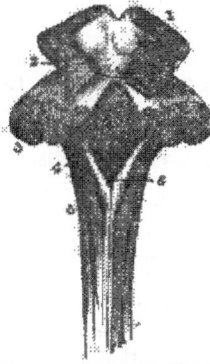

BACK VIEW OF THE MEDULLA.

1, Section of the Optic Thalamus; 2, Corpora quadrigemina;* 3, Section of the *Crura Cerebelli*; 4, Fourth Ventricle; 5, Restiform Bodies; 6, *Calamus Scriptorius*.

Such is the external aspect. Respecting the internal structure little can here be said, since there is probably no anatomical question which can surpass it in complexity and obscurity. The student desirous of pursuing the subject will do well to prepare himself by studying the important works noticed below.** It will

* The two lower bodies are imperfectly distinguished in the engraving.

** The two works of STILLING (*Über die Medulla*, 1843, and *Über den Bau des Hirnknotens*, 1846), form the storehouse whence succeeding writers

suffice for our purpose if we can bear in mind that the Medulla
is really a prolongation of the Spinal Chord, to which there are
some additions both of grey and white matter.* It has ganglionic masses peculiar to it, named the *Olivary bodies* (Fig. 53. 4).
It has also a great variety of commissural fibres, by means of
which an immense variety of actions are co-ordinated. Sensory
nerves and motor nerves issue from it; but these do not display
the symmetry of arrangement noticed in the nervous pairs issuing
from the Chord. It is also the ganglionic centre for the nerves of
Hearing and Taste.

If we now ask what are the functions of this complex part
of the Encephalon, we shall find that the ever-recurring question as to whether the Brain is or is not the exclusive sensorium, may here receive considerable illustration. We shall also
find that there was something more than a mere question of
naming involved in the doubt as to whether or not the Medulla
belonged to the Brain. For observe, the Medulla is now almost
unanimously declared to be a seat of sensation and volition. If,
therefore, it be *not* included in the term Brain, there can be no
longer any question as to the Brain being the exclusive sensorium; and if the upper part of the Spinal Chord can be a seat of
sensation and volition, there can be no valid argument against
the evidence which proves that the rest of the Spinal Chord is
also a sensorial seat.

Müller says: "*It is the seat of volition.*   The experiments of

have gratefully drawn their chief materials, the only considerable additions
being due to SCHRÖDER VAN DER KOLK (*Bau und Functionen der Medulla
Spinalis und Oblongata*); and LOCKHART CLARKE (*Philosophical Transactions,
1858*), whose admirable researches have been duly appreciated by the few
persons in Europe competent to estimate them. In citing the last-named
anatomist, I cannot here forbear acknowledging how much I owe to the
readiness with which he initiated me into his method of making microscopic
preparations.

* "It is well known that in the spinal chord the columns of white and
grey substance are parallel to each other, and preserve the same relative position throughout their entire course; but in the Medulla Oblongata these parts
not only assume a different arrangement, by becoming more or less blended
with each other, and with new structures, but frequently pursue a curvilinear
direction in different planes, inclined at varying angles." — LOCKHART
CLARKE.

Flourens show that animals in which the cerebral hemispheres have been removed, though in a state of stupor, are still capable of executing voluntary movements; they have still this power after the removal of the cerebellum also." *   I am not sure that I rightly understand this; but we may suppose him to mean that the Medulla is *a* seat of volition; that it is not *the* exclusive seat, will be evident when I narrate my own experiments, which show that animals manifest volition after removal of the whole Brain, including the Medulla.   Müller thus continues: —

"*It is the seat of the faculty of sensation.* This is not merely shown by the anatomical fact that all the cerebral nerves, with the exception of the first and second (olfactory and optic), are connected with it, or with its prolongations into the Brain; it is proved also by experiment."

The reader is requested to pay particular attention to the passage just quoted, and to the assertion that the Medulla must be the seat of sensation because nerves are connected with it. Schröder van der Kolk, who also maintains that the Medulla and the ganglia at the base of the Cerebrum constitute the sole sensorium, ** is more specific than Müller, for he says that the Medulla must be "the seat of Perception, the spot where sensory *impressions* become *sensations*," because it is there (as he supposes) that the sensory nerve-fibres terminate in ganglionic cells.   Now I ask, if the fact that nerves are connected with ganglionic centres is a proof that these centres must be the seat of sensation; how can we deny that *similar* ganglionic centres lower down the Spinal Chord, which are *similarly* connected with sensory nerves, must also be the seat of sensation?   And this question becomes still more pressing when we learn, as we shall presently, that the same kind of experiments as those which indicate the Medulla Oblongate to be a seat of sensation, no less decisively indicate the Spinal Chord to be one.   The only *possible* answer which occurs to me is this: The nerves which issue from the Medulla Oblongata, and the ganglia above it, are nerves of *special* sense — namely, the auditory, gustatory, olfactory, and optic; each of these nerves, being in connection

* MÜLLER: *Physiology*, I. 823.
** SCHRÖDER VAN DER KOLK: *Bau und Functionen*, p. 68.

with a special apparatus, is capable of producing a different effect from that of all other nerves. It is only the nerves of special sense which can create sensation.

Easy as it is to refute such an answer, I have thought it worth while to adduce it, because Logic irresistibly forces us to conclude, that unless sensation be the product of a *particular* group of nerves and their ganglia, it must be the product of *all* nerves and their ganglia. Unless some reason can be shown why the apparatus of Sight, Smell, Taste, and Hearing, has the peculiar privilege of awakening sensation, the mere connection of a nerve with its ganglion must suffice for sensation. Now, that these special organs of sense have no such peculiar privilege is very evident, when we consider the facts. Without here insisting on muscular sensations and visceral sensations, on the multitudinous forms of sensation I have grouped under the head of Systemic consciousness, it is enough to refer to the sensations of Touch, Temperature, and Pain. No one will be hardy enough to deny that these are veritable sensations; yet these are not capable of being produced at all by the nerves of Sight, Smell, or Hearing. They have no special apparatus. There is no one tactile nerve and tactile ganglion: all the skin-nerves are nerves of touch, all produce sensations; and these sensations, there is ample evidence to believe, are produced when the whole of the brain, including the Medulla, is removed.*

This view of the relation of nerves to centres, and the consequent extension of sensation to all parts of the cerebro-spinal axis, is not so entirely novel as it may at first appear. The only real novelty is in its anatomical precision. Sir Charles Bell, to cite only one example, had a strong though dim conviction that it was an error to limit sensation to the action of the special senses. "It appears to me," he says, "that the frame of the body, exclusive of the special organs of seeing, hearing, &c., is a complex organ, I shall not say of sense, *but which ministers, like the external senses, to the mind;* that is to say, as the organs of the five senses serve to furnish ideas of matter, the framework of the body contributes, in certain conditions, to develop

* The attempt to explain away such evidence, on the Reflex Theory, will be refuted by-and-by.

various states of the mind."* Although this is very vague, and,
because of its vagueness, has found little acceptance, we see
that the phenomena had not escaped Bell's attention. As he
proceeds, he becomes still more vague; and thinks that because
a blow on the eye will produce the sensation of a flash of light,
which proves that the organs of the senses can be exercised
when there is no *corresponding* outward impression, we can com-
prehend how other organs of the body may have a relation
established with the mind without reference to outward impressions. As an anatomist, it behoved him to indicate by what
kind of mechanism this relation was established. I have done
so, by referring to the one mechanism which, in the case of the
external senses, we know to be operative — namely, the connection of nerves with their ganglia: wherever a nerve excites a
ganglion, there will be sensibility. The visceral-nerves excite
their ganglia, the muscle-nerves excite their ganglia, the skin-
nerves excite their ganglia, and the nerves of special sense
excite their ganglia: the physiological process is in each case similar, although the sensations produced are necessarily various.
Bell seemed to be very near the truth at one time, as may be
gathered from the following passage: — "It is a singular fact
in the history of physiological opinions, that the heart, an
organ the most susceptible of being excited by the agitations or
derangements of the body, should have been considered at one
time as insensible. And yet in one sense it is true that it is so.
To actual touch the heart is insensible, as was exhibited to the
illustrious Harvey, in the person of a young nobleman who had
the heart exposed by disease. This single circumstance, had
there been no other evidence, should have earlier directed physiologists to a correct view of the matter; from its proving that
the *internal organs are affected and united by sensibilities altogether different in kind from those bestowed upon the skin.* The
sensibility of the external surface of the body is a special endowment adapted to the elements around, and calculated to protect
the interior parts from injury. But though the heart has not
this common sense of touch, yet it has an appropriate sensibility,
by which it is held united in the closest connection and sympathy

* BELL: *The Anatomy and Philosophy of Expression*, 4th edit. p. 83.

with the other vital organs."* Had Bell not shared the universal prejudice respecting the Brain as the exclusive seat of sensation, such considerations would have led him, I think, to the
truth.

In the course of our demonstration that every ganglionic
centre must be a seat of Sensibility, we have found that the majority of physiologists now regard the Medulla Oblongata as a
sensational centre; and their reasons for so regarding it, both
anatomical and experimental, we have said, apply with equal
force to the whole of the Spinal Chord, of which, indeed, the
Medulla is but the upper part. Having elicited this, we will now
call attention to another interesting hypothesis which has been
advanced respecting the Medulla.

IV. Is THERE A VITAL POINT? — It has been demonstrated
that the Medulla Oblongata is the centre for the nerves of Respiration. The various actions involved in speech, in swallowing,
sneezing, &c., are also co-ordinated here. It is because the
actions concerned in Respiration have their centre here, that
any other part of the spinal axis may be destroyed without
destroying life; but destruction of the Medulla in mammals has
been known, since the time of Galen, to bring with it instantaneous destruction of life. This fact was lighted up with sudden
interest when Flourens announced that he had discovered a particular spot, a mere point, the extirpation of which caused instant death. He called this the *nœud vital*, or vital point, because every other part of the organism might be removed without
death.

In that part of the grey substance of the Medulla called the
"floor of the fourth ventricle," and, because it is shaped like
a V, called the *calamus scriptorius* (nib of the pen), there is a
smaller v to be seen (Fig. 54, c, p. 99). The point of this second
v, not larger than a pin's head, is the "vital point," according
to Flourens. When experiment had verified the assertion that
death instantly followed the destruction of this point, physiologists quickly perceived that the explanation of the fact was

* BELL's *Anatomy, and Philosophy of Expression*, p. 86.

not that here life had its special centre, but that here was the
special centre for the co-ordination of the breathing mechanism.
Indeed, the fact that reptiles will live for months without their
heads, sufficed to disprove this notion of a "vital point."

Since this passage was originally written, I have learned
that the very fact upon which Flourens rests his hypothesis, is
not correctly conceived by him. Schiff and Brown-Séquard
have both removed this "vital point" without destroying life —
the animal continuing to breathe and live for five or six days.
Their conclusion is, that when extirpation of the point causes death, it is because of the irritation of the neighbouring parts
in the Medulla suddenly checking the action of the heart. *

V. INFLUENCE OF ONE CENTRE ON ANOTHER. — The reader will
perhaps have felt some surprise in learning that the irritation
of a nerve-centre arrests, instead of exciting, the action of the
heart. The fact is indubitable, whatever may be the explanation. The heart, as we formerly learned (vol. i. p. 230), possesses
its own independent ganglia, in virtue of which it continues
pulsating long after death, and even after removal from the
body. But if the pneumogastric nerves be galvanised, these
nerves, although they send filaments to the heart, will not cause
the heart to beat faster — they will arrest its beating. This was
first shown in an experiment devised by Weber. He transmitted
an electric current through the pneumogastric, and the heart
suddenly stopped; after allowing it to resume its beats till they
reached the normal rapidity, he again stopped them by another
current. **

That which is effected by the electric current may be effected
by irritation of the Medulla Oblongata. The galvanic stimulus
acts in the same way as the stimulus of the nerve-centre. There
is one point, however, to which especial attention should be
called. Although the electric current arrested the beating of

* SCHIFF: Lehrbuch der Physiol., I. 583. BROWN-SÉQUARD: Journal de la
Physiol., I. 217, et seq.
** This experiment has since been repeated in various ways. See ECKHARD,
Beiträge zur Anatomie und Physiologie, p. 147. LONGET failed when he tried
the experiment, owing to an incorrect application of the method.

the heart, in the experiments just noticed, it would have *quickened* the pulsation had the current been slighter. The same phenomena will follow a powerful and a moderate excitement of the Medulla: the powerful excitement arresting, and the moderate accelerating, the pulsations. Hence it is that sudden death may result from the "shock" of grief or of joy. Hence it is that a strong emotion makes the heart palpitate. Every one knows the effects of a burst of strong emotion: there is a momentary cessation of the pulse, followed by an agitation: at first our "breath is taken away," and then we shout, or cry, or tremble. Some faint under a powerful shock; others die.

While noticing this influence of the Medulla on the heart, we must not omit to mention the important fact that *pain* diminishes the heart's action. Indeed, pain will sometimes cause death in this way. When patients die under an operation, it is seldom from the loss of blood; it is from the effect of pain on the heart's action, combined with the previous weakening effect of the hemorrhage. This has been proved by experiment. On the other hand, Wilson Philip found that when a rabbit had been stunned by a blow on the head, its Medulla might be destroyed without an arrest of the heart ensuing. * Claude Bernard also found that if rabbits were rendered insensible by etherisation, their Medulla could be destroyed without destroying life; whereas, if the Medulla be even irritated without previous etherisation, death inevitably ensues from cessation of the heart's action. ** The immense importance of chloroform, and other anæsthetic agents, in severe operations, is thus made physiologically apparent.

It is a consequence of the wonderful complexity of our organism, in which each part plays on another, that remote and unsuspected influences produce important results. Mental agitation will suddenly arrest or increase the secretions; imperfect, or too abundant, secretion will depress, or confuse the mind. An idea will agitate the heart, and disturb the liver; a languid liver will disturb the serenity of the mind; a worm in the intestine will

* WILSON PHILIP: *Experimental Inquiry into the Laws of the Vital Functions*, 1817, p. 72.
** CLAUDE BERNARD: *Système Nerveux*, I. 384.

produce melancholy, and even madness. — So indissolubly is our mental life bound up with our bodily life.

VI. SUMMARY OF THE FUNCTIONS OF THE BRAIN. — We have now gone over, one by one, the cardinal facts which have been ascertained respecting the functions of the various parts of the Brain; and these are the chief results to which the inquiry has led: —

1. All the ganglionic masses have one property in common, which is Sensibility; and they differ only in their functional manifestation of this property, according to their connections with different organs.

2. The Cerebral hemispheres have the functions of Intelligence and Emotion. Probably also some other functions.

3. The Cerebellum has functions which remain at present undetermined.

4. The Medulla Oblongata has the functions of ministering to the respiratory and many other reflex actions. The special senses, Hearing and Taste, have their centres in this organ; as Sight and Smell have their centres in the corpora quadrigemina and olfactory lobes. *

5. Inasmuch as all these centres have Sensibility, they must all be organs of the Mind, because they must all minister to the general Consciousness.

6. The facts and arguments which establish the conclusion that the Mind cannot be localised in any *one* part of the Brain, such as the Cerebrum, Cerebellum, the ganglia at the base, or the Medulla Oblongata, but that each of these parts has its own special functions, and contributes its own special forms of consciousness, lead to the suspicion that other parts of the nervous system may also contribute other special forms of consciousness.

It is this suspicion we shall examine minutely in the ensuing section.

* There are grave doubts respecting the olfactory lobes, which will be discussed in the next chapter (OUR SENSES AND SENSATIONS), but for the present we may follow the doctrine of the schools.

CHAPTER IX.

(Continued.)

THE MIND AND THE BRAIN.

SECTION III. — THE SPINAL CHORD AND ITS FUNCTIONS.

Structure of the Spinal Chord — Imperfection of our microscopical knowledge — Difference between an organism and a mechanism: the organic
mechanism is vital and sensitive — Theory of Reflex-Action: Marshall
Hall, Müller, and Prochaska — Error of excluding sensation — Grainger's
advocacy of the theory — Schröder's reflex-fibres — Sensation without the
brain: experiments on insects — Marshall Hall's experiments — Spontaneous motion in headless animals — Reflex-action in the Brain — Hydrophobia — Voluntary and involuntary actions — What is volitional control?
— Volition dependent on sensation — Growth of a volition — Control over
our thoughts — Involuntary actions becoming voluntary — Spinal Chord a
sensational centre; views of earlier writers; the deductive evidence; the
inductive evidence — Evidences of spontaneity and choice in decapitated
animals — Two centres of sensibility established in one animal — Are
walking and swimming reflex-actions? — Experiments on puppies and rabbits — Examination of the evidence against the sensibility of the chord —
What share has the Spinal Chord in our actions?

I. STRUCTURE OF THE SPINAL CHORD. — Formerly the Spinal
Chord (or Spinal Marrow, as it is still sometimes called) was held
to be a large nerve-trunk issuing from the brain, and giving off
numerous branches which supplied the body. Although this idea
is now completely abandoned, and the Chord is known to be a
great centre, or series of centres, intimately connected, as the
several vertebræ are connected into one spinal column, yet men
still cling unconsciously to some of the old conceptions, and are
disposed to regard the Chord as a *conductor*, rather than as a
centre of Sensibility. It is this conception we must irrevocably
dismiss from our minds.* If the Chord seems to act sometimes

* It seems to me that the recent experiments of SCHIFF, BROWN-SÉQUARD,
and others, which have excited so much discussion, and which attempt to
determine the conductibility of different parts of the chord, are all vitiated by
this initial mistake.

as a conductor only, it is merely because nerve-centres once
excited play upon each other; and in this sense the brain is also
a conductor.   Every segment of the Spinal Chord *may* act separately as an independent centre; every segment is a little brain.

The Chord commences at that imaginary line where the Medulla Oblongata is supposed to end.   It terminates in man about
the second lumbar vertebra; in most animals it extends along the
whole length of the spinal column; but there are great varieties
in this respect.   It is composed of six *external* columns of white
fibrous matter — namely, two anterior, two posterior, and two
lateral; and of four *internal* columns of grey, ganglionic matter,
called respectively the two anterior, and the two posterior, horns
(*cornua*).   A minute canal runs through the centre, which may
be regarded as a prolongation of the fourth ventricle of the
brain.

Fig. 55 represents the anterior and posterior aspects of the
Chord with the double origin of its nerves.

Fig. 55.

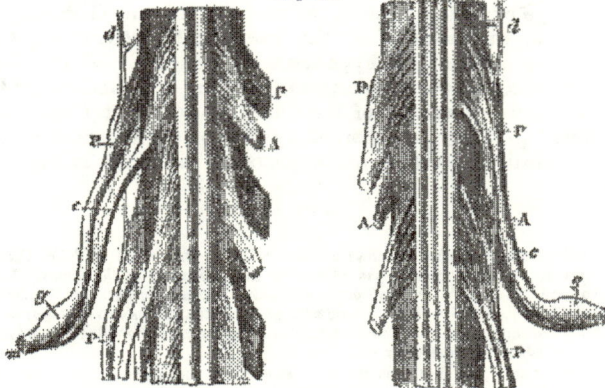

SPINAL NERVES AND SPINAL CHORD. — (After Bernard.)
1, Anterior view; 2, Posterior view.   A is the anterior root of the
nerve, and P the posterior root.   One pair in each figure is represented
with the division made below the ganglion (*g*).   The other pairs are
divided above the ganglion.   At *c* and *d* are filaments connecting two
posterior roots.

As we are not here called upon to understand the whole anatomy of this organ, further details would be superfluous. The student will find ample information in the works named below. *

Of late years there has been an immense expenditure of labour in the attempt to unravel the microscopic structure of the Spinal Chord; but so excessively difficult is this task, that one may fear it will be a long while before Physiology will be in a condition to base safe conclusions on the results ascertained. This remark is especially addressed to students, as a warning against their being misled by the confident and plausible statements and deductions to be met with in modern works. I have been led to pay great attention to this subject; and have not only made a vast quantity of preparations of the chord of man, oxen, sheep, pigs (adult and newly born), cats, kittens, puppies, moles, rats, lizards, frogs, and fishes, many of which have been prepared according to the various methods employed by Stilling, Kölliker, Schröder van der Kolk, Gratiolet, and Lockhart Clarke, so as to test the various statements of these authorities; but I have also had the advantage of seeing some of the best English and German preparations: the result of all this has been the conviction, that whoever propounds an hypothesis on the basis of the facts hitherto ascertained, is in danger of building on a sandbank. **

A transverse section of the Chord, if sufficiently thin, and rendered properly transparent by any of the accepted modes of preparation, presents the appearance indicated in Figs. 56, 57, 58.

---

* ROLANDO: *Richerche anatomiche sulla struttura del Midollo Spinale* GRAINGER: *Observations on the Structure and Functions of the Spinal Chord.* TODD and BOWMAN's *Physiological Anatomy.* TODD: *Anat. of the Brain, Spinal Chord, and Ganglions.* LEURET et GRATIOLET: *Anat. Comparée du Système Nerveux,* tome II. HIRSCHFELD and LEVEILLE: *Nervologie.* QUAIN's *Anatomy,* edited by SHARPEY and ELLIS.

** KÖLLIKER, in his last edition, expresses the same scepticism. His words read like a sarcasm against SCHRÖDER VAN DER KOLK, whose confidence is astonishing, and whose published figures represent, I venture to say, what he *imagines*, not what can be *seen*. This will be evident to any one who adopts the method prescribed by SCHRÖDER; still more so, when we find that anatomist giving up his method in favour of LOCKHART CLARKE's, which most certainly does not show what SCHRÖDER represents.

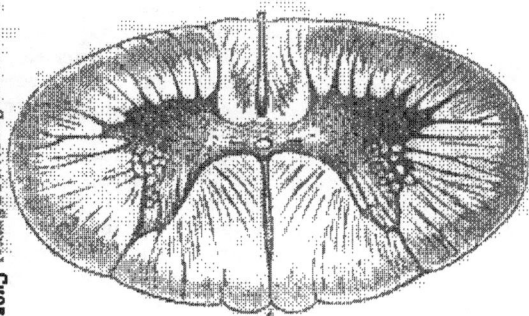

TRANSVERSE SECTION OF SPINAL CHORD
IN MAN (Cervical region).

a. Fissure of the anterior columns;
b. Fissure of the posterior columns. The
central masses are the anterior and
posterior horns of grey matter.

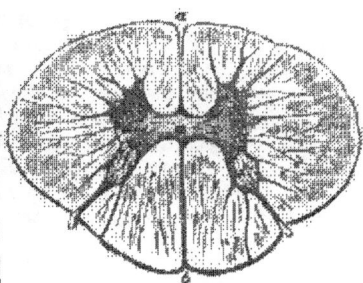

TRANSVERSE SECTION OF THE
SPINAL CHORD (Dorsal region).

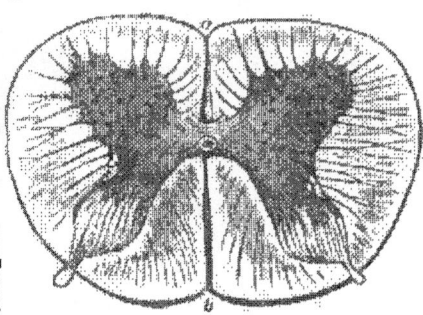

TRANSVERSE SECTION OF THE SPINAL
CHORD (Lumbar region).

Fig. 56.

Fig. 57.

Fig. 58.

These figures are copied from Gratiolet's Atlas. By way of comparison, we may consider Fig. 59, which is copied from Kölliker, and represents one-half of a section made in the lumbar enlargement of a child's chord.

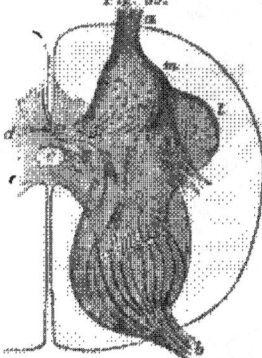

Fig. 59.

TRANSVERSE SECTION OF SPINAL CHORD IN A CHILD (Lumbar region).

a, Root of anterior nerve entering the columns of ganglionic cells m and f; c, Central canal; d and e, Anterior and posterior commissures; b, Root of posterior nerve entering the posterior horn of grey matter.

Having made ourselves acquainted with these aspects of the internal structure, we may look a little closer at the groups of large ganglionic cells to be found in the anterior horns of grey matter. They vary considerably in shape and size. A general idea may be gained from Fig. 60.

These ganglionic cells are identical with those found in the brain; but because they are larger than the majority of those found in the posterior horn, they have been supposed to be motor-cells, by a logical process not very admirable, as it seems to me. The anterior roots of the nerves are, as you know, held

Fig. 60.

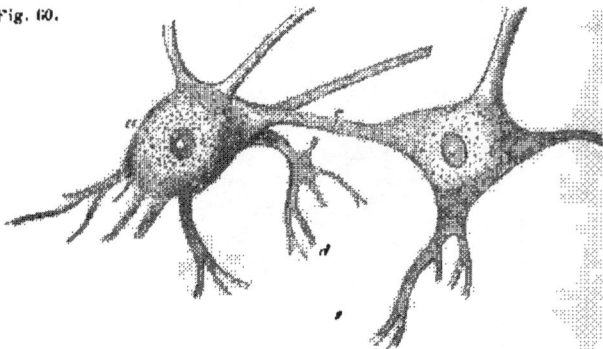

NERVE-CELLS FROM SPINAL CHORD. — (After Gratiolet.)

to be motor only; the posterior roots sensory. We have already seen that this is a misconception; but even on the supposition that it is correct, we shall need some other evidence for believing that the anterior horn of grey matter is *therefore* motor. The notion seems to me entirely baseless. Still less can I accept the notion of Jacubowitch that the largest cells are motor, those of the second size sensory, and the smallest sympathetic. What may be seen, or imagined, in preparations which are imperfectly transparent, must yield to what is seen in preparations made on a better method, * and so transparent that one may read such characters as in a well-printed book. In such sections I affirm that so far from there being any necessary connection between large cells and the motor function, there is no constancy whatever as to size. In the ganglia of two indubitable motor-nerves — the *spinal accessory* and the *hypoglossus* — the size varies greatly. In the posterior horn there are not only large cells ** (less abundant, indeed, than in the anterior), but the largest cell I have ever seen, was one with seven processes in the posterior horn of an ox. And while there are large cells in the posterior, there are abundance of small cells in the anterior horn. Indeed, the idea of properties so widely separated, as Sensibility and Motility, being dependent on slight differences in the size of identical cells, is eminently unphilosophical.

But we must pause no longer on this microscopic structure; ***

---

* See note at the conclusion of this chapter.

** BIDDER and KUPFFER deny the existence of these cells in the posterior horn. The same denial is made by OWSJANNIKOW: *De Medullæ spinalis textura*, p. 87; and by METELKA: *De Medullæ spinalis avium textura*, p. 80, who declares that what have been mistaken for nerve-cells are nothing but lacunæ in the web of connective tissue. In LOCKHART CLARKE's preparations, and in my own, the cells are unmistakable, and their well-defined nucleus prevents any possibility of doubt. From this one statement it is certain that the preparations of the Dorpat School must be very inferior in distinctness to ours; yet these writers profess to see, and they give drawings of, appearances which can by no means be made out in our preparations; whence it is easy to conclude that they describe what they imagine to be the real structure, not what can positively be seen.

*** The student is referred to BIDDER and KUPFFER: *Untersuchungen über die Textur des Rückenmarks*, and KÖLLIKER'S reply in the *Zeitschrift für wissenschaftliche Zoologie*, ix. 1; also KÖLLIKER: *Gewebelehre*, 3d edit.; LEYDIG: *Histologie*; LOCKHART CLARKE: *Philos. Transactions*, 1851 and 1853; LEBwe have ascertained that the spinal chord is a series of centres, having ganglionic substance in its interior, which is in connection with the roots of the motor and sensory nerves.   In a word, it has the essential characters of a series of ganglia; and minute investigation discloses that these ganglia are essentially similar to those of the Brain.   We shall never understand the functions of the nervous system unless we fix firmly in our minds the conception of the cerebro-spinal axis as one whole, the functions of the various parts differing from each other, only as they are differently related to the rest of the organism.   Bergmann and Leuckart do not hesitate to define the "brain as the anterior enlargement of the spinal chord;" and this definition, they remark, makes it less paradoxical to find the brain so slightly developed in the lower vertebrate animals, and not existing at all in the Amphioxus. *   In the invertebrate animals, there can be no shadow of doubt that the ganglia which represent the brain of higher animals are absolutely, and in all respects, identical with the other ganglia, which represent the spinal chord.

But our attention is now demanded by the important questions raised respecting the functions of the Spinal Chord.   The chief of these functions (by most writers regarded as the sole function) is the production of movements in the trunk and limbs.   These movements may either be produced in obedience to the mandates of the Brain — as in voluntary motions; or independently of the Brain — as in involuntary motions, which take place by what is called the Reflex-Action of the chord.

II.   THE VITAL MECHANISM. — What is meant by Reflex-Action, and what is the Reflex-Theory, so continually invoked by modern writers?   Several times already we have been forced to use these terms; ** and now we have reached a stage in our in-

---

ROSSER: Annales des Sc. Nat., 1857, vii.; LEURET et GRATIOLET: *Anat. Comp.*, ii.; SCHRÖDER VAN DER KOLK: *Bau und Functionen der Med. Spinalis und Med. Oblongata;* OWSJANNIKOW: *lle Med. spin. textura;* METZLER: *De Med. spin. avium textura.* STILLING's last work I have not seen; but it is said to be the most encyclopædic treatise yet produced.

 * BERGMANN und LEUCKART: *Vergleichende Anatomie*, p. 515. Compare also TODD: *Anat. of Brain and Spinal Chord*, pp. 2, 77.

 ** See the explanation given at p. 40-43, Vol. II.

quiry when a distinct understanding of them becomes indispensable. But inasmuch as the Reflex-Theory implies the conception of the animal *organism* being to a great extent a *mechanism;* and further, inasmuch as our ordinary conception of a mechanism carries with it the idea of actions performed unconsciously, without sensation; it is absolutely necessary that we should accurately determine the sense in which we are to use, and understand, such a phrase as " the vital mechanism."

The results of scientific investigation during many centuries have been gradually, and of late rapidly, tending to the conclusion that the animal organism is constructed on principles analogous to those which determine the construction of a mechanism. It acts like a mechanism; and differs from one, only in the greater *complication* of its parts and its effects. On the other hand, many persons feel a very natural repugnance to such a conception. Life seems to them the antithesis to mechanical action; the very notion of a mechanism is not that of life, but of a simulacrum of life. Without life, the organism is without action. We cannot imagine the watch performing its actions prompted by any sensation; we cannot imagine the organism performing its actions *without* life. This is the source of the repugnance, often felt, against conceiving the organism as a mechanism; but this repugnance will subside, if we reflect on the wonderful adjustment of part to part, in a complicated whole, and compare it with the somewhat similar adjustments of a mechanism; bearing in mind that this *similarity* is not *sameness*, and that the organism, although a mechanism, is a *vital* mechanism, this vitality being the source of profound differences. Some theorists have overlooked the important element of vitality; and have imagined that a vital, *sensitive* machine, can act like an *ordinary* piece of mechanism, which is not sensitive; but this error should not force us to give up a very useful analogy. We may still cling to the fact that the *adjustments* of the complex organism determine its activities: the muscles set moving by a peculiar stimulus, are as necessarily determined by their organic adjustments, as the wheels of a watch are set moving in a particular way, and are determined in their particular action by the peculiarity of *their* adjustments. When a

8*

stimulus to the respiratory nerves brings into play the group of
muscles which expand the chest, and these, in turn, bring into
play the group which contracts the chest — when the stimulus of
food to the nerves of the alimentary canal determines the action
of the digestive mechanism, muscular and secretory — when the
stimulus of pain sets going the actions of flight, struggle, or
shrieking, — we have a series of actions which are *mechanical*,
inasmuch as they depend on the adjustment of parts, like the adjustment of cogged wheels; and are *vital*, inasmuch as they
depend on vitality for their performance.   With this quali-
fication, the idea of a mechanical construction becomes important.   We perceive how the various actions of an animal are
dependent on the adjustment of its organs. Once set this mechanism going, and it can only act in the determinate direction
permitted to its peculiar adjustments; and in so far it acts like
a watch, or a steam-engine.   The organism of the chick is so adjusted that it can peck up the grains; and it does so immediately the stimulus given to its sensational centre, through the
optic apparatus, sets going the first of the necessary movements.   It will do this as soon as it leaves the shell, or even before it leaves the shell.   In like manner the Snapping Turtle,
according to Agassiz, snaps as fiercely when it is still a colour-
less and undeveloped embryo, wrapped up in the fœtal membranes, as it does in after-life.   This surprises ut as first, because we are accustomed to attribute such actions to "a conscious and voluntary" effort.   On getting over our surprise, and
learning to regard these actions not as prompted by any distinct
ideas, but simply as the results of an organism peculiarly constructed to act in this way — what we have to guard against is
the error of those who, fixing their attention on the *mechanical
adjustment*, overlook the fact of the *sensational guidance*.   It is
true that the animal mechanism, when set going, acts like the
mechanism of a watch; but to *set* it going, and to *keep* it going,
there is needed the constant presence of sensation.   This has
been frequently forgotten, and even denied.   The mechanism
has been credited with the whole phenomenon.   That sensation
is a necessary part of the mechanism — the mainspring of the
watch — the fuel of the steam-engine — seems, singularly

enough, to have been overlooked. The marvellous way in which the sensational element is bound up with the mechanical element, so that our very sensations may be said to be organised in us, is illustrated in a thousand examples of what are called "automatic actions." A piece of music with which we are familiar may be performed "mechanically," without any "effort" or "attention;" indeed, while we are talking to some one, or thinking of something else. This we are said to do "unconsciously;" and if Consciousness be restricted to Thought-Consciousness, there is no objection to calling these automatic actions unconscious; but there is every objection to calling them actions independent of sensation. The sensations excited by each note, and determining each movement of the muscles, are indispensable to the performance of music; the presence of *guiding sensations* suffices; but without this presence, the action is impossible. Although the mechanism of the fowl, whose cerebrum has been removed, is uninjured except as regards one of its sensational centres, this mechanism will not suffice to keep the bird from starvation amidst heaps of grain; because to set going the necessary train of actions which would result in pecking, there is needed the stimulus from the cerebral centre. If the grains be placed within the beak of this bird, they will not be swallowed, unless they roll near the sensitive part of the throat, and *then*, the stimulus of the sensation being given, the swallowing actions are set going, and on these follow the digestive actions. The theorists whom I have chiefly in view at present, deny that swallowing depends upon sensation — they call it simple reflex-action; an opinion which we shall presently examine. Enough, in this place, if we have made clear to ourselves the following positions: —

An organism is a mechanism, and acts mechanically, inasmuch as its actions are *necessarily determined by the adjustment of its organs*. But the organism differs from the mechanism in being vital, in having Sensibility as its mainspring; and its actions, which are called mechanical or automatic, are all *determined by the impulse of guiding sensations*. It further differs from a mechanism in its development of new adjustments and new capabilities. No machine has any self-development. What

its parts could perform last week, they perform this week, and
no more.   But the organism develops.   New adjustments are
formed, so that a combination of actions, which to-day is impossible, will become easy, perhaps, at the end of a month.   I
do not, however, conceive it to be rational to suppose that
a group of muscles which originally required the stimulus of a
nerve-centre, as a guiding sensation, to move them, will at
any time move without that stimulus; although it is very conceivable that *secondary* sensations which the movements, when
they were difficult, necessarily excited, should frequently be
absent, now the movements are so easy that they claim no attention.   I can conceive the possibility of *having* a sensation without *thinking* of it, and I conceive automatic actions to be determined by guiding sensations, although the mind may not be
"conscious" of them.

III. THE THEORY OF REFLEX-ACTION. — The muscular movements have from time immemorial been grouped under two
heads: the voluntary, and involuntary.   We shall have to consider the nature of this distinction presently, but must now
inquire into that principle of Reflex-Action which, I conceive,
underlies all the nervous phenomena, but which Marshall Hall
conceived was characteristic of only a particular class.   There
were, he thought, four distinct classes: the *voluntary*, dependent on the brain; the *involuntary*, dependent on the irritability of the muscular fibre; the *respiratory*, wherein "the
motive influence passes in a *direct line* from one point of the
nervous system to certain muscles;" and the *reflex*, dependent
on the "true spinal system" of *incident-excitor* nerves, and of
reflex motor nerves.   These last-named actions are produced
when an *impression* on the sensitive surface is conveyed, by an
excitor-nerve, to the spinal chord, and is there *reflected* back on
the muscles by a corresponding motor-nerve.   In this process *no*
sensation whatever occurs.   The action is purely reflex, purely
excito-motor — like the action of an ordinary mechanism. *

* MARSHALL HALL. In *Philos. Trans.*, 1833. *Lectures on the Nervous
System and its Diseases*, 1836. *New Memoir on the Nervous System*, 1843.

Müller, who shares with Marshall Hall the glory of having established this classification, thinks that although the absence of sensation is a characteristic of the reflex-actions, these actions may be, and are at times, accompanied by sensation. "The view I take of the matter is the following: Irritation of sensitive fibres of a spinal nerve excites primarily a centripetal action of the nervous principle, conveying the impression to the spinal chord; if the centripetal action can then be continued to the *sensorium commune*, a true sensation is the result; if, on account of division of the chord, it cannot be communicated to the sensorium, it still exerts its whole influence upon the chord; in both cases a reflex motor-action may be the result."[*]

This is, in brief, the Reflex Theory, which Marshall Hall and Müller have succeeded in making an European doctrine. There has been much discussion, often exploding on both sides into anger and injustice, respecting Marshall Hall's claims to originality. He has been accused of plagiarism from Prochaska; but I think that whoever attentively traces the history of the doctrine, will find that although Prochaska undoubtedly described the reflex-actions, and called them reflex, long prior to Marshall Hall — and, as it seems to me, conceived the whole phenomenon with far greater accuracy than was ever attained either by Marshall Hall or by Müller — yet it is very probable that Marshall Hall was unacquainted with his predecessor, who had long been dead, and whose theory had excited no attention; and it is certain that the theory propounded by Marshall Hall was *not* that propounded by Prochaska, but differed in essential points from it. This, however, is what neither Hall nor his adversaries seem to have known. So entirely had Prochaska's theory escaped attention, that even Müller, in announcing Hall's theory, and giving him the credit of priority over his own nearly contemporaneous discovery, never once alludes to Prochaska; and Arnold, in the historical sketch in which he enumerates those who before Hall had knowledge of the facts of reflex-action, is evidently unaware of Prochaska's claims.[**] When, therefore, Hall and Müller took up this subject, it was new to

[*] MÜLLER: *Physiology*, i. 721.
[**] J. W. ARNOLD: *Die Lehre von der Reflex Function*, 1842.

the scientific world; they succeeded in making the world accept their theory.

The one fundamental point in this theory which seems to me wholly inadmissible, is the supposition that the reflex-mechanism is independent of Sensibility — that reflex-actions take place *without* sensation. And, unless I have wholly misunderstood Prochaska's general views, this is the point which he also would have considered erroneous. The reader may be glad to have Prochaska's exposition of the reflex-actions. We must premise that he always means to indicate the whole of the Spinal Chord, Medulla Oblongata, Optic Thalami, and the *crura Cerebelli et Cerebri*, when he speaks of the *sensorium commune:* "The reflexion of sensorial into motor impressions which takes place in the sensorium commune, is not performed according to mere physical laws, where the angle of reflexion is equal to the angle of incidence, and where the reaction is equal to the action; but that reflexion follows according to certain laws, writ, as it were, by Nature on the medullary pulp of the sensorium, which laws we are able to know from their effects only, and in nowise to find out by our reason. The general law, however, by which the sensorium commune reflects sensorial into motor impressions, is the preservation of the individual; so that certain motor impressions follow certain external impressions calculated to injure our body, and give rise to movements having this object, namely, that the annoying cause be averted and removed from our body; and *vice versâ* internal, or motor impressions follow external or sensorial impressions beneficial to us, giving rise to motions tending to the end that the agreeable condition shall be maintained.

"Very many instances which might be adduced, undoubtedly prove this general law of the reflexions of the sensorium commune, of which it may be sufficient to mention a few. Irritation being made on the internal membrane of the nostrils excites sneezing, because the impression made on the olfactory nerves by the irritation is conducted along them to the sensorium commune, there by a definite law is reflected upon motor nerves going to muscles employed in respiration, and through these produces a strong expiration through the nostrils, whereby the air passing with force the cause of irritation, is removed and rejected. In like manner it happens that when irritation is caused in the windpipe by the descent of a particle of food or a drop of fluid, the irritation excited is conducted to the sensorium commune, and there reflected on the nerves devoted to the movement of respiration, so that a violent cough is excited; a most suitable means for expelling the cause of the irritation, which does not cease till the irritant be ejected. If a friend brings his finger near to our eye, although we may be persuaded that no injury is about to be done to us, nevertheless the impression carried along the optic nerve to the sensorium commune, is there so reflected upon the nerves devoted to the motion of the eyelids, that the eyelids are involuntarily closed, and prevent the offensive contact of the finger with the eye. These, and innumerable other examples which might be brought forward, manifestly show how much the reflexion of sensorial impressions into motorial, effected through the sensorium commune, has reference to maintaining the conservation of the body.

"Since the *principal function* of the sensorium commune thus consists in the reflexion of sensorial impressions into motor, it is to be noted that this reflexion may take place either with consciousness or without consciousness."

We must interrupt the quotation here, to remark, that when Prochaska says reflexes may take place with or without consciousness, — or, to use his own phrase, *vel animâ insciâ, vel verò animâ consciâ* — he means "with, or without, *Thought*-consciousness," and not, as so often misinterpreted, "with, or without, *sensation*." This distinction entirely accords with the view I hold, but is different from that generally held.

"The movements of the heart, stomach, and intestines," he continues, "are certainly in nowise dependent on the consciousness of the soul, for whilst no muscular movement can be excited unless a stimulus applied to the sensorial nerves passes by a peculiar reflexion to the motor nerves, and excites contractions of the muscle, it is at the same time certain that the reflexion of the impressions suitable for exciting those movements, if it takes place in the sensorium commune, is effected without consciousness [Thought-consciousness]. But it is a question whether these impressions, in order that they may be reflected, do really travel so far as the sensorium commune, or, without taking this long circuit, are reflected nearer in the ganglia from whence these parts derive many nerves? This matter is to be considered afterwards. But that reflexions of sensorial impressions into motor are effected in the sensorium commune itself, while the mind is altogether unconscious, is shown by certain acts remaining in apoplectics deprived entirely of consciousness; for they have a very strong pulse, breathe strongly, and also raise the hand, and very often apply it unconsciously to the part affected. The sensorium commune also acts independently of consciousness in producing the convulsive movements of epileptics, and also those which are sometimes observed in persons buried in profound sleep, namely, the retractions of pricked or irritated limbs, to say nothing of the motion of the heart and the respiratory acts. To this category also belong all those motions which remain some time in the body of a decapitated man, or other animal, and are excited when the trunk, and particularly the medulla spinalis, are irritated, which motions certainly take place without consciousness, and are regulated by the remaining portion of the sensorium commune existing in the medulla spinalis." *

It is clear, from this passage, that Prochaska, in explaining the actions which take place "without consciousness," did not mean that they took place without *sensation;* he meant that they were neither determined by, nor followed by, *thought.* He uses the word Consciousness as equivalent to Thinking; and this is a very general use of the term, nowadays, as we find in writers who declare that we cannot have sensations unless we *know* that we have them. In strict physiological language, this is tantamount to saying that we cannot have spinal Sensibility unless we have at the same time cerebral Sensibility — that the spinal chord cannot act independently of the Brain; whereas we know that it *can,* and does, act independently of the Brain; and it is to distinguish such actions that the term "reflex" has been invented. To suppose, as is commonly supposed, that the cerebrum *endows*

* UNZER and PROCHASKA *On the Nervous System.* Translated by Dr. LAYCOCK, p. 430-2. The original may be seen in PROCHASKA: *Opera Minora,* pars II., cap. 2.

the spinal chord with sensibility — that an impression only becomes a sensation when it reaches the Brain — is to suppose what the whole course of modern investigation tends to refute, namely, that the spinal chord is simply a conductor, and not itself a centre; and it is also to suppose that the Brain is *essentially different* from the Chord.   Prochaska seems to have understood that the sensorium must first be called into activity before a motion can be produced; the sensations excited in this sensorium are quite independent of any thought which they may, or may not, excite in the Brain.

It is here that Marshall Hall diverges from Prochaska, and, as I think, it is here his error begins.   Yet, in common with his antagonists, he imagined Prochaska held reflex-action to be wholly divorced from sensation.   His distinguished ally, Mr. Grainger, whose work * is far more philosophical than anything Marshall Hall ever wrote, also insists on this absence of sensation as the distinguishing peculiarity of reflex-action.

Mr. Grainger seems fully impressed with the philosophical canon to which we have constantly referred, that similarity of structure necessarily implies similarity of properties; but instead of concluding that the brain and spinal chord, being similar in structure, must have sensibility in common, he assumes a diversity of structure to correspond with an assumed diversity of function.   The Reflex-Theory, he truly remarks, wants an anatomical basis: "unless a set of nerves distinct from those of sensation and volition be capable of demonstration, it is impossible to establish the correctness of what, without such evidence, is merely an hypothesis."   Accordingly he set himself the delicate task of demonstrating this distinct class of nerves.   Sharing the prejudices of that day against the use of the microscope, and refusing to use a lens for fear of deception, his task became impossible.   In the twenty years which have since elapsed, men have learnt to use the microscope with more security, and in the last ten years they have learnt how to make preparations, which, if they have not taught us the whole structure of the spinal chord, must in

* GRAINGER: *Observations on the Structure and Functions of the Spinal Chord*, 1837.

the course of time lead to accurate knowledge. Anatomists have long rejected the supposed system of excito-motory fibres.

[While these sheets are passing through the press, I find Schröder van der Kolk, whose statements, as I have before hinted, are to be received with extreme caution, describes a system of reflex-fibres, with a confidence rather surprising when we scrutinise his evidence. He maintains that each posterior root, on entering the white columns of the chord, divides into two bundles; the one bundle, containing purely sensory-fibres, runs straight up to the brain; the other bundle, containing purely reflex-fibres, runs into the grey matter of the chord, where the fibres terminate in the ganglionic cells. It is, he says, because the posterior root contains these two kinds of fibres, that it is larger than the corresponding anterior root. On this I have to remark, first, that the facts on which this hypothesis is based are excessively questionable; secondly, that the supposed confirmation drawn from the larger size of the posterior root is worthless, inasmuch as the fact is only true with regard to some animals — in the frog, for instance, the posterior root is *smaller* than the anterior; and finally, that if the anatomical facts were as he states them, his conclusion would not be less rash and hypothetical. For let us grant that one fibre enters the grey substance of the chord, and there terminates in a ganglionic cell, whereas another fibre runs up to the Medulla Oblongata, and there terminates in a ganglionic cell (which is the real statement of his position, stripped of equivocal language), what difference, of an essential kind, is here established, such as could justify the distinction of sensory and reflex fibres?]

The anatomical basis for the Reflex-Theory is still to seek. Indeed, were a distinct set of nerves to be discovered, they must be in connection with nerve-centres; and inasmuch as the reaction of a nerve-centre is Sensibility — inasmuch as *all* nerve-centres must have the *same property*, in spite of any difference in their *functions*, — it is clear that the reflex-fibres would excite Sensibility, if they excited the centre.* Let us, however, see what

---

* A friendly critic objects: "How, in this case, do you explain one nerve-centre appreciating only sound, and another light, and another flavour? Rigorously interpreted, your position would involve that all sen-

physiological observations can be adduced in favour of the reflex-theory..

"We have lastly to inquire," says Müller, "how far true sensation is engaged in the production of reflex motions. Volkmann inclines to the opinion of Whytt, that the motions consequent on impressions are the result of sensations conveyed to the sensorium, giving rise to spontaneous reactions. That this is in many instances the case, appears to me indubitable, particularly with those reflex phenomena which occur in an unimpaired state of the brain and spinal chord. Thus I regard, for example, the closure of the eyes under the stimulus of a strong light, and the action of the respiratory muscles induced by irritation of the mucous membranes of the respiratory organs, or intestinal canal." Note this admission, and then consider the counter-argument he brings forward: "But when we remember that, if we divide the trunk of a salamander into several portions, each part, if it contain a fragment of the spinal chord, will still evidence the reflex motions, we can scarcely maintain the applicability of this view to all cases." *

Here the question naturally rises: Why can we *not* suppose the segments of the chord to be sensitive, and its actions to be determined by sensations, as well when the brain is absent, as when the brain is present? The only obstacle is in the prejudice respecting the brain being the sole seat of sensation (compare page Vol. II, p. 64). But look at the facts. We etherise a frog, and cut off its head; after which we divide its spinal chord, in the region of the back. We have then two segments of a headless animal. When the effect of the ether has disappeared, we pinch, or prick, the fore-leg, and it is at once withdrawn; we do the same to the hind-leg, and it is withdrawn; we irritate the posteriors, and the hind-legs vehemently push the instrument away. Another frog, also decapitated, hops away when thus irritated; but this one,

---

sations are the same." By no means; my position is, that all sensations are forms of Sensibility, and their differences result from variations in the nature or degree of the stimulus. The same skin-nerve yields to different stimuli the very different sensations of touch, warmth, cold, tickling, pressure, pain, &c. The subject will be treated more fully in the next chapter.

* MÜLLER, 720.

with the divided chord, cannot hop. All these actions of the decapitated animal are, we are told, purely reflex, totally without
sensation; "because sensation is only possible when the brain is
present." In the uninjured frog these actions result from sensations, because the impressions on the skin are *conducted* to the
brain. All this seems clear enough until we extend our observations. Let us decapitate a frog, and see whether the head, separated from the body, will not exhibit the same signs of Sensibility which are exhibited by the body separated from the head.
We touch the eye, and the eyelid closes; we throw a strong light
on the eye, and the pupil contracts and the lid closes; we touch
the tongue, or the inside of the mouth, and the larynx makes a
motion of swallowing. All these are precisely similar to what
occurs in the uninjured frog, and are clearly allied to the actions
of the headless trunk; yet Physiologists would have us believe
that these actions, both of head and trunk, which indicate sensation when the animal is entire, do *not* indicate sensation when the
head is separated from the body; they would have us believe that
the motions of the eyelid, pupil, and larynx, in the separated
head, are purely reflex, wholly destitute of sensation. I confess
this seems to me very arbitrary. The headless trunk is first said
to be incapable of sensation, because the brain cannot be
reached; and then the head itself is said to be incapable of sensation, although impressions on it *do* reach the brain. Does,
then, sensation depend on the union of the spinal chord with the
brain?

But however arbitrary it may seem to deny sensation to the
separated head, and to consider its actions as purely reflex, there
is absolute necessity for such a position, if the Reflex-Theory is
to be upheld; because, if we grant sensation to the *separated head*,
when we see it responding in the usual manner to stimuli, we can
have no grounds for denying sensation to the *separated body*, when
we see it responding in the usual manner to stimuli.

In the numerous experiments I have made with a view to a
right understanding of this subject, those on insects have furnished decisive examples. When a wasp is cut in two, both
halves live, and manifest Sensibility (if we assume that a wasp
ever manifests it, and is not a mere machine) during three or four

days. If you irritate one half — the head — it will *bite;* if you irritate the other half — the tail — it will *sting.* Take a beetle, such as the large water-beetle, *Dytiscus marginalis,* and remove its head. Here is one, which was decapitated eleven hours ago. At first the head twittered its antennæ, and moved its mandibles, just as it had done before decapitation: this was evidence of *spontaneous* action. It also frequently moved the larynx. Sometimes it spun round on the table by means of its long antennæ. When quiet, if I touched it, these motions were resumed. It seized any object with its mandibles, and bit fiercely. About ten hours ago all spontaneous action ceased; but any irritation produced the reactions of sensibility. All this while the *headless trunk* was swimming rapidly, and, if irritated, behaved precisely as the trunk of an *uninjured* insect behaves.

Once more, I ask, How can we refuse this evidence of sensibility, unless we boldly deny that the insect has sensibility at all? If we accord sensibility to the entire beetle, we must accord it to the separated head; and if to the separated head, then, on the same grounds, to the separated body.

Cast a glance at the nervous system of the beetle, and you observe that the ganglia in the head are similar to those in the trunk, and are only united with them by two threads of nerve-fibres. Is it rational to suppose that the mere fact of union of such threads can endow actions with sensation, when we know that the actions themselves are the same whether the union exist or not; and the only difference created by a division is, that the actions of the fore-part are no longer consentaneous with the actions of the hind-part? The nervous communication enables the two parts of the insect to *act together;* it does not, and it cannot, give sensation where no Sensibility existed. According to the view I take, Sensibility is the property of every ganglion, just as Contractility is the property

Fig. 61.

NERVOUS SYSTEM OF GARDEN BEETLE.
(After Milne-Edwards.)

of every muscle. And carrying this idea with us, we shall find
experimental evidence in abundance; for, suppose we cut off one
segment of an animal's body, the loss of this segment will not en-
tail a loss of sensibility in the *rest* of the body; a dog, or a lizard,
may lose its tail without losing its susceptibility to impressions.
Let us now remove another segment. The insect continues to
fly, walk, bite, &c., as before. From this sensitive, though
truncated, insect, we continue to remove segment after segment,
till we reach the last segment, or head. In the course of these
operations we find the insect more and more crippled; but at no
point ceasing to manifest sensibility; the head gives unequivocal
signs, just as the whole body, *minus* one segment, gave unequivocal signs. There is but this alternative: either we must deny
that the insect at any time has sensibility; or we must assert that
only in the ganglia of the head does sensibility reside. The first
of these positions would render Physiology silent altogether, and
indeed would render it impossible for us to draw any conclusions
respecting man; since it is only by the similarity of their actions
with our own that we can conclude men to have feelings similar
to our own: each man can only have direct knowledge of his *own*
consciousness. The second position of the alternative, which
makes Sensibility the exclusive property of the cephalic ganglia,
is an assumption contradicted on the one hand by the *anatomical identity* of all ganglia, and on the other hand by the *physiological identity* of the actions of head and trunk, when separated.

That I am not doing the upholders of the Reflex-Theory any
injustice in asserting that they call the actions of the separated
head purely reflex, without sensation, will be apparent from the
following passage from Marshall Hall's Memoir: — He decapitated a turtle. "The head being placed upon the table for observation, it was first remarked that the mouth opened and shut,
and that the submaxillary integuments descended and ascended
alternately from time to time, replacing the acts of respiration.
I now touched the eye or eyelid with a probe. It was immediately
closed: the other eye closed simultaneously. I then touched the
nostril with the probe. The mouth was immediately opened
widely, and the submaxillary membranes descended. This effect

was especially induced on touching the nasal fringes situated just within the anterior part of the maxilla. Having made these observations, I gently withdrew the medulla and brain. All the phenomena ceased from that moment. The next observations were made upon the other parts of the animal. The limbs, the tail, were stimulated by a pointed instrument or a lighted taper. They were immediately moved with rapidity. The sphincter was perfectly circular and closed: it was contracted still more forcibly on the application of a stimulus. On withdrawing the spinal marrow gently out of its canal all these phenomena ceased." The conclusions drawn from these observations are not a little surprising to any one who has a sense of logical proof. "This experiment," he continues, "affords evidence of many important facts in physiology. It proves that the presence of the medulla oblongata and spinalis is necessary to the contractile function of the eyelids, the submaxillary textures, the larynx, the sphincters, the limbs and the tail, on the application of stimuli to the cutaneous surfaces or mucous membranes [which no one doubted]. It proves (!) the reflex character of this property of the medulla oblongata and spinalis, and the dependence of these motions upon the reflex function. It proves that the tone of the limbs, and the contractile property of the sphincter, depend upon the same reflex function of the medulla spinalis — effects not hitherto suspected by physiologists." *

Now what is the proof here afforded? The facts are, that the limbs and tail contract, when stimulated, although the head be removed from the body. This is assumed to be a proof that such contractions take place without sensation, because the Brain is assumed to be the sole seat of sensation. "In decapitated animals the *very organ* of sensation and volition, and the other mental faculties, is removed." ** But unhappily for this argument, the facts cited by him show, that when the "very organ" itself is present — in the severed head — precisely similar phenomena are observed. If the brain is the very organ of sensation, it will manifest sensibility as long as any vitality remains, whether joined to the body or severed from it: just as muscles manifest

* MARSHALL HALL: *Philos. Trans.* 1833, p. 644.
** MARSHALL HALL: *New Memoir on the Nervous System*, p. 33.

contractility, and the heart beats, when separated from the body:
it is but a feeble manifestation, I admit, but as long as there is
any manifestation, it will be of the *organic function peculiar to the
organ*. In most animals, the loss of blood, and the shock, destroy
at once all manifestation of sensibility in the severed head; * but
in reptiles, batrachians, and insects, the property still endures
for a short period.

Does not the reader perceive that if the head, containing the
" organ of sensation," after being severed from the body, manifests any of those signs of sensibility which it manifests when
joined to the body, we can have no right whatever to say these
identical effects are due to *different causes* ?   Does he not further
see that if the phenomena observed in the *body separated from the
head*, are precisely similar to those observed in the *uninjured animal*, and to those observed in the *severed head*, these identical
phenomena cannot be due to different causes?   Deny that the
separated body manifests sensibility, and you must deny that the
separated head manifests it; but you cannot stop here, you must
also deny that the uninjured animal manifests it.

That is the interpretation I put upon the facts.   The one
suggested by Marshall Hall rests on the double assumption that
the Brain is the exclusive seat of Sensibility (an assumption of
the very point in question), and that unless the Brain be in vital
connection with the rest of the body, all Sensibility is impossible.
Of *proof* there is not a shadow.   Indeed, I cannot help an expression of surprise at the weakness of the evidence on which this
celebrated Reflex - Theory is based.   Except the striking facts
noted of human beings, with injured spines, who were insensible
to prickings and burnings — facts which we shall hereafter see
do not in any way contradict the views put forth in these pages,
and do not, when properly considered, give the Reflex-Theory
any countenance — there is not a single fact, or experiment,
which can make us pause.   As to Marshall Hall's few experiments,
the facts are so inaccurately stated by him, or, when accurate,
are so illogically interpreted, that a feeling of the ludicrous is

---

* Were it not so, the sufferings of a man beheaded would be frightful.
But we know, from experiments on mammals, that the loss of blood causes
death before the shock passes away.

irresistible when we hear him declare: "*Nothing can affect my view* of the subject, which is, as I have stated, the *simple expression of the facts.*"

Let us give Marshall Hall due honour for his ingenuity and his steady pertinacity against all opposition, but let us also rigidly question the claims even of the most honoured. I do not think that accuracy of observation, or of reasoning, were his strong points; and in the course of the following pages the reader will see grounds for this judgment. Meanwhile two important mis-statements call for notice. One of the cardinal "facts" in Hall's theory is, that decapitated animals never move unless *excited* to motion by an *external* stimulus. This fact I positively deny. Had he kept frogs and tritons for days after decapitation, or weeks after division of the spinal chord, he would have observed frequent refutations of his hasty conclusion. Had he even remembered Redi's account of the tortoise, which, after the whole cranial cavity had been completely emptied, *walked* about as usual, and lived for five months,[*] he would never have ventured on such a statement.

Some time ago I removed the brain from a frog, and left it on a plate to recover from the effects of ether. The next morning the servant came to me, with suppressed alarm, assuring me my frog would escape. "No, there's no danger. It can't escape, its head is off." "But I assure you, sir, it's quite lively; I thought it would jump off the table." On going upstairs, I found the animal in the middle of the room. Such things are of frequent occurrence. Dr. Inman, of Liverpool, writes me word that he has witnessed it on several occasions. He completely emptied the cranial cavity of a frog, yet found the animal quite vivacious: "There is no lack of spontaneous movement, and the reflex-actions are distinct enough in the eye, eyelid, and other places." Indeed, no one has investigated this subject without seeing abundant evidence of spontaneous movements after removal of the brain. These movements are, it is true, less evident when the Medulla Oblongata has also been removed; but that is simply because lung-respiration depending on the Medulla, and vital energy on respiration, the removal of the Medulla is too serious

* REDI: *Observ. circa Animal. Vivent.*, p. 209.

an interference with the relations of the organism to permit more
than feeble evidences of spontaneity. Nevertheless, when the
spinal chord is divided, the *direct* influence of the Medulla is
removed from the nervous centres behind the section, but its
indirect influence, in keeping up an active nutrition of those
centres, enables the parts behind the section to move spontaneously. A Triton, or Lizard, with a divided chord, will be seen to
move its tail and hindlegs spontaneously; *i. e.*, without any
external stimulus being applied.

When I use the phrase external stimulus, it is in the sense
implied by Marshall Hall and Mr. Grainger, meaning some irritation from the contact of a hard substance, an acid, or the flame
of a taper. But as a change in the temperature of the room, a
current of cold air, or the effect of exposure on the wound, may
equally well range under the category of external stimuli, I think
it important to show that a decapitated frog will move spontaneously when there is no external stimulus possible. The frog
is first etherised; and then, its brain having been carefully removed, the whole of its skin is stripped off. The effect of the
skinning is to render it totally insensible to any external impressions: you may pinch, prick, tear, burn the flesh, or cut off the
limbs bit by bit, without producing the slightest sign of sensation.
Yet this frog will hop spontaneously; and if you draw its hind-
legs from under it, and leave them outstretched, it will draw them
up again in a few minutes; thus proving that motions may take
place in a brainless animal when all external impressions are
rendered powerless. Moreover, I found that a triton, *divided in
two*, had spontaneous movement in *both* halves; I placed the
tail-half under a glass, and kept the air within moist, to prevent
evaporation from the skin, yet even here this fragment of an
animal occasionally moved.

So much for the cardinal fact in the Reflex-theory— a fact
which is to prove that the motions of a decapitaded animal are
excited, but not *felt*. I conceive that *all* actions, in all animals,
are excited, and all are felt: an unexcited motion is inconceivable;
but some motions are excited by *external*, and others by *internal*
stimuli.

The second point to be noticed here, illustrates Hall's some-

what loose manner of conducting experiments which require
rigid caution; and the equally loose manner in which he drew
conclusions. "I divided," he says, "the spinal marrow of a very
lively snake between the second and third vertebræ. The movements of the animal were immediately before extremely vigorous and unintermitted. From the moment of the division of
the spinal marrow, it lay perfectly tranquil and motionless, with
the exception of occasional gaspings and slight movements of the
head. It became quite obvious that this state of quiescence
would continue indefinitely, were the animal secured from all external impressions." So far from this being "obvious," it is
directly counter to fact. The mere division of the spinal chord
gives a "shock," which for a time keeps the animal motionless,
or convulsive, but never prevents subsequent spontaneity of movement. But let us continue his account: "Being now stimulated, the body began to move with great activity, and continued
to do so for a considerable time, each change of position or
situation bringing some fresh part of the surface of the animal
into contact with the table or other objects, and renewing the
application of the stimulus. At length the animal became again
quiescent; and being carefully protected from all external impressions, it moved no more, but died in the precise position and
form which it had assumed."

A closer reasoner would have seen that the snake's movements — if originated by a *sensation* derived from an irritation
— would subside with the subsidence of the sensation; but they
could never subside — while vitality remained — if the mere
excitation, caused by contact of the table, originated each movement; since this excitation must be *renewed* at each movement of
the snake, and thus one movement would necessarily bring on the
next. But Marshall Hall set logic at defiance. On this very
page he declares, that when a decapitated animal has relapsed
into the repose from which it will never rouse itself, unless stimulated externally, "the slightest touch with a hard substance, the
slightest stimulus, will renew the movements;" and he thinks
that these movements *cannot* depend upon sensation, because the
position into which the animal falls may be one which would be
attended with extreme pain if sensibility remained — *e. g.* when

the animal remains suspended over the acute edges of the table.
Had he stopped here, one might have attached some weight to
the argument; but he proceeds—" the infliction of punctures and
the application of a lighted taper did not prevent the animal,
still possessed (?) of active powers of motion from passing into a
state of complete and permanent quiescence."

As the "observation" is one on which Hall lays great stress,
the reader is requested to notice the remarkable confusion in the
statement. First we are told that the slightest touch with a hard
substance suffices to renew the movements; and then we are told
that the proof of these movements not being due to sensation, is
that punctures and burnings produced no such renewal of movements—as if punctures were effected without "the slightest touch
of a hard substance!" The truth of the case, so ill observed by
him, is this, that the snake, when thoroughly exhausted, did not
move, if punctured or burned; but before that exhaustion had
taken place, punctures and burnings could have made it writhe,
and any other stimulus would have made it move. On the whole,
we cannot but agree with Arnold, when he says that Hall one
moment relies on the fact that decapitated animals move, as a
proof that movements may take place without sensation; and the
next moment proves the absence of sensation by the fact that the
animals do not move.*

These examples will suffice to show how little Marshall Hall's
experiments support his theory. Let us glance at another
example which is adduced in favour of the theory: "Mr. Grainger
found," says Dr. Carpenter, "that he could remove the entire
hind-leg of a salamander with the scissors without the creature
moving, or giving any expression of suffering, if the Spinal Chord
had been first divided; yet that by irritation of the foot, especially
by heat, in an animal similarly circumstanced, violent convulsive
actions were excited in the legs and tail. This fact is important,
not only as showing the comparatively powerful effect of impressions on the cutaneous surface, but also as proving how little relation the amount of reflex-action has to the intensity of sensation."

On this we must remark that the fact is altogether mis-stated,

* ARNOLD: *Die Lehre von der Reflex Function*, p. 64.

owing to theoretic preconceptions. When Mr Grainger states
that the creature did not move, or give any expression of suffering,
he means, I presume, that the fore-part of the creature remained
quiet; which is no more than would be expected, since the division
of the spinal chord had divided the creature into two distinct
parts—as regards sensibility. The fore-part was quiet, because tho
fore-part was not touched. But I venture to say, the hind-part was
not quiet; *that* always writhes when the leg is cut off. And although
the leg may be cut off from this hind-part without producing any
considerable writhings, such as are produced by heat or other irritation, yet this by no means warrants the conclusion drawn by
Dr. Carpenter; and for these reasons: the sensibility of a Salamander to external stimuli is almost exclusively cutaneous; stripped of
its skin, *no* amount of cutting, or pricking, produces the slightest
sensation: when therefore the leg is cut off, if the scissors be very
sharp, and the movement rapid, the animal scarcely responds to tho
stimulus; but if the scissors be not very sharp, and the cut be made
slowly, the animal—or a segment of the animal—writhes energetically. An irritation of the skin, by heat or other stimulus, will, of
course, produce greater writhings than cutting off a leg: but this
will be the case with the uninjured animal, no less than with tho
animal whose chord has been divided. Thus we see that the fact
in noway supports the hypothesis of reflex-actions being produced without sensation.

Indeed, I know of no facts whatever which justify the hypothesis, but abundant facts irreconcilable with it. These latter
facts we shall have to consider presently, in treating of the
sensational function of the spinal chord. If we are to limit
sensation to the brain, it is obvious that actions which take place
without a brain, must be actions without sensation. But this is
the point which has to be proved, not assumed; and it cannot be
proved by such facts or arguments as have hitherto been advanced. Actions may be determined by cerebral, or by spinal,
sensibility; to deny sensibility to the spinal chord, because its
sensations may in many respects be unlike those of the brain, is
as unphilosophical as to deny sensibility to the cerebrum,
because its sensations are unlike those of the optic or auditory
centres: *and this has actually been maintained.* Various writers

have denied consciousness to the cerebral hemispheres. Nor, until we adopt language having scientific precision, is there any ground for objecting to such a conclusion; since it is perfectly clear that the same principle of reflex-action takes place in the cerebrum, as that which we have noted in the spinal chord.

IV. REFLEX-ACTION IN THE BRAIN. — It was suspected by Prochaska, and has since become quite ascertained, that reflex-actions would take place from the Sympathetic Ganglia, without the participation of the Spinal Chord. The proof is simple. The whole spinal chord and brain may be destroyed, yet the heart will continue to beat, and the intestines to move.

But a more important step was to be taken: the Brain was to be included among reflex centres, and some at least of its actions reduced under the general law of reflexion. This step was taken by Dr. Laycock in 1840. In a striking paper *.read by him at the British Association in 1844, he brought together the evidence on which his view was founded. The idea has been adopted and illustrated in the writings of Dr. Carpenter, who now calls the action "unconscious cerebration." If the modern reflex-theory be adopted, this extension of it to the brain is inevitable. But it seems to me that unconscious cerebration is nothing more than this: we can have a sensation without thinking of that sensation; and in like manner we can think without thinking that we think—a train of ideas may go on without exciting a particular direction of the consciousness.

"I was led to this opinion," Dr. Laycock says in announcing his view, "by the general principle that the ganglia within the cranium being a continuation of the spinal chord, must necessarily be regulated as to their reaction on external agencies by laws identical with those governing the spinal ganglia and their analogues in the lower animals." If, therefore, the spinal chord is a centre of reflexion, the brain must also be one. It is a matter of regret that Dr. Laycock did not extend this principle, and declare that whatever was true of the *properties* of the cranial centres, must also be true of the spinal centres; if the brain have Sensibility, the spinal chord must also have it.

* Printed in the *British and Foreign Medical Review*, Jan. 1845.

Dr. Laycock refers to the curious phenomena of Hydrophobia in proof that reflex-actions may be excited by the optic nerves, or by a mere idea of water. When a mirror was presented to a patient, the reflection of the light acting on his retina, in the manner of a reflection from the surface of water, produced a convulsive sobbing, as in the attempt to swallow water, and the patient turned aside his head with expressions of terror. Money was given him to induce him to look a second time, but before he had looked in it a minute, the same effect was produced.

The *idea* of water excited similar convulsions. No sooner was it suggested that the patient should swallow a little water than he seemed frightened, and began to cry out. By kindly encouragements, he was brought to express his willingness to drink, but the *sound* of the water, as it was poured out again, brought on convulsions. In another case, "on our proposing to him to drink, he started up, and recovered his breath by a deep convulsive inspiration. On being urged to try, he took a cup of water in one hand, and a spoon in the other. With an expression of terror, yet with great resolution, he filled the spoon, and proceeded to carry it to his lips; but before it reached his mouth, his courage forsook him, and he was forced to desist. He repeatedly renewed the attempt, but with no more success. His arm became rigid and immovable whenever he tried to raise it to his mouth, and he struggled in vain against this spasmodic resistance."

The facts of reflex cerebral action are important illustrations of the law of nervous phenomena, but they do not in any way establish the peculiar assumption of the Reflex-Theory, which is, that actions can take place without the excitations of Sensibility.

Dr. Carpenter, adopting the opinions of Marshall Hall and Dr. Laycock, thus classifies all reflex-actions: 1. Those determined by the Spinal Chord; they are "excito-motor." 2. Those determined by the Sensory Ganglia; they are "sensori-motor." 3. Those determined by the Cerebrum; they are "ideo-motor." In all these consciousness is said to be absent.

Here we must once again call attention to the ambiguity of ordinary language. Consciousness is a word which, although used as equivalent to sensation, is often, and more frequently, used as equivalent to thought. To have a sensation, and to be

conscious, are held as convertible terms: there can be no sensation without consciousness. But there is frequent use of phrases
implying that sensations *may* exist without consciousness, as
when we say, "I heard the clock strike, but was unconscious of
it; I wound up my watch, but did so unconsciously." This is the
meaning which Dr. Carpenter seems to attach to the word; and
with that meaning, there is no impropriety in his speaking of
"unconscious cerebration," which some have ridiculed, as if it
were tantamount to "unthinking thinking." There is no doubt
that we go through many mental processes without any of that
reflex-feeling which is characterised by the phrase "being conscious." The train of ideas may never diverge from the direct
path: a problem may be solved, and the mind will be so intent
on the solution as to be wholly "unaware" of anything else.
During reverie we are not only "unconscious" of the presence
of external objects, but of our own state. The intellectual mechanism acts without interruption from sensation. When the
word consciousness is restricted thus, we may properly say that
there can be unconscious thinking, and unconscious sensation.
It is only saying that some centres of our complex organism may
act, without at the same time calling some other centres into
play.

The perplexing ambiguities which necessarily arise when
different writers use the words sensation and consciousness,
without rigorously defining their terms, I have endeavoured to
avoid, by uniformly employing the word Sensibility as a general
term indicating the property of *all* nerve-centres; and the word
Sensation as a general term including every reaction of Sensibility to a stimulus, external or internal. By so doing, all
nervous phenomena are brought under the same law; as all
muscular phenomena are brought together when Contractility
is assigned to muscular fibre, and Contraction to the activity of
that property. A muscle may be flexor, or extensor, or sphincter;
its function may be to serve expression, respiration, locomotion,
voluntary or involuntary movements; but in all cases the actions
depend on Contractility. The muscular mechanism, like the
nervous mechanism, is so related in its parts, that some of them
cannot be called into action without also playing upon others;

but there are parts which can act with a certain independence. The arm may be moved without any alteration of the muscles of expression, yet it cannot be moved without affecting the muscles of respiration. But whether the parts act separately, or in combination, the necessary condition of all muscular action is Contractility. In like manner, whether the various nerve-centres act separately or in combination, the necessary condition of all ganglionic action is Sensibility.

I have thought it desirable, on many grounds, to make Consciousness an equivalent term for Sensibility, and have grouped the various forms of Sensibility under the heads of Thought-consciousness, Sense-consciousness, and Systemic-consciousness. But this is a point which may be left to the pleasure of the reader. The thesis maintained in these pages does not require assent to such a classification; but it asserts, as a scientific proposition, that Sensibility is the property of all nerve-centres; and that no action can possibly take place in the organism which has not a sensation, *of some kind*, as a basis. The Reflex-Theory, which considers the organism as a mechanism, errs in supposing that this mechanism can dispense with Sensibility. I also hold that the organism is a mechanism — but a vital and *sensitive* mechanism. It was no discovery of Marshall Hall's that many actions could take place, and did take place, without our being "conscious" of them — meaning thereby, without our *attending to*, or *thinking* of them. Every one knew that. His discovery purported to be, that whereas *some* actions have a sensational origin, and can only be performed in virtue of a sensitive mechanism; there are *other* actions which have *no* such origin, but which, like the actions of a steam-engine, depend on the reflexion of impressions into motions, one cogged wheel moving another. In this he made the immense mistake of forgetting that in the *vital mechanism each cog is a sensation*. Unless his purely mechanical view be adopted, the Reflex-Theory is merely a new name; and the reader has already seen how little evidence there is in favour of such a view, how much against it. The evidence against it will become more and more coercive as we proceed. But it is necessary for a right understanding of the claims of the Spinal Chord to the title of a sensational and *volitional* centre

that we should examine with some attention what constitutes —
in a physiological sense — a volition.

V. Voluntary and Involuntary Actions. — It seems an easy
thing to distinguish a voluntary from an involuntary action; and
yet this seemingly easy thing sorely perplexes the cunning of
philosophy. It seems also an easy thing to distinguish between
an animal and a plant; yet when we come to seek for the one
distinctive characteristic which marks the animal world, and
separates it decisively from the vegetable world, we are sorely
puzzled. There is no difficulty in saying that a cow is an animal,
and a cabbage is a plant: but when we descend to the simpler
forms of animal life, we find them so nearly allied to plants that
our classification is troubled. Still greater is our perplexity when
the simpler actions are presented for analysis; positive as we
may be that some actions have a volitional element, we are at a
loss to mark out *what* that element is.

In popular language, those actions are called voluntary over
which we can exercise control, either in the way of restraining,
or of prompting them. I can move my arm, or keep it motionless,
if I will to do so. But there are other actions which are beyond
control; no effort of Will suffices to prompt, or to restrain them.
The heart beats without my control. The eyelid winks, the
wounded muscle quivers, the stomach digests, involuntarily. I
can control the movement of my arm, unless a sharp pain forces
me to withdraw it; and when I withdraw it under sudden pain,
the action is said to be involuntary.

This is a rough classification, which suffices for our daily
needs. We want a term to mark a certain group, and the term
voluntary satisfies that want. But the severer exigencies of
Science are not satisfied so easily. A rigorous examination shows
that in most, if not in all, the so-called involuntary actions (as
we shall see presently) this very volitional element of control may
find a place. Although breathing is an involuntary act, it can
be, and often is, restrained or accelerated by the will; but the
controlling power soon comes to an end — we cannot voluntarily
suspend our breathing for many seconds; the urgency of the

sensation at last bears down the control. In like manner, we can partially, but not wholly, restrain the shrinking and trembling which accompany pain and terror. It has been said that these partial influences of control are due to the fact that the apparatus involves some of the voluntary muscles, and these are, of course, under the control of the will; but that inasmuch as the apparatus is not wholly constituted by voluntary muscles, it is not wholly under control. Yet this is only a re-statement of the fact in different terms. The muscles are styled voluntary, because they are under control. Nevertheless, it is easy to prove that an apparatus of purely voluntary muscles will furnish an involuntary act — an act quite beyond all influence of the Will. The act of winking is an example. It is performed by voluntary muscles, and may be a purely voluntary act — as when we wish telegraphically to warn one of our hearers that we are jesting. Yet this act, which is as purely voluntary as any we perform, is habitually an involuntary act; the contact of the air with the eye causes a loss of temperature by evaporation, and the sensation caused by this dryness urgently insisting on being remedied, we wink. Not only is winking one of the typical examples of involuntary action, but we find that it occurs in spite of the most obstinate effort to restrain it: no resolution on our part *not* to wink will prevent our winking, after a certain time, or if a hand be passed rapidly before the eye.

This example shows that the partial control which the will exercises over what are called involuntary acts, does not depend on the nature of the muscles involved. The *same* action which is voluntary at one moment will be involuntary at another, according to the urgency, or intensity, of the stimulus. We laugh because we are tickled, or because some ludicrous image presents itself: both of these are involuntary actions, although both are capable, within certain limits, of control; but we may also laugh because we pretend to be tickled at the great man's joke — secretly felt to be a very feeble effort of humour. We cough because there is a tickling in the throat; and we also cough because we desire to drown the too buoyant platitudes of a remorseless orator. We yawn because we are weary, and we yawn because we determine to set others yawning. It seems clear, therefore, that the *volitional* element we are in search of, cannot lie *in the act* itself, but in something which *precedes or accompanies* the act. According to the popular opinion, an act is called voluntary if the mind has determined it by a conscious conception of the object to be attained; and if we were to say that volition is an action determined by a distinct idea, we should express the current opinion pretty accurately. Is that opinion tenable?

It is not tenable, because on the one hand actions may be determined by distinct ideas, and yet be "involuntary;" and because on the other hand actions may be voluntary, yet not determined by distinct ideas, but determined simply by sensations. Let a friend pass a finger rapidly before your eye, and although he has solemnly assured you that he will not touch you, and you have profound confidence in his word, yet no effort of Will prevents your winking. It is in vain you resolve to be firm — the eyelid drops as the finger approaches. This winking is, according to ordinary conceptions, an involuntary act, since it is performed in spite of the will; yet it is an act determined by an idea, the idea of *danger;* and the proof of this is seen when you approach a finger to the eye of an animal, or infant, in whom no such idea of danger is excited: it does not wink. Nor do you wink when you approach your own finger to your eye, because then the idea of danger is absent. We have here an action eminently *controllable*, and obviously determined by an *ideal stimulus*, having therefore the two cardinal characters of a voluntary act, yet being unmistakably involuntary. To reconcile such a contradiction we must suppose that the Will oscillated — one instant it resolved that winking should not take place, and the next instant resolved that it should. This explanation would, however, force the admission that the act of winking was not involuntary; after which, it would be puzzling to say *what* acts are involuntary. If the will can thus oscillate, and thus rescind its orders, why may it not in all the assumed cases of involuntary action be in a state of oscillation?

What is the process of control? Every action is a response to a sensitive stimulus. Muscles are moved by motor-nerves which issue from nerve-centres; these nerve-centres are excited by impressions carried there, either by sensory nerves going from a sensitive surface, or by impressions communicated from some other centre. A stimulus applied to the skin excites a *sensation*, which being reflected on a muscle excites a *contraction*. But instead of the sensation exciting a muscle, it may be reflected on some nerve-centre, and excite a reflex-feeling. This secondary, or reflex-sensation, may either play upon a muscle, or upon some other centre, and *this* will excite an action. Thus it is that the same external stimulus may issue in very different actions. We decapitate a frog, and half an hour after prick or pinch its leg: the frog hops, or suddenly draws up its leg. We now prick, or pinch, an uninjured frog in the same way, and we mostly (not always) observe that its leg is motionless; it does not hop away, it only lowers its head, and perhaps closes its eyes; a second pinch makes it hop away. In the decapitated frog, the action was reflex; the stimulus transmitted from the skin to the spinal chord was directly answered by a contraction of the leg. In the uninjured frog, the stimulus was also transmitted to the Spinal Chord; but from thence it ran upwards to the brain, exciting a reflex-feeling of alarm; but though alarmed, the animal was not forced into any definite course of action to secure escape; and while thus hesitating, a second prick came, and the urgency of the sensation then caused it to hop away. This hopping was reflex, but it was indirectly so: it was prompted by the reflex-feeling, which in turn had been excited by the original sensation. In like manner, if a dog's tail be pinched by a stranger, the dog cries out, and turns suddenly round to bite his tormentor. If the tormentor happen to be the dog's master, or friend, the dog will cry out, start away, or perhaps even turn round to bite — but he will not bite; should he get so far as to seize the hand with his teeth, he checks himself in time. This control is often touchingly seen in removing a thorn from a dog's foot: the pain causes a reflex-action, which brings the dog's head down upon the operator's hand; but instead of biting, the grateful animal licks that hand.

These are cases of control. They are possible only because reflex-feelings are excited; one sensation being rapidly followed by another, so that before one action, directly reflex, can occur, *another action* is set going, which interferes with it, controls it. An examination of the Nervous System discloses a number of centres, all capable of independent action, yet all connected with each other, and thus brought into some dependence on each other; it is through this dependence that control becomes possible. A sensation, instead of issuing in the action which usually follows it, sometimes issues in another sensation; this in turn may issue in a third sensation, instead of in an action; just as, when a row of billiard-balls is struck, the impetus is transmitted from one ball to the other, the *last* in the row flying off, and all the others remaining in their original position. At some point or other, could we follow its course, we should observe that the original sensation issued in an action, although, because the final stimulus to this said action is a reflex-*feeling*, the action itself is very unlike what it would have been if *directly* reflex. Tickle the face of a sleeping man, and by a reflex-action his hand is raised to rub the spot; tickle the face of that man when awake, and instead of this reflex-action, there will be one of vocal remonstrance, or perhaps one guiding a pillow in its descent upon your head.

Inasmuch as all actions whatever are the products of stimulated nerve-centres, it is obvious that all actions are reflex — reflected from those centres. It matters not whether I wink because a sensation of dryness, or because an idea of danger, causes the eyelid to close: the act is equally reflex. The nerve-centre which supplies the eyelid with its nerve has been stimulated; the stimuli may be various, the act is uniform. At one time the stimulus is a sensation of dryness, at another an idea of danger, at another the idea of communicating by means of a wink with some one present; in each case the stimulus is reflected in a muscular contraction. Sensations excite other sensations; ideas excite other ideas; and one of these ideas may issue in an action of control. But the restraining power is limited, and cannot resist a certain degree of urgency in the original stimulus. I can, for a time, restrain the act of winking, in spite of the sensation of dryness; but the reflex-feeling which sets going this restraining action will only last a few seconds; after which the urgency of the external stimulus is stronger than that of the reflex-feeling —

the sensation of dryness is more imperious than the idea of resistance — and the eyelid drops.

If a knife be brought near the arm of a man who has little confidence in the friendly intentions of him that holds it, he will shrink, and the shrinking will be "involuntary" — in spite of his will. Let him have confidence, and he will not shrink, even when the knife touches his skin. The idea of danger is not excited in the second case, or if excited, is at once banished by another idea. Yet this very man, who can thus repress the involuntary shrinking when the knife approaches his arm, cannot repress the involuntary winking when the same friend approaches a finger to his eye. In vain he prepares himself to resist that reflex-action; in vain he resolves to resist the impulse; no sooner does the finger approach, than down flashes the eyelid. Many men, and most women, would be equally unable to resist shrinking on the approach of a knife: the association of the idea of danger with the knife, would bear down any previous resolution not to shrink. It is from this cause that timorous women tremble at the approach of firearms. An association is established in their minds which no idea is powerful enough to loosen. You may assure them the gun is not loaded; "*that* makes very little difference," said a *naïve* old lady to a friend of ours. They tremble, as the child trembles when he sees you put on the mask. These illustrations show that the urgency of any one idea may, like the urgency of a sensation, bear down the resistance offered by some other idea; as the previous illustrations showed that an idea could restrain or control the action which a sensation or idea would otherwise have produced. According to the doctrines current, the Will is said to be operative when an idea determines an action; and yet all would agree that the winking which was involuntary when the idea of danger determined it, was voluntary when the idea of communicating with an accomplice in some mystification determined it.

The reader will have gathered already that we admit no real and essential distinction between voluntary and involuntary actions. They are all voluntary. They all spring from Consciousness. They are all determined by feeling. It is convenient, for common purposes, to designate some actions as voluntary; but this is merely a convenience; no psychological, nor physiological, insight is gained by it; an analysis of the process discloses no element in a voluntary action which is not to be found in an involuntary action. In ordinary language it is convenient to mark a distinction between my raising my arm because I will to raise it for some definite purpose, and my raising it because a bee has stung me; it is convenient to say, "I *will* to write this letter," and "this letter is written against my will — I have no will in the matter." But Science is more exacting when it aims at being exact; and the philosopher, analysing these complex actions, will find no element answering to the "will," in one, which is absent from the other: he will find this only, that in each case certain muscular groups have been set in action by certain sensational or ideational stimuli.

It is a very general mistake to suppose that every act of volition implies a distinct idea of its object. Unless such an intellectual element be present, guiding the movement, the voluntary character is said to be wanting. But it is well said by Müller, that "the ultimate source of voluntary motion cannot depend on any conscious conception of its object; for voluntary motions are performed by the foetus before any object can occur to the mind — before any idea can possibly be conceived of what the voluntary motion effects. . . . The foetus moves its limbs at first, not for the attainment of any object, but solely because it can move them. Since, however, on this supposition, there can be no particular reason for the movement of any one part, and the foetus would have equal cause to move all its muscles at the same time, there must be something which determines this, or that, voluntary motion to be performed. The knowledge of the changes of position which are produced by given movements, is gained *gradually, and only by means of the movements themselves.* . . . The voluntary excitation of the origins of the nervous fibres, without objects in view, gives rise to motions, changes of posture, and consequent sensations. Thus a *connection is established* in the yet void mind *between certain sensations and certain motions.* When subsequently a sensation is excited from without, in any one part of the body, the mind will be already aware that the voluntary motion, which is in consequence executed, will manifœt itself in the limb which was the seat of sensation; the fœtus *in utero* will move the limb that is pressed upon, and not all the limbs simultaneously. The voluntary movements of animals must be developed in the same manner. The bird which begins to sing is necessitated by an instinct to incite the nerves of its laryngeal muscles to action; tones are thus produced. By the repetition of this blind exertion of volition, the bird at length learns to connect the kind of cause with the character of the effect produced. The instinct of this dream-like and involuntary-acting impulse in the sensorium has some share in the production of certain movements in the human infant, which are in themselves voluntary. In the sensorium of the newly-born child there is a necessitating impulse to the motions of sucking; but the different parts of the act of sucking are themselves voluntary movements."*

In this passage, Müller calls certain actions voluntary which writers usually consider to be reflex (involuntary), and reflex-actions with them mean actions without sensation; but as Mr. Bain remarks, "It may be by a reflex-action that a child commences to suck when the nipple is put between its lips; but the continuing to suck so long as the sensation of hunger is felt, and the ceasing when that sensation ceases, are truly volitional acts. All through animal life, down to the very lowest sentient being, this property of consciousness is exhibited, and operates as the instrument for guiding and supporting existence. To whatever lengths the purely reflex instincts, or the movements divorced from consciousness, may be carried on in the inferior tribes, I can with difficulty admit the total absence of feeling in any being we are accustomed to call an animal; and with this feeling I am obliged also to include this property, *which links the state of feeling with the state of present movement.*"** It is this link of feeling with action, which according to Müller, constitutes Volition.

This idea of the nature of Volition has been adopted and developed by Mr. Bain, *** with a fulness and suggestiveness of

* MÜLLER: *Physiology*, II. 835.
** BAIN: *The Senses and the Intellect* , p. 290.
*** BAIN: *The Emotions and the Will.*

treatment which leaves little to be desired. There are questions he leaves untouched, and points on which I do not find myself able to agree with him; but, on the whole, I have received more light from his work, than from that of any other psychologist; and shall therefore expound his views, in preference to those of any other. He considers the Will as the generalised expression of our power to perform voluntary actions; and by voluntary actions he means those which have an *established* connection with certain sensations. A sensation of pain excites the active organs: the animal struggles till it has escaped the pain; these struggles are involuntary, and they are so because beyond definite control, beyond the guidance of any one feeling; they belong to what Mr. Bain calls the "diffusive wave of emotion;" whereas voluntary actions are *isolated*, and directed to a *particular* end. In the course of its struggles, the animal accidentally makes one movement which is followed by an alleviation or cessation of the pain; this makes it discontinue all the other movements, and continue that which alleviates. If any of the other movements are set going, the pain recurs, and warns the animal to cease. The continuance of an alleviating movement, Mr. Bain regards as the volitional element.

"We must in the first instance clearly and broadly separate the diffusive wave, accompanying all emotions as their necessary embodiment, from the active influence now under discussion. This is the more necessary as the two classes of movements are very apt to coexist. A blow with a whip, inflicted on a sentient creature, produces, as a part of the emotional effect, strictly so called, a *general* convulsive start, grimace, and howl; it also produces, in the case of the mature animal, an exertion *in some definite course* to avoid the recurrence of the infliction. The first effect is entirely untaught, primitive, instinctive; being intimately and indissolubly connected with feeling in the very nature of it. The other effect is based likewise on an original property, but brought into the shape that we usually find it in, after some experience and considerable struggles. The element just mentioned, of aim or purpose, in no sense belongs to the movements of the diffused wave, or those constituting the manifestation or expression of the mental state. The ecstatic shout of hilarious excitement, the writhings of pain, are energetic movements, but they belong neither to the class of central spontaneity above described, nor to the voluntary class now under consideration."

When a very young infant is in pain, it struggles and squalls. That is all it can do; it does that lustily. Mr. Bain considers it due to the diffused wave of emotion. Suppose the cause of the pain to be a needle pricking its foot; the child will make no effort to remove that needle, because the link between such a pain and such an action has not yet been established, and this voluntary effort cannot be made. Before it can make such an effort it must have learned to *localise its sensations*. Every surgeon knows that the young infant may be allowed to have his hands free, when operated on, because it cannot with its hands interfere with the knife, not as yet knowing *where* the seat of pain is. When, later on, it has learned to localise its sensations, it may learn what actions alleviate them. A baby in discomfort from some itching of the nose is at first simply restless; it learns to rub that nose with its little fist, only after much experience of rubbings.

Mr. Bain relies on the primary fact that when pain coexists with an accidental alleviating - movement, or when pleasure coexists with a pleasure-sustaining movement, such movements become subject to the control of the respective feelings which occur in their company. It is a primordial law that we shrink from pain and cling to pleasure; as long as the pain is unalleviated, movements are kept up; as soon as one particular movement brings cessation of pain, that movement is kept up. An infant lying in bed has the painful sensation of chilliness. This feeling produces the usual emotional display, namely, movement, perhaps cries and tears. In the course of a variety of spontaneous movements of arms and legs, there occurs an action that brings the child in contact with the nurse lying beside it; instantly warmth is felt, and this alleviation of painful feeling becomes immediately the stimulus to sustain the movement going on that moment. That movement, when discovered, is kept up, in preference to the others. In this way the child learns to connect certain sensations with certain movements, and at a year old will draw close to its nurse whenever the sensation of cold comes on, even during sleep. "It is an original property of our feelings to

prompt the active system one way or another, but there is no
original connection between the several feelings and the actions
that are relevant to each particular case.   To arrive at this goal,
we need all the resources of spontaneity, trial and error, and the
adhesive growth of the proper couples, when they can once be
got together.   The first steps of our volitional education are a
jumble of spluttering, stumbling, and all but despairing hope-
lessness.   Instead of a clear curriculum, we have to wait upon the
accidents, and improve them when they come."

No one will withhold his assent from the proposition that a
pain increasing in company with any movement must tend to
cause the arrest of that movement; or that pleasure increasing
in company with a movement must tend to cause the continuance
of that movement.

"The spontaneous action that brings a limb into a painful
contact, as when the child kicks its foot upon a pin in its dress,
is undoubtedly from the earliest moment of mental life arrested.
Without this I see no possible commencement of voluntary
power.   So a movement that mitigates a pain already in operation is maintained, as long as the creature is conscious of diminished suffering.   In this way, the arms, hands, and fingers work
for abating sharp agony, provided only the right member has
found its way into action.   No provision, as I have often said,
exists at the dawn of life for getting the right member into play.
The infant being must go through many a cycle of annoyance,
because, among numerous stimulants to action that have occurred, the right one has been omitted.   But the true impetus
once arising, the mind is alive to the coincidence of this with
decreasing or vanished pain; just as, on the other hand, we must
suppose it alive to the coincidence of some other movement with
an aggravation of the evil.   The greater the pain, the more
strongly is the alleviating movement sustained when once under
way.   For the next stage of the process, the establishment of a
connection between the pain and the special action, we must fall
back upon the foundation of all our acquisitions, namely, the
force of contiguous association.   The concurrence of a particular
sensation, as a prick in the arm, with that retracting movement
which rids us of the pain, leads to the rise of an adhesive bond

between the two, if a sufficient number of repetitions have occurred. We cannot say how many instances of chance conjunction are requisite to generate an association so strong as to take away the uncertainties attending the spontaneous discharge; all the circumstances governing the rapidity of contiguous adhesion would have to be taken into account in this case. The excitement of strong pain on the one hand, or of strong pleasure on the other, is a favourable moment for the growth of an association: and probably not a great number of those occasions would be necessary to convert an inchoate into a full-formed volition. Full-formed, I say, because when the supposed pain can bring into play the proper movement, in the absence of all spontaneous tendency, we have a case of voluntary power complete for all the purposes of the living being. The example that I am now discussing, namely, the retractation of any part of the body from a painful contact, implies a very numerous set of coincidences between local pains and local movements. For all contacts on the back of the hand, there must be an association with the muscles of flexion; for the palm, the extensor muscles must be affected. For the outside of the arm, the tendency to draw it towards the side has to be prompted. And so in like manner for every part of the body, under an irritating smart, there must be a formed connection between painful sensation arising in the locality and the corresponding movements of retractation. This is one department of voluntary acquisition, and consists of a multitude of couples of individual sensations and individual movements, joined by association, after being commenced by spontaneity. For the class of acute pains supposed the acquirement is perfect, owing in a great measure to the simplicity of the case. It is not so with many of those muscular pains, which we are professedly considering at present, although in the foregoing illustration we have departed from them, and somewhat anticipated the subject of sensation at large. The cramps of the limbs do not ordinarily suggest the alleviating action. Owing partly to the rarity of the feeling, we have not usually a full-formed volition which enables the state of suffering to induce the alleviating action, and consequently we are thrown upon the primitive course of trial and error. This instance shows,

by contrast with the preceding, how truly our voluntary powers
result from education. An established link between a cramp in
the ball of the leg, and the proper actions for doing away with
the agony, is quite as great a desideratum as drawing up the foot
when the toe is pinched or scalded; yet no such link exists, until
a melancholy experience has initiated and matured it. The connection in the other case is so well formed from early years, that
almost everybody looks upon it as an instinct, yet why should
there be an instinct for the lighter forms of pain, and none for the
severest? The truth is, that the good education in the one is
entirely owing to our being more favourably situated for making
the acquisition."

Hitherto we have seen voluntary actions under the guidance
of sensations only; let us now observe the ideal guidance. A
child is seated at table. He places his hand upon the bright
teapot, and the pain of the burn makes him withdraw his hand;
again the brightness attracts his curious fingers, and again the
pain makes him desist. After a certain number of trials the idea
of the pain is so associated with that of the teapot, that the child
no longer burns himself. But he has thrust his hand into the
biscuit-plate, and finds this action rewarded with a biscuit
instead of a burn. On repeating it he is scolded, or slapped, or
put into the corner — made to suffer pain; and if this pain be
always inflicted when he acts thus, he will soon learn to restrain
his forays upon the biscuits. This link which is established between an action and a pain, is an ideal link, and finds its place in
memory; it is nearly as firm as a sensational link. The supposition, however, that this ideal link makes the action voluntary,
as distinguished from an action which is guided by a sensational
link, will not withstand criticism.

At first our actions are guided by sensations; then by the
ideal representatives of those sensations.

"Instead of an actual movement seen, we have for the
guiding antecedent a movement conceived, or in idea. The association now passes to those ideal notions that we are able to form
of our various actions, and connects them with the actions themselves. All that is then necessary is a determining motive, putting the action in request. Some pleasure or pain, near or

remote, is essential to every volitional effort, or every change from quiescence to movement, or from one movement to another. We feel, for example, a painful state of the digestive system, with the consequent volitional urgency to allay it; experience, direction, and imitation, have connected in our minds all the intermediate steps, and so the train of movements is set on. On the table before us we see a glass of liquid; the infant never so thirsty could not make the movement for bringing it to the mouth. But in the maturity of the will, a link is formed between the appreciated distance and direction of the glass, and the movement of the arm up to that point; and under the stimulus of pain, or of expected pleasure, the movement is executed."

It often happens that we are conscious of "an interval of suspence between the moment of painful urgency and the moment of appeasing action;" because the reflex-feelings are many, and these cross and recross each other, so that no one of them issues in action. This was the case with the frog which we cited just now; instead of hopping away when pinched, it cowered and seemed hesitating as to its escape.

And this leads us to consider how thoughts, no less than actions, can be controlled; how the mind has power over its actions, no less than over the actions of the body. The fact that we can, in some degree, control the thoughts, is indisputable; *how* we do so is not so clear.

The power of keeping up one train of thought, is analogous to that of keeping up one course of muscular action. We cling to certain ideas because they are pleasant, or interest us, or because some remote pain or pleasure stimulates us; and we repress all other thoughts as they arise, just as we should repress movements which disturbed a pleasurable sensation. It is notorious that we cannot call up any one idea at will; but having once got hold of the idea, we can keep it before the mind. What Mr. Bain has said when treating of the intellectual process named by him "constructive association," seems to us the true explanation of *all* command over the thought: —

"When Watt invented his 'parallel motion' for the steam-engine, his intellect and observation were kept at work, going out in all directions for the chance of some suitable combination

rising to view; his sense of the precise thing to be done was the
constant touchstone of every contrivance occurring to him, and
all the successive suggestions were arrested, or repelled, as
they came near to, or disagreed with, this touchstone. The
attraction and repulsion were purely volitional effects; they
were the continuance of the very same energy that, in his baby-
hood, made him keep his mouth to his mother's breast while he
felt hunger unappeased, and withdraw it when satisfied, or
that made him roll a sugary morsel in his mouth, and let drop
or violently eject what was bitter or nauseous. The promptitude
that we display in setting aside or ignoring what is seen not to
answer our present wants, is volition, pure, perennial, and
unmodified; the power seen in our infant struggles for nourish-
ment and warmth, or the riddance of acute pain, and presiding
over the last endeavours to ease the agonies of suffering. No
formal resolution of the mind, adopted after consideration or
debate, no special intervention of the 'ego,' or the personality,
is essential to this putting forth of the energy of retaining on
the one hand, or repudiating on the other, what is felt to be
clearly suitable, or clearly unsuitable, to the feelings or aims
of the moment. The inventor sees the incongruity of a proposal,
and forthwith it vanishes from his view. There may be extra-
neous considerations happening to keep it up in spite of the
volitional stroke of repudiation, but the genuine tendency of
the mind is to withdraw all further consideration, on the mere
motive of unsuitability; while some other scheme of an opposite
nature is, by the same instinct, embraced and held fast. In all
these new constructions, be they mechanical, verbal, scientific,
practical, or æsthetical, the outgoings of the mind are necessarily at random; the end alone is the thing that is clear to the
view, and with that there is a perception of the fitness of every
passing suggestion. The volitional energy keeps up the attention, or the active search, and the moment that anything in
point rises before the mind, springs upon that like a wild beast
on its prey."

Nowhere has Mr. Bain expressed himself categorically respecting the difference between voluntary and involuntary actions; but he assumes the difference, and, implicitly at least,

he makes it depend on the establishment of the link of feeling. "Voluntary actions," he says, in the nearest approach to a definition we can recall, "are distinguished from reflex and spontaneous activity by the *directive intervention of a feeling in their production.*" In denying the intervention of sensation in reflex-actions, he only follows the current theory; but unless he separates the involuntary from reflex and spontaneous actions, he falls into manifest contradiction with his own principles, in making the intervention of feeling *the* mark of a voluntary act. We have endeavoured to show that both voluntary and involuntary actions are reflex, following upon the stimulus given to their centres, that stimulus being sensational or ideational. Nor is this all: they are both capable of being brought under *control* — that is to say, of being restrained or originated by the influence of some other centre. That we do not habitually control (that is, *interfere* with) the action of the heart, the contraction of the iris, or the activity of a gland, is true; it is on this account that such actions are called involuntary; they obey the immediate stimulus. But it is an error to assert, as most physiologists and psychologists persist in asserting, that these actions *cannot* be controlled, that they are altogether beyond the interference of other centres, and cannot by any effort of ours be modified. It is an error to suppose these actions are essentially distinguished from the voluntary movement of the hands. We have acquired a power of definite direction in the movements of the hands, which renders them obedient to our will; but this acquisition has been of slow laborious growth. If we were asked to use our toes as we use our fingers — to grasp, paint, sew, or write with them, we should find it not less impossible to control the movements of the toes in these directions, than to contract the iris, or cause a burst of perspiration to break forth. Certain movements of the toes are possible to us; but unless the loss of our fingers has made it necessary that we should use our toes in complicated and slowly acquired movements, we can do no more with them than the young infant can do with his fingers. Yet men and women have written, sewed, and painted with their toes. All that is required is that certain links should be established between sensations and movements; by continual practice these links *are* established; and what is impossible to the majority of men, becomes easy to the individual who has acquired this power. This same power can be acquired over what are called the organic actions; although the habitual needs of life do not *tend* towards such acquisition, and without some strong current setting in that direction, or some peculiarity of organisation rendering it easy, it is not acquired. In ordinary experience the number of those who can write with their toes is extremely rare, the urgent necessity which would create such a power being rare; and rare also are the examples of those who have any control over the movement of the iris, or the action of a gland; but both rarities exist.

It would be difficult to choose a more striking example of reflex-action than the contraction of the iris of the eye under the stimulus of light; and to ordinary men, having no link established which would guide them, it is utterly impossible to close the iris by any effort. It would be not less impossible to the hungry child to get on the chair and reach the food on the table, until that child had *learned* how to do so. Yet there are men who have learned how to contract the iris. The celebrated Fontana had this power; which is possessed also by a medical man now living at Kilmarnock — Dr. Paxton — a fact authenticated by no less a person than Dr. Allen Thomson.* Dr. Paxton can contract or expand the iris at will, without changing the position of his eye, and without an effort of adaptation to distance.

To move the ears is impossible to most men. Yet some do it with ease, and all can learn to do it. Some men have learned to "ruminate" their food; others to vomit with ease; and some are said to have the power of perspiring at will. ** That many glands are under the influence of the Will — in other words, that we can stimulate them to secretion by a mere ideal stimulus — is too well known to need instance here. Even the beating of the heart can be arrested. The heart has its own nervous system. The minute ganglia imbedded

* *Glasgow Medical Journal*, 1857, p. 451.
** MAYER: *Die Elementarorganisation des Seelenorgans*, p. 12, is the authority for the last statement.

in its substance regulate its rhythmic movements; and long after
death the heart is seen to beat. But although thus independent,
it is also dependent: its nervous system is in connection with the
spinal chord and brain; and influences from these will act upon
it (see p. 105). Thus it is that emotions agitate the heart; the
disturbance of its movements comes from the interference of
brain or chord. Now, if once we recognise a channel of sensation, we recognise a possible source of control; and if the daily
needs of life were such that to fulfil some purpose the action of
the heart required control, we should learn to control it. Some
men have, without such needs, learned how to control it. The
eminent physiologist, E. H. Weber of Leipzig, found that he
could completely check the beating of his heart. By suspending
his breath, and violently contracting his chest, he could retard
the pulsations; and after three or five beats, unaccompanied by
any of the usual sounds, it was completely still. On one occasion he carried the experiment too far, and fell into a syncope.
Cheyne, in the last century, recorded a case of a patient of his
own who could at will suspend the beating of his pulse, and always fainted when he did so.

It thus appears that even the actions which most distinctly
bear the character recognised as involuntary — uncontrollable
— are only so because the ordinary processes of life furnish no
necessity for their control. We do not learn to control them,
though we could do so, to some extent; nor do we learn to control the motions of our ears and toes, although we could do so.
And while it appears that the involuntary actions can become
voluntary, it is familiar to all that the voluntary actions tend,
by constant repetition, to become involuntary, and are then
called secondarily automatic.

The conclusion at which we arrive is this: Popular language
conveniently classes actions as voluntary when a distinct conception of the object to be achieved accompanies or originates
them. But Psychology and Physiology, descending deeper
than such classifications, and analysing the process which takes
place in the organism, declare that all actions whatever are the
responses of organs to the stimulus of their nerve-centres.
Whether the action be the movement of a muscle or the secre-

tion of a gland, it is finally determined by the centre from which
the organ is supplied. This centre may be stimulated by a sensory nerve going from the surface — as when the salivary gland
pours out its secretion after the stimulus of food, or the limb
contracts on the stimulus of pain. The centre may also be stimulated by the action of some *other* centre: as when the *idea* of
food causes a flow of saliva; or an irritation of the salivary gland
causes a flow of gastric juice. But whether the action result
from a direct or an indirect stimulus, it is always the same response of an organ to its centre; whether the starting-point be
an idea, or a sensation, the final issue is an excitation of the
particular centre, and the response of a particular action.* We
cannot separate some actions from others, and call them
voluntary merely because they are dependent on a link of feeling, since all actions are dependent on sensation. And if any
reader objects to such a conclusion on the ground that it makes
the Soul animate the *whole* body, and preside over all its actions,
not simply over a few of them — if he objects that we are thereby
retrograding towards the doctrine of Stahl — our reply is: we
must follow Logic whither Logic leads. Any reader who is uncomfortable at the idea of retrograding, who is unwilling to
believe that all the phenomena of his sensitive organism have
one common source, one kindred nature, and one common
name — the soul — is at perfect liberty to try and reach some
other conviction which, besides being more agreeable to his
feelings, will better explain the facts. It is a topic on which no
man will, wisely, dogmatise. The veil of mystery will never
be lifted. We who stand before that veil, and speculate as to
what is behind it, can but build systems; we cannot see the truth.

VI. The Spinal Chord as a Sensational, Volitional Centre.
— The ground has now been fairly cleared for a most important

* In the valuable work by M. LANDRY — *Traité des Paralysies*, the first
part of which appeared while these sheets were at the printer's — there is a
view of voluntary, involuntary, and reflex actions, almost identical with the
one given above. Indeed, although M. LANDRY's language, and his psychological opinions generally, accord with current doctrines, the physiological
conclusions to which his researches have conducted him agree, in the main,
with those I have endeavoured to establish.

inquiry, one not only essential to the argument against the Brain as the exclusive organ of the Mind, but also essential to the right understanding of most questions relating to nervous phenomena. It was necessary that we should first come to a distinct understanding about the Reflex-Theory; because while, on the one hand, that Theory relied for support on the facts which showed that the Spinal Chord was an independent centre, acting as well without the Brain as with it—and hence its actions were assumed to be independent of sensation; — on the other hand, the facts which unequivocally declare that the Spinal Chord *is* a sensational centre, were set aside, and explained away, as being "merely reflex." To prove that reflex-actions are independent of sensation, it is first necessary to prove that the actions of the Spinal Chord *are* independent of sensation. This has never been proved: it has been assumed; and assumed in the face of opposing evidence. I shall now endeavour to show that the Spinal Chord is a sensational centre; a conclusion which would give the final blow to the Reflex-Theory.

1. *Views of earlier Writers.* — Although the reasons for the opinion maintained in these pages respecting the fundamental agreement of all nerve-centres, have not, I believe, before been applied to the functions of the Spinal Chord, the opinion itself, of the sensational functions of the chord, is by no means new. Robert Whytt maintained it. Prochaska, as we have seen, held that the spinal chord formed the greater part of the *sensorium commune;* and he adduced, in proof, the familiar fact of sensibility manifested by headless animals. The next writer whom I can discover to have held this opinion is J. J. Sue — the father of the celebrated French romance-writer — who, in 1803, conceived that his experiments proved the Spinal Chord to be capable of replacing, to a certain extent, the functions of the Brain.* Next came Legallois,** who undertook to show, by

* Sue: *Recherches Philosophiques sur la Vitalité et le Galvanisme*, p. 9. He was not consistent, however, but adopted Bichat's opinion respecting the sensibility of the viscera, p. 68.

** Legallois: *Expériences sur le principe de la vie.* Published, I conclude, in 1811; the edition I use is the one printed in the *Encyclopédie des Sciences Médicales*, iv.

a series of experiments, that the principle of sensation and movement, in the trunk and extremities, has its seat in the Spinal
Chord. The mere division of the chord, he said, produces "the
astonishing result of an animal, in which the head and the body
enjoyed separate vitality, the head living as if the body did
not exist, and the body living as if the head did not exist.
Guinea-pigs, after decapitation, seem very sensitive to the pain
caused by the wound in the neck; they alternately carry first
one hind-leg, and then the other, to the spot, as if to scratch
it. Kittens also do the same."

A few years afterwards, 1817, Dr. Wilson Philip concluded
that "the spinal marrow possesses sensorial power, as appears
from very simple experiments;" but he held the Brain to be the
chief source of sensorial power.* The following year, Lallemand
supported this opinion by the very curious phenomena exhibited by infants born without brains: these infants breathed,
swallowed, sucked, squalled, and gave very unequivocal signs
of sensibility. The value of such observations consists in dis-
proving the objection frequently urged against the evidence of
decapitated animals, namely, that in the animals the Spinal
Chord preserves the remains of a sensibility endowed by the
Brain.

Longet here places an observation recorded by Beyer. A
new-born infant, whose brain, during the birth, had been completely extirpated (to save the mother's life), was wrapped in
a towel, and placed in the corner of the room, as a lifeless
mass.   While the surgeon was giving all his care to the
mother, he heard with horror a kind of murmur proceeding from
the spot where the body had been placed. In three minutes a
distinct *cry* was heard. The towel was removed, and, to the
surprise of all, this brainless infant was seen struggling with
rapid movement of its arms and legs. It cried, and gave other
signs of sensibility for several minutes. **

In 1828, Calmeil arrived at the same conclusion as that
reached by Legallois, Wilson Philip, and Lallemand. Indeed

* WILSON PHILIP: *Experimental Inquiry into the Laws of the Vital Functions*, pp. 209, 210.
** LONGET: *Traité de Physiologie*, ii. 106.

when, in 1833, the Reflex-Theory appeared, this opinion was
so firmly rooted, that we find Mr. Grainger combating it as the
established error of the day. He takes as much pains to show
that physiologists are wrong in attributing sensation to the
Spinal Chord, as I am here taking to show that they were right.[*]
"It is, indeed, apparent," he says, "that the whole question
concerning the truth or falsehood of the theory which attributes
the reflex power to the Spinal Chord, hinges upon the correctness or incorrectness of the received doctrines respecting the seat
of sensation and volition; so that until those doctrines are proved
to be false, it is impossible to establish the hypothesis of Dr.
Hall."[**]

The reader is requested to take note of this, because when
we come to the evidence which proves the Spinal Chord to be a
centre of sensation, we shall find that the *only* ground for re-
jecting that evidence is the assumed truth of the Reflex-Theory,
coupled with the assumption of the Brain being the exclusive
seat of sensation. Whereas if the evidence proves that the
Spinal Chord *is* a sensational centre, then the Reflex-Theory is
destroyed, and cannot be urged against such evidence.

Thus many of the facts which prove the sensational function
of the Spinal Chord were known, and even a vague conception
of their real significance was general, until the Reflex-Theory
came to explain all such facts as the results of mechanical adjustment, and of a new nervous principle called "Reflexion."
For twenty years this theory has reigned, and met with but
little opposition. Yet the true doctrine has not wanted de-
fenders in Germany. Nasse[***] denied that decapitated animals
showed no spontaneity, and asserted that they exhibited clear
signs of mental activity. Carus sarcastically pointed out that
the *word* "reflex" was replacing "irritability," as a key to un-
lock all puzzles; and he took up a position which is very similar
to the one occupied in these pages, namely, that the Spinal
Chord being formed of grey matter as well as of fibres, it must

---

[*] He cites Cuvier, Majendio, Desmoulins, and Mayo as maintaining this
error.
[**] GRAINGER: *Structure and Functions of the Spinal Chord*, p. 66.
[***] NASSE: *Unters. zur Physiologie und Pathologie*, vol. II. part. 2.

have sensibility and power of reacting on nervous stimulus, no
less than conductibility: in fact, it is a centre, and must act like
all other nerve-centres.* J. W. Arnold refuted the Reflex-Theory
in a very remarkable little work, in which he vindicates the claim
of the Spinal Chord as a sensitive and motive centre, although
denying to its actions any volitional character.** This was in
1844. Eleven years elapsed without any further opposition,
when Edward Pflüger, in 1853, published his work on the Sensorial Functions of the Spinal Chord.*** In this work he recurred
to the old views of Prochaska and Legallois; but although he
attacked Marshall Hall with merciless severity, he did not point
out the fundamental error of the Reflex-Theory, which theory
he seems to accept. Nor did he give his views that philosophical
and anatomical basis which could alone render his interpreta-
tions acceptable. Added to this, the tone of asperity in which
his work was written, created a prejudice against him; and
thus, while many admitted his facts, all rejected his conclusions.†

In 1858 Professor Owen read a paper of mine at the Leeds
meeting of the British Association, on "The Spinal Chord as a
Centre of Sensation and Volition," in which a rapid indication
of my point of view, and an account of some experiments to
illustrate it, were given — not, I believe, conclusive to any of
the audience. Indeed, the subject was too vast to be discussed
in such a paper; and my object was rather to excite new inquiry, than to make converts to a view which could only be
embraced after a thorough reinvestigation of the dominant
theories.

In 1859 appeared Schiff's work, to which so many references
have already been made; †† and here we find a large space
allotted to the discussion of Pflüger's doctrine. Schiff, whose

* Carus: *System der Physiologie*, iii. 101.
** J. W. Arnold: *Die Lehre von der Reflex-Function*, 86.
*** Pflüger: *Die sensorischen Functionen des Rückenmarks der Wirbel-
thiere*.
† Except. Auerbach, who repeated and varied the experiments; and
Funke, who partially adopted the conclusions in his systematic treatise on
Physiology.
†† Schiff: *Lehrbuch der Physiol.*, 208.

immense experience as an experimentalist, and whose acuteness and caution, every one will highly estimate, frankly pronounces in favour of the sensational character of spinal actions; but he denies that they are volitional, and objects strongly to the introduction of any such idea as that of "psychical activity." He thinks it utterly untenable to suppose that impressions have reactions in the brain which they have not in the Spinal Chord: — if one has sensibility, the other must have it; and he thinks that, so far from the actions of the chord being distinguishable from those of the Brain by the character of "reflexion," and depending on a mechanical arrangement — *all* actions, cerebral or spinal, are reflex; *all* depend on a mechanical arrangement. *

From this sketch of the history, let us now pass to the evidence on which the sensational character of the Spinal Chord may be founded. The evidence may be considered under two aspects — argument and experiment; deduction and induction.

2. *The Deductive Evidence.* — In the course of our inquiry we have had so many occasions to notice incidentally the various points of the deductive evidence which establishes the fundamental similarity of the brain and chord, that it will not be necessary here to do more than resume them.

Similarity in structure implies similarity in property; and the ganglionic substance of the Chord being of a similar structure to the ganglionic substance of the Brain, there must necessarily be a community of *property* between them.** It is true

* The very latest writer on the spinal chord — LANDRY: *Traité des Paralysies* — maintains that it is a centre of sensation, and that there is in it a faculty *analogous* to the perception and judgment of the brain. Compare pp. 163 *et seq.* and 305. He also cites an essay by Dr. PATON of Edinburgh (*Edinburgh Medical Journal*, 1846), in which the sensational and volitional claims of the spinal chord are advanced.

** While these sheets are passing through the press, I have read OWSJANNIKOW's dissertation — *De Medulae Spinalis Textura* — in which he briefly but distinctly expresses the opinion so often urged in these pages, that ganglionic cells must everywhere have the same property; and the brain, being nothing but a mass of such cells and fibres, must resemble every other mass of such cells and fibres. "Mihi enim cerebrum non videtur esse nisi massa, imprimis, ex ingenti cellularum nervearum numero fibrisque ex illis

that there are some considerable differences in the arrangement
of the tissues, in the cerebral and spinal centres; and this, at
first, might raise the suspicion that the properties of the two
would correspondingly differ. But the nervous system of animals
reveals that the mere presence of nerve-fibres and gangliouic
substance is all that is requisite for the production of sensibility
and volition, quite irrespective of any arrangement of these
elements. And further, we know that the Medulla Oblongata
is a seat of Sensibility, yet the arrangement of its elements is
extremely unlike that of the Brain.

It has already been seen that the Medulla Oblongata is admitted by physiologists to be a seat of sensibility. But we have
also seen that this Medulla is a part of the Spinal Chord, having
the same constituent parts, with a surplus of grey matter, the
two forming one indistinguishable whole.* The Medulla is as
much a part of the Spinal Chord as the skull is a part of the
cranio-spinal axis. No anatomist now finds any difficulty in
conceiving how the various separate bones which constitute
the vertebral column may differ so widely in form, as at one
end to become a tail, and at the other a skull; nor does he for
an instant suppose that the *properties* of these bones differ at one
end of the column and the other; nor that the functions or uses
of these bones — protecting the enclosed nerve-centres, and
affording attachment to muscles — are not fundamentally similar. A man would incur ridicule if he were to assert that the *os*

originem ducentibus composita. Itaque in hisce cellulis altiores functiones
tum corporis tum animi reposita sunt. *Quae cellulae utrum in unam catervam,
pluresve easque majores collectae sint, an per totum corpus dispersae reperi-
antur, tanti non interest, dummodo facultas, qua praeditae sunt, eadem maneat,*"
— p. 93. If the anatomical fact announced by him at page 17 should be established — namely, that the same cell by its two processes is the origin of both
anterior and posterior fibres — it would complete my view of the identity of
the so-called sensory and motor nerves. But although the fact would suit my
theory, I cannot convince myself of its accuracy.

* If any one, misled by certain unimportant differences, is inclined to dispute this identity of the Medulla and the Chord, he is recommended to study
the comparative anatomy of the cerebro-spinal axis, and he will find on
reaching the frog, triton, lizard, and probably all other reptiles, that all trace
of the Medulla as a *distinct* organ has disappeared: it is then nothing but the
upper part of the chord.

frontis was essentially unlike the *os coccygis*, in properties as bone. Yet men do not scruple to maintain that the upper part of the Spinal Chord has the property of Sensibility, which they deny to the lower part; although the difference between the two is merely one of form, and is considerably *less* than the difference between two bones. No one is bold enough to assert that the upper part of a muscle is contractile, while the lower part is not so at all. Yet this is really very little more than asserting that the Medulla has sensibility, but the Spinal Chord has none.

Mr. Grainger is the only writer whom I can remember to have avoided this grave logical error. He maintains, and justly, that the difference between the Medulla and the chord is one of degree only, not of kind; and it is on this ground that he *denies* the Medulla to be a seat of sensation, because the chord, he thinks, is proved not to be sensitive. I hold that both are seats of sensation; or else, as he says, that neither is.

The only ground for denying that the actions of decapitated animals are determined by sensation, is because the Brain, or encephalon, is believed to be the sole seat of sensation. To explain the resemblance between the actions of animals with and without their brains, a theory is invented, which says: These actions are reflex; but in the uninjured animal there is reflex-action *plus* the transmission of an impression to the brain, and it is *this* which produces sensation; in the headless animal we see reflex-action, *minus* the transmission to the Brain.

As a logical deduction from the assumption that *only* the brain can be the seat of sensation, this theory is perfect. Unhappily for it, the facts contradict the assumption; they show that sensation and volition *are* manifested where there is no Brain. Moreover, the assumption of reflex-action taking place without sensation, is made on a false analogy of the vital mechanism with an ordinary mechanism. When facts show, as we shall presently see, that decapitated animals manifest the *same* kind of evidence of sensation and volition, as is manifested by the same animals with their heads on, the assumption that they *cannot* feel, because their heads are off, is rather arbitrary.

A gentleman was one day stoutly asserting that there were

no gold-fields except in Mexico and Peru. A nugget, dug up in
California, was presented to him, as evidence against his positive assertion. He was not in the least disconcerted. "This
metal, sir, is, I own, extremely *like* gold; and you tell me
that it passes as such in the market, having been declared by
the assayers to be undistinguishable from the precious metal.
All this I will not dispute. Nevertheless, the metal is not gold,
but *auruminium*; it cannot be gold, *because* gold comes only
from Mexico and Peru." In vain was he informed that the geological formation was similar in California and Peru, and the
metals similar; he had fixed in his mind the conclusion that gold
existed *only* in Mexico and Peru: this was a law of nature; he
had no reasons to give why it should be so; but such had been
the admitted fact for many years, and from it he would not
swerve. He was not fond of newfangled notions, which, after
all, would only lead us back to the exploded errors of the past.
To accept the statement that gold was to be found elsewhere
than in Mexico and Peru, would be to return to the opinion of
the ancients, who thought there was gold in the upper regions of
Tartary!

Sensation is not tangible, assayable, like gold. We can
understand, therefore, that the very men who would make
merry with the *auruminium*, would accept easily such a phrase
as "reflex-action." The decapitated animal defends itself
against injury, gets out of the way of annoyances, cleans itself,
performs many of its ordinary actions, but is said to do these
things without that Sensibility which, if its head were on, would
guide them. Even before the Reflex-Theory was invented this
line of argument was used. Gall, referring to the experiments
of Sue, previously noticed, says that "Sue confounds the effects
of Irritability with those of Sensibility." * Not gold, dear sir,
but *auruminium!*

This denial of sensation to the decapitated animal is something like what the missionary Williams tells us of the Fijian
philosophy. The body of a dying man in Fiji is laid out several
hours before actual death. "I have known one take food afterwards; and another who lived eighteen hours after. All this

* GALL et SPURZHEIM: *Anal. et Physiol. du Système Nerveux*, I. 83.

time, in the opinion of a Fijian, the man was dead. Eating, drinking, and talking, he says, are the involuntary actions of the body — of the 'empty shell,' as he calls it — the soul having taken its departure." [*]

3. *The Inductive Evidence.* — We have now to consider the proofs furnished by observation. In using the word *proof*, as applied to such investigations, we must be understood as implying the kind of proof which, in the nature of things, *can* be had, and not the kind of proof to be had in physics, or chemistry. Schiff is right in saying that no demonstration is possible in such cases. Feeling is purely subjective. That others feel, as we feel, is to us a matter of positive conviction, but can never be a matter of demonstration. We conclude that other men feel as we feel, because they act as we act. This conclusion is extended to animals: the resemblance of their acts to our own, under similar conditions, forces on us the conviction that they also resemble us in feeling. This conclusion, although purely inductive, is so strong that there are few theorists, even for the sake of a theory, who can believe animals to be machines destitute of all sensation. Nevertheless, we have no *proof*, rigorously speaking, that any animal feels; none that any human being feels; we *conclude* that men feel, from certain external manifestations, which resemble our own, under feeling; and we conclude that animals feel — on similar grounds.

Now, inasmuch as the actions of animals furnish us with our sole evidence for the belief in their feeling, and this evidence is universally considered as scientifically valid, it is clear that similar actions in decapitated animals will be equally valid; and when I speak of *proof*, it is in this sense. *Spontaneity* and *choice* are two signs which we all accept as conclusive of sensation and volition. The dog rising from the ground, and walking away, not being called or driven away, is justly supposed to manifest spontaneity and volition. He is doubtless moved by some internal stimulus, of sensation or idea; but because the stimulus is not external, we call the action spontaneous. No action can be self-determined. The law of Causation forces us to assume

[*] WILLIAMS: *Fiji and the Fijians*, I. 88.

that every action is preceded by *some* stimulus, internal or external. Without entering on a metaphysical discussion of spontaneity, we may conveniently class all actions which are determined by some *internal* stimulus, sensational or ideational, as spontaneous, in distinction from actions determined by some *external* stimulus: the dog leaps from a chair spontaneously; but when pushed from it, the action is not spontaneous.

Choice is another sign peculiar to conscious organisms. In a ' mechanism, without sensation to determine its actions, there is absolute *uniformity:* the same note always responds to the same key, the same wheels are set going in the same order; there is no suspension of one course of action, and substitution of another, such as we observe in the vital mechanism. It is difficult to determine what choice is, but if we say that whenever an animal brings new actions into play, to accomplish an end which it has previously missed, whenever it ceases one set of actions, and *substitutes* several others, until a successful issue is reached, it manifests volition. Indeed this, as we previously saw, constitutes a voluntary action. Philosophers have not yet agreed on the nature of volition; but all men will admit that when they observe a monkey, who has burnt his paws, seize an unsuspecting cat, and with *her* paws reach the chestnuts, a voluntary action is before them. If a tickling in your throat excites the action of coughing, and when this coughing does not succeed, if you swallow some water, this choice of now means is assuredly the sign of a voluntary act.

Thus, escaping from all metaphysical ambiguities, we may assume that *spontaneity* and *choice* are two palpable signs by which to recognise the presence of sensation and volition. Without pretending to know what takes place within an animal, wo may feel confident that if its actions manifest spontaneity and choice, they are not the mere results of mechanical adjustment, but have in them the elements of sensation and volition. Our task, then, is to ascertain whether animals, after decapitation, manifest these palpable signs.

It is emphatically asserted by the advocates of the Reflex-Theory that spontaneity is utterly absent in decapitated ani-

mala.* This statement I have already shown to be erroneous
(p. 131); but I will here add further evidence. I decapitated a
toad and a triton; and merely divided the spinal chord of a frog
and another triton. The four were placed in the same pan. At
first the spontaneous movements of the decapitated pair were insignificant; but on the second day the headless toad was quite
as lively and restless as the frog with a head; and the headless
triton little less so than his companion with a head. I have at
this moment a frog whose chord has been divided for some weeks:
he remains almost immovable unless touched; he is generally
found in the same spot, and in the same attitude to-day as
yesterday, unless touched, or the table is shaken. I notice that
he occasionally moves one of his fore-legs; occasionally one of
his hind-legs; but without changing his position. If he were
headless, this quiescence would be cited as a proof of the absence
of spontaneity; whereas I have had a headless companion with
him, who very frequently moved about.

It should be observed that an animal without its head is without
the various stimuli which can be received through sight, smell,
and hearing, each of which will determine movements; it is
therefore necessarily quiescent, unless some of its visceral sensations stimulate it. And it is to the variety of states which may
be determined by changes in the circulation, and the conditions
of the viscera, that the great variety in the actions of decapitated animals must be attributed· Some never move, but die
quietly on the spot where they were left; others are restless;
others move occasionally. Nevertheless I affirm that attentive
and repeated examination of decapitated animals will furnish
abundant evidence of spontaneous action.**

Let us now pass on to *choice*. Place a child of two or three
years old upon his back, and tickle his right cheek with a
feather. He will probably move his head away. Continue
tickling, and he will rub the spot with his right hand, *never*
using the left hand for the right cheek, so long as the right hand

---

* MARSHALL HALL: *New Memoir*, 35. GRAINGER, 149.
** LANDRY: *Traité des Paralysies*, p. 305, also believes the Spinal Chord
to originate spontaneous movements.

is free; but if you hold his right hand, he will use the left. Does any one dispute the voluntary character of these actions?

Now contrast the actions of the sleeping child under similar circumstances, and their sequence will be precisely similar. This contrast is the more illustrative, because physiologists generally assume that in sleep consciousness and volition are *suspended*. "The brain sleeps, the spinal chord never; volition and sensation may be suspended, but not reflex-action." This proposition is extremely questionable; yet it is indispensable to the reflex-theory; because unless sensation and volition *are* suspended during sleep, we must admit that they can act, without at the same time calling into activity that cerebral sensibility, which, in ordinary language, is supposed to constitute all consciousness. The child moves in his sleep, defends himself in his sleep; but he is not "aware" of it: that is to say, the actions are not combined with those cerebral sensibilities, which would come into play in waking moments. The spinal sensibility acts without the cerebral sensibility; but the actions are nevertheless determined by sensation and volition.

"Children," says Pflüger, "sleep more soundly than adults, and seem to be more sensitive in sleep. I tickled the right nostril of a three-year-old boy. He at once raised his right hand to push me away, and then rubbed the place. When I tickled his left nostril he raised the left hand. I then softly drew both arms down, and laid them close to the body, imbedding the left arm in the clothes, and placing on it a pillow, by gentle pressure on which I could keep the arm down without awakening him. Having done this I tickled his left nostril. He at once began to move the imprisoned arm, but could not reach his face with it, because I held it firmly though gently down. He now drew his head aside, and I continued tickling, whereupon he raised the *right* hand, and with it rubbed the *left* nostril — an action he never performed when the left hand was free."

This simple but ingenious experiment establishes one important point, namely, that the so-called reflex-actions observed in sleep are determined by sensation and volition. The sleeping child behaves exactly as the waking child behaved; the only difference being in the energy and rapidity of the actions. If

the waking child felt and willed, surely the sleeping child, when
it performed precisely similar actions, cannot be said to have
felt nothing, willed nothing? It is not at one moment a conscious organism, and at the next an unconscious mechanism.

It is possible to meet this case by assuming that the child was
nearly awake, and that a dim consciousness was aroused by the
tickling, so that the cerebral activity was in fact awakened.
But, plausible as this explanation may be, it altogether fails
when we come to experiments on decapitated animals. If any
one will institute a series of such experiments, taking care to
compare the actions of the animal before and after decapitation,
he will perceive that there is no more difference between them
than between those of the sleeping and the waking child. *

The following may serve as a sample: I placed a large and
very vigorous triton in an empty cigar-box, and noted down in
my note-book the various actions it performed. After running
about, and vainly trying to escape, it seemed to resign itself to its
prison, and with the apathy characteristic of these creatures,
remained quite motionless for some time. While thus resting, it
occasionally moved its tail, or raised its head, and turned it
round. Then it took a single step forwards, and stood still again.
It then moved three steps forward, and rested. I touched its foot
gently with the scissors, and the foot was slowly withdrawn, but
the animal never moved. I touched it three times rapidly, but
gently, and this produced a slow crawl. I *pressed* the scissors,
and it at once started off in a rapid run. I next touched its flank
with acetic acid. It ran about manifesting great discomfort, but
showed no intention of rubbing the acid away with its foot — as
the frog always does — indeed it seemed as unable to protect
itself against the unpleasant sensation, as a baby is when a needle
in its frock is pricking it: the pain produced a *general agitation*,
but no voluntary act. At length, however, on a second appli-

* It is better simply to remove the brain, than to remove the whole head,
which causes a serious loss of blood. An etherised animal may be operated
on with ease and accuracy. For many experiments, mere division of the
spinal chord is better than decapitation. Great variations in the results must
be expected, because the condition of the animal, its age and sex — whether
fasting or digesting — whether the season be spring or summer — and a hundred other causes, complicate the experiment.

cation of acid, while running about, its flank came accidentally
in contact with the side of the box, and the sensation seemed to
guide the animal to a voluntary act, for it now continued crawling
along, rubbing its flank against the rough wood, until the acid
was all rubbed off, or the sensation had abated. Here was the
link of feeling — the continuance of an action once begun —
which we have already seen to characterise voluntary actions.

I now cut off its head, at the articulation of the occiput with
the atlas, sparing the lower jaw, to save the loss of blood. It
dropped on the left side, with the fore-legs pressed close to its
body. Three-and-twenty minutes after the operation, it began
to move the left hind-leg feebly; still, however, lying on its side.
Four minutes after, the right leg began to move. Presently it
rose on all fours, and turned round the remnant of its head,
raising it also in the air, as if seeking something. It then relapsed
into motionlessness. After eighteen minutes of rest it once more
raised neck and shoulders, and began to move forward. After a
pause the tail began to move backwards and forwards. It then
crawled two steps. Finally its movements became sufficiently
energetic for it to crawl a distance of two inches without pausing.
Having allowed it to recover itself, I repeated the tests of
sensibility, which had been employed before decapitation. The
reactions were precisely similar. When the foot was gently
touched, it was languidly withdrawn; when irritated, the animal
moved; when the foot was pressed on by the scissors, an energetic
movement followed; and when acetic acid was applied, the
animal almost ran. I now waited half an hour, and then touched
its flank with acetic acid; as on the former occasion, this made it
very agitated; but its movements were disorderly, and helpless.
In vain I watched, expecting to see it rub its flank against the
side of the box; it curled itself in the centre, and there writhed.
I now gently pushed it towards the side, but it remained motionless; when, however, I slowly pushed it forwards, so that its flank
might rub the side, the "sensational link" seemed established,
for the animal now crawled slowly along, pausing at intervals,
its body curved inwards towards the wood, and thus rubbed the
acid away. *

* This was the only triton I ever observed to get rid of the acid by rub-

The evidence of spontaneity and choice, of sensibility and volition, is unmistakable in the foregoing case. *Even more striking is the following experiment, devised by Pflüger, which I have verified, and varied, many times: A frog is decapitated, or, better still, its brain is removed. When it has recovered from the effect of the ether, and manifests lively sensibility, we place it on its back, and touch, with acetic acid, the skin of its thigh (just above the *condylus internus femoris*). Let the reader imagine his own shoulder burnt at the point where it can be reached with the thumb of the same arm, and he will realise the operation. No sooner does the acid begin to burn, than the frog stretches out the *other* leg, so that its body is somewhat drawn towards it. The leg that has been burnt is now bent, and the back of the foot is applied to the spot, rubbing the acid away — just as your thumb might rub your shoulder. This is very like the action of the tickled child, who always uses the right hand to rub the right cheek, unless it be held; but when the child's right hand is prevented from rubbing, the left will be employed; and precisely this do we observe with the brainless frog: prevent it from using its right leg, and it will use its left!

To show this we decapitate another frog, and cut off the foot of the leg we are to irritate. No sooner is the acid applied, than the leg is bent as before, and the stump is moved to and fro, as if to rub away the acid. But the acid is not rubbed away, and the animal becomes restless, as if trying to hit upon some other plan for freeing himself of the irritation. And it is worthy of remark that he often hits upon plans very similar to those which an intelligent human being adopts under similar circumstances. Thus, the irritation continuing, he will sometimes cease the vain efforts with his stump, and stretching that leg straight out, bends the *other* leg over towards the irritated spot, and rubs the acid away. But, to show how far this action is from one of unconscious mechanism, how far it is from being a direct reflex of an impression on a group of muscles, the frog does not *always* hit even on this plan. Sometimes it bends its irritated leg more energetically, and likewise bends the body towards it, so as to permit the spot

bing its body against anything accidentally coming in contact with it; but this one did so almost as well without as with its head.

to be rubbed against the flank — just as the child, when both his hands are held, will bend his cheek towards his shoulder and rub it there.

It is difficult to resist such evidence of *choice* as is here manifested. The brainless frog chooses a new plan when the old one fails, just as the waking child chooses. And an illustration of how sensations guide and determine movements,. may be seen in another observation of the brainless frog, when, as often happens, it does not hit upon either of the plans just mentioned, but remains apparently restless and helpless; if under these circumstances we perform a part of the action for it, it will complete what we have begun: if we rub the irritated leg, at some distance from the spot where the acid is, with the foot of the other, the frog suddenly avails itself of this *guiding sensation*, and at once directs its foot to the irritated spot.

In these experiments on the triton and the frog, the evidence of sensation and volition is all the stronger, because the reactions produced by irritations are not uniform. If when a decapitated animal were stimulated it always reacted in *precisely the same way*, and never chose *new means* on the failure of the old, it would be conceivable to attribute the results to simple reflex-action — *i. e.*, the mechanical transference of an impulse along a prescribed path. It is possible so to conceive the breathing, or the swallowing mechanism: the impression may be directly reflected on certain groups of muscles. But I cannot conceive a machine suddenly striking out new methods, when the old methods fail. I cannot conceive a machine thrown into disorder when its accustomed actions fail, and in this disorder suddenly lighting upon an action likely to succeed, and continuing *that;* but I can conceive this to be done by an organism, for my own experience and observation of animals assures me that this is always the way new lines of action are adopted (see p. 148). And this which is observed of the sentient, conscious animal, I have just shown to be observed of the brainless animal; wherefore the conclusion is, that if ever the frog is sentient, if ever its actions are guided by sensation, they are so when its brain is removed. Ergo the Spinal Chord is a sentient centre.

Schröder van der Kolk thinks that Pflüger was deceived in

attributing sensation and volition to the frog, because the reflex-
actions are, he says, so nicely adapted to their ends, that they
are undistinguishable from voluntary actions. The mechanism
is such that, by means of the communications established between
various groups of cells, all these actions adapted to an end may
be excited by every stimulus. But I deny the fact. I deny that
all the actions are awakened by every stimulus. Only some few
are awakened, and those are not always the same, nor do they
follow the same order of succession. One decapitated frog does
not behave exactly like another; does not behave exactly like
himself on different occasions; but, on the contrary, exhibits
great variety in his actions; and, above all, exhibits spontaneity
and choice in his actions.

For a proper comparison of cerebral with spinal sensibility,
the following experiment is well adapted: I divided the spinal
chord of a triton as at Fig. 62. Had a physiologist been present,

Fig. 62.

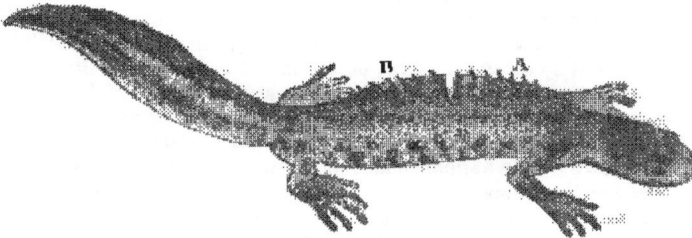

TRITON WITH SPINAL CHORD DIVIDED.

when the animal recovered, he would have noticed, as a confirmation of the reflex-theory, that when the animal crawled,
it dragged its hinder legs, and indeed the whole of the segment
B, like a log after it; yet when the segment B was touched,
the tail, or legs, moved. "Here," he would say,[*] "you perceive all voluntary movement in segment B is paralysed; it no
longer responds to the mandates of the brain; yet its reflex-
action is not destroyed; prick it, and this segment, incompe-

* Compare FLOURENS: *Recherches*, p. 50.

tent to obey the will, obeys the laws of reflex-action, and moves.
All sensibility, you perceive, has departed from segment B.   In
vain you prick or burn it; the animal feels nothing, as you assure
yourself by noticing the complete stillness of the segment A."

These arguments, which may be found in numberless trea-
tises, seem victoriously conclusive, till we discover the fallacy
involved in them.   The cerebro-spinal axis is a compound centre:
it is *one*, only in the sense that a government or army is one: it is
the union of several individual centres.   When that axis is
divided, the effective unity is destroyed: instead of one centre,
two centres are established; and these two, being no longer
united, cannot act in union, but must act separately.   The limbs
of A will obey the volition of A, but not the volition of B, with
which they are no longer united.   Nor will the limbs of B obey
the volition of A.   There is no longer one seat of government,
but two seats.   There has been a "repeal of the union."   Parlia-
ment sits in Dublin, as well as in Westminster.

Let us, with this new light, examine the phenomena.   When
we irritate the segment A, the animal crawls; but in crawling, it
is only A that is active; B is *dragged* along, does not voluntarily
move.   Why should it move, unless it felt a stimulus?   But we
irritate segment B, which five minutes ago seemed so lifeless, so
incapable of voluntary movement; and instantly the legs of B
begin the crawling action, *while A remains perfectly motionless.*
The body of the animal is moved sideways, and not forwards,
because the quiescence of the head and shoulders renders forward motion impossible.   Still the indifference of A to a stimulus
applied to B, is as great as the indifference of B formerly was to
the stimulus applied to A.   If the tail-end was said to be deprived
of voluntary motion and sensibility, because it was separated
from the brain, and would not feel with or act with the fore-part
of the body; so must we now say, that the fore-part of the body
is deprived of voluntary motion and sensibility, since it will not
act with, or feed with, the tail-end.

In fact, division of the cerebro-spinal axis is tantamount to a
division of the animal into two halves; and each half obeys its
own nerve-centres.   The soldiers under Cromwell do not obey
the orders of Rupert, nor do those under Rupert obey the orders

of Cromwell. But the soldiers of each army obey their respective generals. It is thus with the triton whose chord has been divided: each half moves when irritated, and each moves independently of the other. The tail-end gives precisely the same indication of sensibility, whether united with the brain, or separated from it; and it gives precisely the same indication as the brain-end gives.

If the triton be watched for weeks, the truth of this will become irresistible. Although the animal is generally quiet, it moves spontaneously the segment A, and the segment B; *but never together*. If a lighted taper be brought near segment A, the fore-legs set to work, and the segment crawls, *dragging* B after it. If the taper be brought near B, the hind-legs set to work, and the segment moves sideways. If the tail be touched or gently pinched, it curls up; if the hind-leg be touched, it is raised in the air; but A feels nothing of this, and therefore does not move.

It should be observed that similar facts have long been known; but since the Reflex-Theory has been established they have been misinterpreted; and even before that epoch, the prejudice in favour of the Brain as the sole centre of volition, was so strong, that Mr. Mayo could thus write: — "The physiological experiment of making separate nervous centres, by division of the spinal marrow, admits of explanation, on supposing the *principle of volition to continue for a short period* extended to the portions separated from the brain; a conjecture consistent with, perhaps, but far from established by, the very curious fact, that the convulsive movement of the leg of an animal thus circumstanced, when the sole of the foot is irritated, is accurately the gesture which the animal employs when, in undisputed possession of sensation, it retracts its limb from a similar aggression, and not, to appearance at least, a mere convulsive throe." * The explanation falls to the ground, when we learn that the same phenomena are exhibited weeks and months after division of the chord.

Among my notes of observation there is remarkable evidence of volition in the tail-half of a triton whose chord had been

* Mayo: *Anat. and Phys. Commentaries*, 1823, part. II. p. 19.

divided. It was lying, high and dry, in the wooden bowl in which
it was usually kept, the small amount of water having almost entirely evaporated. I poured in a little water, slowly. In a few
seconds after the water had reached the tail and one of the hind-
feet, the whole segment B began to move, the legs were slowly
raised, as for crawling, the back elevated, and thus the segment
sidled into the water — the segment A remaining perfectly motionless all this time. The volitional character of this action was
the more evident, because, had the act been purely reflex, excited
by contact with the water, and not by a sensation, it would *always* occur when water touched the skin, whereas I had several
times before added water, when the triton was lying high and dry,
but never before did it seek the water with its hinder segment.

    Once clearly apprehend the principle here expounded, name-
ly, that division of the chord produces two independent centres,
and all the recorded facts of experiment and pathology receive a
simple explanation. Mr. Grainger records the results of two experiments which deserve mention here. He removed a portion
of the chord in a very young rabbit: "The peculiar fact noticed
was that from time to time, *without any stimulus being applied,*
the hind-legs were forcibly and repeatedly thrown back, *as if the
animal were running quickly;* whilst at these times the fore-limbs,
which were still under the control of the animal, remained motionless. These movements were so decided and so long continued, that it would have been difficult to have rejected the idea
of sensation and volition still remaining in the hinderpart of the
body, if" — and here the reader is particularly requested to follow the reasoning — "if it had not been distinctly observed that
when the same animal attempted to walk it could only move its
two forelegs; by whose power the hinder ones and the trunk below the division of the chord, which were perfectly motionless,
were dragged along the table."*

    Surely the reader will agree with me that the facts by no
means bear out this inference? If, as we have stated, division of
the chord establishes two independent centres, we can no longer
expect these to act in unison. When the hind-legs were agitated,
the forelegs were motionless; when the fore-legs moved, the

* GRAINGER, p. 55.

hind-legs were motionless. After relating other similar experiments, Mr. Grainger insists on the motionlessness of the hinder limbs, adding, "Now, as the very idea of volition implies a perfect control over any muscle which an animal may wish to stimulate, this utter want of such power is the most decisive proof which could be adduced to show that in this and similar cases the empire of the will was destroyed by the section of the chord." *

This decisive proof, however, rests, I think, on a misconception. The animal is spoken of as if its *organic integrity remained* after division of its chord; whereas, as we have seen, division of the chord is equivalent to cutting the animal in two; and no one would expect the muscles of the separated half to move in obedience to the brain from which it was separated. The body of an animal with a divided chord may still be one, inasmuch as it is nourished with the same food, and sustained by the same circulation; but the nervous mechanism is no longer one; and each half of the body is regulated by its own centres.

To prove this, I performed the following experiment. A triton, whose chord had been divided some weeks, was completely cut in two. The head-half immediately began crawling away with great activity; which, as this half contained the heart, and almost all the viscera, was not surprising. The tail-half remained for some time in a standing posture, and then began to crawl forward. After three stops it paused; remained quiet during five minutes, and began again. but feebly. The tail moved spontaneously, but with great slowness. When it was touched, both tail and legs moved. I then placed it under a glass, with a moistened sponge inside, to prevent evaporation from the skin, and left it there for two hours, watching its spontaneous, though very languid, movements.

If any reader remains still unconvinced, I can only recommend him to divide the spinal chord of a frog a little below the shoulders, and keep the animal for some days or weeks, ** watch-

* Compare also MARSHALL HALL: *Philos. Trans.*, 1833, p. 650, where a similar fact is adduced as decisive.

** Care must be taken to prevent water getting to the chord, as that soon kills the animal.

ing it, and testing its Sensibility. The evidences of spontaneous action, and of sensation, exhibited by both halves, the one no less than the other, will have more weight than pages of argument. Marshall Hall had observed some of these evidences, observed the decapitated animal defending itself variously against various irritants, but his *interpretation* of what he observed, is not, perhaps, the most convincing of inferences: "The *design* in all this is obvious," he says; "but is it design in the decapitated or divided animal? Certainly not; but of its omniscient Creator! It *coincides* with what would be design in the animal."[*] Now of two things, one: either *every* act in an animal must be the design of its Creator: in which case sensation and volition cannot endow the actions of the perfect animal with a design already endowed; or else the Creator has designed none of these actions, but only designed that a sensitive mechanism shall execute them: in which case the actions of the perfect and the decapitated animal being found to *coincide* — being, indeed, undistinguishable by us — what ground have we for assuming that they are not the results of similar causes?

This flying to design for refuge, merely to save an assumption, reminds me of objections which have sometimes been made in private. When I have narrated the experiments on the decapitated frog, I have been told that the frog whose foot had been amputated, and who therefore had recourse to *other* means to get rid of the acid, *felt* nothing: "He did it all from *habit*. It was *instinct*." If frogs are in the *habit* of being irritated by drops of acetic acid, and are in the habit of having their feet amputated, which teaches them to seek other means of escape, all I can say is, that their education takes place in *other* ponds than those I have dredged. Schröder van der Kolk refers to some experiments by Szokalski, on puppies and young rabbits, from which the brain — *i. e.*, the cerebrum, cerebellum, the corpora quadrigemina, optic thalami, and corpora striata — had been removed; these animals cried out when their tails were pinched, rubbed their noses when acids were applied, and made swallowing movements when bitters were placed in their mouths. "Szokalski thinks these were instinctive rather than reflex actions,"

* *New Memoir*, p. 31.

says Schröder, "but in this I cannot agree with him." What
was meant by the word instinctive we are left to guess; but if
sensation is excluded from instinct, and if sensation is excluded
from actions such as those of the brainless puppy and rabbit, I
know not *what* evidence of sensation can be entertained.

It is maintained by many writers that the actions of walking
and swimming are reflex — due solely to the contact of the sole
of the foot with the ground in walking, and the contact of the
skin with the water in swimming. The impression of this contact
is reflected on the muscles; but no sensation originates, or
guides the actions. My experiments do not confirm this. When
I touched the segment A (Fig. 61) of the triton, it dragged the
segment B after it; but although in the dragging the feet of B
were rubbed along the surface, they very rarely set going the
walking actions: sometimes they did so; but contact was by no
means sufficient to *excite* this action; whereas during their tran-
sit, while they were being dragged like paralysed limbs, a prick,
or a pinch, immediately roused them into walking movements.
I placed a frog, with divided chord, in a pan of water; the fore-
legs immediately set going an energetic swimming action, but
the hind-legs remained motionless, although they too were in
contact with the water, and the impression ought to have been
reflected on their muscles. I then decapitated another frog: on
being thrown into the water it swam vigorously with both fore
and hind legs. Presently it ceased swimming, and floated quietly
on the surface; but on being touched again began swimming.
This was repeated many times. It shows that mere contact of
the water is not enough to excite swimming actions; whereas a
sensation *is* enough. Claude Bernard found that a frog, whose
skin had been removed from all its legs, swam as well as before.
But when the whole skin had been removed, I found the frog
capable, indeed, of swimming, since its power of muscular adjustment was unaffected, but making no attempt to swim.

These observations respecting the sensibility of the Spinal
Chord may be closed with the following fact recorded by Volkmann. Young rabbits and puppies when taken from their mothers, manifest their discomfort by restless movements; the
puppies also whine. No one doubts that sensation is present in

such cases. Now, if the brain be removed from rabbits and puppies, precisely similar phenomena are observed, when these young animals are taken from their mothers. "I observed the motions, which seemed the result of discomfort, quickly cease when I warmed the young rabbit by breathing on it. After a while it was completely at rest, and seemed sunk in deep sleep; occasionally, however, it moved one of its legs without any external stimulus having been applied, and this not spasmodically, but in the manner of a sleeping animal."* Is this cessation of the restlessness, when warmth is restored, not evidence of sensation? We see an infant restless, struggling, and squalling; and we believe that it is hungry, or that some other sensations agitate it; it is put to the breast, and its squalls subside; or a finger is placed in its mouth, and it sucks that, in a peaceful lull, for a few moments, to recommence squalling when the finger yields no satisfaction. If we accept these as signs of sensation, I do not see how we can deny such sensation to the brainless infant, or animal which will also cease to cry, and will suck the delusive finger!

VII. EVIDENCE AGAINST THE SENSIBILITY OF THE SPINAL CHORD. — Having at some length adduced the evidence which, to my mind, is conclusive in favour of the sensibility of the Spinal Chord, it is now necessary to examine the evidence which can be adduced against it. We have already seen that the main argument against it has been drawn from the universal preconception of the Brain being the exclusive sensorium; and we have also seen that this begs the question. Another argument has been drawn from the indisputable fact that many actions take place without awakening any distinct "consciousness" or attention — these are, breathing, winking, digesting, and many others. But we have seen, in the Chapter on FEELING and THINKING, that this proves nothing, or proves too much. An action may be sensational, without producing that secondary feeling, usually styled "consciousness;" and, in this sense, thinking may be proved unconscious — nay, sensations themselves may be so.

* VOLKMANN, quoted by PFLCOE.

There remains only the striking fact of human patients with injured or diseased spines, feeling nothing below the injury. This fact we have more than once referred to as the *cheval de bataille* of the Reflex-Theory, which, we have also affirmed, turns out on close inspection to be the sorriest of Rozinantes. Let the fact be stated in all its force. A man with an injured spinal chord may lose all power of voluntary movement in the limbs below the injury; and also lose all power of feeling any impressions made on them. Pricks, burns, pinches, leave *him* unaffected. Hunter's celebrated patient, on being asked whether he *felt* the pain which caused his leg to kick out, answered, "No; but you see my leg does." And thus might all such patients reply. These limbs have not lost their power of movement, only their power of obeying the brain. They will not move when the patient endeavours to move them; but they are withdrawn, or convulsed, if pricked or tickled. Marshall Hall reports the case of a man in whom accident had destroyed all sensation and voluntary motion, yet who drew up his legs when they were tickled, without once feeling the sensation of tickling; and he drew them up when sprinkled with cold water, without feeling the slightest sensation of cold. This case is constantly cited, and is indeed very striking. It seems to have a far greater value than any experiments on animals can have, because we cannot question animals as to their sensations, we do not *know* whether they feel or not; we can only infer: whereas we can interrogate the human patient, and he distinctly *denies* being conscious of any impression whatever. "Do you feel this pin which is pricking you, and making your leg jerk?" — "No, I do not." Nothing seems less equivocal. We *must* accept his statement. Do I then doubt it? *Not in the least.*

Dr. Baly, in the notes to his admirable translation of Müller's *Physiology,* records that he has a patient under his care attacked with complete loss of sensation and motion in the left upper and lower extremity, in whom, nevertheless, pinching or even slightly touching the sole of the foot or ankle of the paralysed leg, causes the limb to be retracted and the toes extended, the patient being unconscious both of the stimulus and the movement. When I first read this statement, having entire reliance on Dr. Baly's accuracy in observing and reporting, it seemed to me to overthrow all the evidence on the other side; and this idea was further strengthened by the cases collected by Dr. Budd. * It is unnecessary to occupy space here by citing these cases: they all point in the same direction, and we may therefore accept the conclusion, namely, —

That injury to the Spinal Chord wholly or partially destroys the power of obeying the Brain by voluntary movement, and the power of transmitting sensory impressions to the Brain, in the parts *below* the seat of injury; while in those *above* the seat of injury, sensation and voluntary motion remain.

Such is the conclusion rigorously deduced from numerous facts. I accept it, without reserve. But I shall now prove that it does not in the least affect the question under discussion, does not throw a shadow of doubt on the sensational and volitional character of the Spinal Chord. That it should ever have been thought to do so admits of easy explanation. Let us disclose the fallacy it involves.

On the supposition that the whole cerebro - spinal axis is everywhere the seat of Sensibility, it has already been shown that division of this axis would create two independent centres. In this case we have no right to suppose that the *cerebral* segment will be affected by impressions made on the *spinal* segment; nor, conversely, that impressions made on the cerebral segment will affect the spinal segment. The anterior limbs will obey the Brain, because they are in organic relation with it; but the posterior limbs *cannot* obey the Brain after they have ceased to be in organic relation with it. This has been fully explained (p. 175 *et seq.*)

Now, when a man has a diseased spinal chord, the seat of injury causes, for the time at least, a division of the cerebrospinal axis into two independent centres. For all purposes of sensation and volition it is the same as if he were cut in half; his nervous mechanism *is* cut in half. How then can any cerebral volition be obeyed by his legs; how can any impression on his legs be felt by his cerebrum? As well might we expect the man whose arm has been amputated, to feel the incisions of the

* BUDD: in *Medico-Chirurg. Trans.*, xxii., cited by Dr. CARPENTER.

scalpel, when that limb is conveyed to the dissecting-table, as to feel in his brain impressions made upon parts wholly divorced from organic connection with the brain.

But, it may be objected, this is the very point urged. The man himself does not feel the impressions on his limbs when his spine has been injured; he is as insensible to them as to the dissection of his amputated arm. Very true. *He* does not feel it. But if the amputated arm were to strike the anatomist who began its dissection, if its fingers were to grasp the scalpel, and push it away, or with the thumb to rub off the acid irritating one of the fingers, I do not see how we could refuse to admit that the *arm* felt although the *man* did not. And this is the case with the extremities of a man whose spine is injured. *They* manifest every indication of sensibility. In the frog they manifest unmistakable volition. It is true that the man himself, when interrogated, declares that he feels nothing; the cerebral segment has attached to it organs of speech and expressive features, by which *its* sensations can be communicated to others; whereas the spinal segment has *no* such means of communicating *its* sensations; but those which it *has*, it *employs*. You can ask the cerebral segment a question, which can be heard, understood, and answered; this is not the case with the spinal segment; yet if you *test* its sensibility, the result is unequivocal. You cannot ask an animal whether it feels, but you can test its sensibility, and that test suffices.

In our examination of the triton and the frog, after division of their spinal chord, we saw that the limbs which could convey no impression to the brain, and could obey no impulse from the brain, exhibited the same evidences of sensibility as when they were in connection with the brain. Yet if the animal could have spoken, it would have assured us that it felt nothing in its hinder limbs. The limbs themselves told a different story.

The question we have to decide, therefore, is not whether a patient, with an injured spine, can feel impressions on, or convey voluntary movements to, limbs below the seat of injury — for as respects the nervous mechanism these limbs are separated from him, no less than if actual amputation had taken place — the question is, whether these separated limbs have any sensibility? And the answer seems to me unequivocally affirmative. I assert, therefore, that if there is ample evidence to show that the spinal centres have sensibility, when separated from the cerebral centres, such evidence can in no respect be weakened by the fact that a man with an injured spine is unconscious of impressions made below the seat of injury; since such a fact necessarily follows from the establishment of two centres: the parts above are not sensitive to impressions on the parts below; nor are the parts below sensitive to impressions on the parts above; but each segment is sensitive to its own impressions.

It should be borne in mind that although all vertebrate animals are constructed according to one general type, and all their organs have a certain general homology, the very great variations in their mechanisms will necessarily bring about corresponding variations in their functions. Hence, we may expect to see actions performed by one segment of a frog, which cannot be performed by the corresponding segment of man. And as a part of this variation in structure may be noticed the fact that in man the Spinal Chord is insignificant in comparison with the Brain, whereas in reptiles the Brain is less than the Chord. Anderson[*] estimates the weight of the triton's chord at one-fourth of a grain; that of the brain being one-seventh — showing a proportion of 100 to 180. From the figures given by Sharpey and Ellis,[**] it appears that while the weight of the human brain is 40 ounces as an average, that of the Spinal Chord is less than 2 ounces, sometimes only 1 ounce. The proportion is therefore 40 or 33 to 1. In animals the proportion is much less. In the mouse it is 4 to 1; in the pigeon, $3\frac{1}{4}$ to 1; in the triton, $\frac{1}{4}$ to 1, and in the lamprey, $\frac{1}{14}$ to 1.

VIII. WHAT PART IS PLAYED BY THE SPINAL CHORD? — The reader may now ask what part is to be assigned to the Spinal Sensibility, supposing its existence granted? Do we think with our Spinal Chord? Is it a centre of Intelligence? "Why no, sir," as Dr. Johnson would say.

Our previous investigations conducted us to the conclusion that the cerebrum was the centre of intelligence and emotion —

* ANDERSON: *Comp. Anat. of Nervous System.* 31.
** QUAIN'S *Anat.*, 6th edit., ii. 455.

at least in those animals which have a cerebrum. In the Amphioxus, which has no brain at all, the intelligence and emotion it may possibly have, must necessarily be performed through the agency of the Spinal Chord. Nor is there anything in such a supposition which is at variance with the principles laid down in these pages, however at variance with ordinary theories. For in the Amphioxus the spinal chord must be the centre in which the reflexes of sense are combined, as they are combined in the cerebrum of higher animals.

But quitting all such questions inaccessible except to inference, let us consider the probable share taken in our actions by the Spinal Chord. The intimate *consensus* which exists between every part of the vital mechanism renders it impossible very accurately to define the share of each. But if we look to the anatomical connections of the Spinal Chord, and assume that the Brain is the organ of intellectual action, we may consider that Spinal Sensibility regulates all those actions which are not set going by cerebral Sensibility.

A few illustrations will suffice. The brain of a sleeping man is supposed to be disconnected from all participation in the activity of the chord. Either the man is in profound sleep, and his brain is at rest, or he is dreaming, and his brain being cut off from almost all external stimuli, is occupied exclusively with its own excited activity — with its dreams. The man during this state breathes, swallows his saliva, coughs if any gets into the windpipe, and turns in his bed; the organic processes go on, and his brain has little if any share in all these various actions. From this sleeping man we remove the bed-clothes; the cold air soon produces a sensation of uneasiness; he turns and seeks a warmer spot; perhaps he stretches out his hand and pulls the clothes over him again. The evidence of sensation and volition here is unmistakable. If he did not *feel* the cold he would not move; if he did not *will* to move, and to pull the bed-clothes over him, he could not do it.

There are very cogent reasons for believing that in these cases the sensation and volition have their seat in the Spinal Chord, and not in the Brain. Firstly, the actions very closely resemble those of animals when the entire Brain has been removed. Secondly, brain-prompted actions — *i. e.*, those which spring from a distinct idea, or train of ideas — never seem possible in sleep. The sleeping man, who immediately moves his arm to rub his tickled cheek, or draws the bed-clothes when the cold air reaches him, or turns if he bo touched, *cannot move a muscle when, in dreams, his mind is assailed with terror at danger*, or with desire to rescue his children. It is usual to account for this familiar fact by saying that in sleep "the will is suspended": a mere phrase, and a false one; for the will is not suspended when it permits the man to pull the bed-clothes over him, or to seek a warmer spot in the bed.

When the Brain is actively engaged in thought — as in profound meditation, or reverie — the volitions emanating from the Spinal Chord seem to suffice for all regular and continuous actions, such as walking or eating; or for the relief of particular discomforts, as when the tickling of a fly causes the hand to move towards the spot, or the position of the limbs is changed. We may walk through crowded streets absorbed in thought, yet every obstacle is avoided, and our destination reached with unerring accuracy. It is probable that from time to time the Brain interrupts its course of thought to glance at the houses, and assure us we are not in the wrong track; but although it is probable that, even during the profoundest meditation, the Brain does in general take cognisance of surrounding objects (for when it does *not* we miss our way), yet it seems tolerably certain that the guiding sensations of the Chord suffice during the intervals when then Brain is otherwise occupied. Indeed, men have been known to sleep on horseback, and soldiers have marched during sleep — facts which bear a close resemblance to the phenomena exhibited by decapitated animals.

Here, however, we are once more treading on the confines of Psychology, and must pause ere we get entangled in its labyrinths. If we have indicated in a general way the physiological relations of the MIND and the BRAIN, our object has been achieved. Nor will we here venture into an examination of the Sympathetic system, although we hold that here also the ganglia are centres of Sensibility. But the reader's attention will be more readily secured by the questions to be examined in our next chapter.

NOTE TO CHAPTER IX., SECTION III.

For the sake of any student who may desire to investigate the microscopic structure of nerve-centres, I will describe the best methods of preparation. Take a perfectly fresh brain or chord, and having removed its membranes, cut it in small sections, and harden them in alcohol, in chromic acid, or in bichromate of potass. Whichever solution is used should be very weak at first, and gradually strengthened. Lockhart Clarke's plan is to use a mixture of one part alcohol and three parts of water, for the first twenty-four hours; this is then thrown away, and replaced by equal parts of alcohol and water, for another twenty-four hours; and this again is replaced by pure alcohol. In ten or fourteen days it is ready. Stilling uses chromic acid; Kölliker, bichromate of potass, beginning with a solution of 1 per cent, and increasing it gradually to 4 per cent, constantly changing the solution. Clarke also now generally employs chromic acid, or bichromate of potass. He suggests a solution of ½ per cent of chromic acid for two or three weeks, followed by a solution of ¼ or 1 per cent of bichromate. Both alcohol and chromic acid are excellent, and have different advantages; on the whole, I find it most advantageous, when bichromate of potass is used, to remove the sections, after three weeks, into strong alcohol, which better completes the hardening, and washes out the potass.

Having thus hardened the object, so that it is neither too soft nor too friable to permit of thin sections being made with a very sharp razor (for the spinal chords of small animals I use one of those small razors sold as corn-cutters), the upper surface of which must be previously wetted with alcohol, we have now to render the sections sufficiently transparent. This Kölliker effects by treating them first with soda (Bidder and his pupils use diluted

sulphuric acid), then washing the soda out, and placing the
section on a glass slide, he drops concentrated chloride of calcium on it, and covers with thin glass. This plan has never
seemed to me so effective as the one employed by Lockhart
Clarke. Schröder van der Kolk hardens in alcohol, then placing
a thin section on a glass slide, drops distilled water on it, and
covers with thin glass, and commences a gentle pressure on the
edges of the covering-glass, which pressure causes the water to
rush between the fibres, and wash out the fat. When pressure
no longer makes the water milky (after repeated changes), a drop
of chloride of calcium is added; in six or seven days the section
is clear. This also seems to me very inferior to the plan adopted
by Clarke, who places the section in alcohol for a few minutes,
according to its thickness, and then floats it on oil of turpentine.
On the turpentine it rapidly becomes transparent. It is then removed to a glass slide, on which is a drop of Canada balsam,
and allowed to remain, if not everywhere transparent; or if
transparent, is covered with thin glass, and is ready for inspection.

The simplest of all plans is to harden the chord in alcohol,
make a thin section, place it on a glass slide, add turpentine,
and cover with thin glass; the turpentine penetrates slowly, and
the section gradually clears; you may watch it day by day.

If the cells are to be exhibited, Gerlach's plan is to place the
fresh chord, or the section just made from a hardened chord, in
a very weak filtered solution of carmine, dissolved in weak
ammonia: it is allowed to remain there a few minutes or a few
hours, according to the strength of the solution. It must then
be washed, and placed in alcohol.

By varying the plans, and giving the requisite patience, preparations may be produced of great distinctness; but the complexity of the structure renders it excessively difficult of comprehension, even with the best preparations.

CHAPTER X.

OUR SENSES AND SENSATIONS.

How many senses have we? — Definition of terms — New classification of the
sensations — ORGANIC-SENSATIONS — The Muscular Sense: proofs of its
existence; experiments to show that its seat is not the skin, but the muscles
— Electrical disturbance causing nervous-action — SURFACE-SENSATIONS:
various sensibilities of the skin — TOUCH: tactile corpuscles not organs of
touch; how we localise all our sensations: all sensations referred to the surface;
feelings in amputated limbs; some parts of the skin more sensitive than others
— Feeling of "pins and needles" in the leg — TASTE: organ of; savoury substances must be soluble; dare we trust our instinct in taste? after-tastes —
SMELL: organ of; are the olfactory nerves the nerves of smell? — Are they
nerves at all? — Example of perfect sense of smell in the absence of the
olfactory nerves — Odorous substances — Variations and uses of smell —
HEARING: organ of; cases of perforated tympanum; varieties in sounds; a
musical ear; effect of sounds on the emotions; subjective sounds; direction
of sounds, and how discriminated — SIGHT: organ of — Are images transmitted to the brain? — Description of the Retina — Is it nervous? — It is
insensible to Light; vision commences in a change of temperature — Subjective vision: curious examples — Single vision with two eyes: the paradox
explained — Why are objects not seen inverted? — Colour-blindness —
Psychological importance of the new view of the senses.

"How many senses have you?" inquired the traveller from
Sirius, in Voltaire's exquisite satire; upon which the inhabitant
of Saturn replied, "Seventy-two; but every day we live, we
lament that we have so few."

The European has been taught to be so well satisfied with five
senses, that he is apt to regard as an absurdity the attempt to
alter, or enlarge that sacred number. Yet, if we look closely
into the matter, we find that five is either too few, or too many:
too few, if every distinct source of special sensations is to be
called a Sense; too many, if only that is worthy to be called an
organ of Sense which — as in the case of the eye or the ear —
ministers to a single function, and yields only one group of
special sensations. When it is said, "Man has only five senses,"

it is said that over and above the sensations of touch, sight, hearing, smell, and taste, he has nothing to be called sensation. This is manifestly wrong. "The division of our external senses," says Hutcheson, "into five common classes, is ridiculously imperfect. Some sensations, such as hunger and thirst, weariness and sickness, can be reduced to none of them; or if they are reduced to feelings, they are perceptions as different from the other ideas of touch — such as cold, heat, hardness, softness — as the ideas of taste or smell." *

Gerdy thinks the reduction of our senses to five, one of the most ridiculous of notions. "A sense," he says, "is nothing but a part of our body which gives different sensations from those of other parts. Is it not on the ground of such differences that men have admitted the five senses?" ** Sir W. Hamilton also, after laying down the proposition that all our senses are modifications of touch, or contact, adds "that if Sight and Hearing, if Smell and Taste, are to be divided from each other, and from Touch Proper, under Touch there must, on the same analogy, be distinguished a plurality of special senses."

It is impossible that there can be any philosophic agreement, unless we come to a distinct understanding of terms. We cannot leave undecided what is to be understood by the words "sensation" and "sense." It is clear that there is a great variety of sensations; but this does not imply a corresponding variety in our Senses. The same organ necessarily furnishes a great diversity of sensations, if it is capable of being acted on by a diversity of stimuli. Let us therefore settle our terms; since if the inquiry be, "How many distinct and special sensations have we?" the answer will not be five, but probably five-score; whereas, if the inquiry be, "How many distinct organs of sense have we?" the answer can only be settled by a profound anatomist.***

---

* Quoted by Sir W. Hamilton: *Lectures on Metaphysics*, II. 156. The language is loose enough, but the idea is intelligible.

** Gerdy: *Physiologie Philosophique des Sensations*, p. 39.

*** On this, as on so many other subjects, the philosophical student is referred to the important work by Victor Carus: *System der thierischen Morphologie*; see also Gegenbaum: *Grundzüge der vergleichenden Anatomie*; and Bergmann and Leuckart: *Vergleichende Anatomie*; or the course of development of the senses in the animal series.

A sensation, properly so called, is the reaction of Sensibility, stimulated by an impression — the activity of a nerve-centre awakened by the Neurility of a nerve. This we have seen to be the rigorous definition. Those writers who complicate the idea of Sensation with the idea of Thought, and assert that there can be no sensation unless it be *recognised* as such by the sentient being, may equally accept our definition, since, according to them, Sensibility never *is* awakened by a stimulus unless the brain be also affected.

The stimulus may be external, or internal. It may arise from contact with agents outside, or from agents inside the body: the pressure of a pin on a sensitive surface, the chemical changes going on in the substance of an organ, or the pressure of a blood-vessel, may equally produce sensations, but the sensations produced will not be similar. For while, on the one hand, the *kind* of sensation is determined by the nature and degree of the stimulus, it is, on the other hand, determined by the peculiar structure and organic disposition of the part affected.* The same degree of temperature which, acting on a nerve through the skin, will produce the sensation of cold, will produce no such sensation but one of *pain*, if it act *directly* on this nerve; and I have found, as previously mentioned, that the same nerve which in the frog is sensitive to pricks or cuts through the skin, is not sensitive to them *under* the skin. The ray of light which, falling on the optic *apparatus*, produces a well-known sensation, produces nothing of the kind if it fall on the optic *nerve*, or any other nerve. The wave of air which produces the sensation of sound through the auditory apparatus, produces little appreciable effect on any other part. The sugar which is sweet to the tongue, is merely rough to the gums. Thus each organ of sense *determines* its specific sensations: a blow on the arm causes pain, on the eye a flash of light, on the ear a sound. Electricity causes alkaline, or acid, tastes, phosphoric odours, buzzing sounds, and flashes of light, if applied to tongue, nose, ear, and eye. *One* stimulus is thus transformed into various sensations, according as it acts through various channels.

* Compare VICTOR CARUS: *Morphologie* pp. 61, 62.

Sensibility is the general property of every animal organism. This general property becomes specialised in proportion as the organism itself becomes more special and complex in structure.* Although every animal must feel, it does not follow that every animal must have every *kind* of feeling. The mollusc feels, but it is extremely doubtful whether it feels pain, and still more so whether it feels tickling   Its sense of sight is probably little more than a discrimination of light from darkness; its sense of hearing little more than a susceptibility to vibrations of the air. Nay, even to pass on to higher animals, the cat undoubtedly distinguishes sounds, and does not confound the cry of the cat's-meat-man with that of the dustman; but its susceptibility to musical intervals will be very doubtful to those who have "assisted" at gutter-concerts.   And among men, there are those who cannot distinguish the colours red and blue; others who have no distinct appreciation of odours and savours; others who can scarcely follow a melody; others who are very ticklish, or not at all so; others exquisitely sensitive to pain, and others very much less so.   All these *specialities* of the general Sensibility depend on specialities of the nervous system and the organs of sense.

The precise number of our senses is a question not easily answered.   If every distinct part of the organism, which is the source of distinct sensations, is to be called a Sense, we must necessarily include the Muscles and Viscera among the Senses, for the sensations derived through the muscles—sensations of adjustment, weariness, cramp, &c.—are as *specific* as those derived through the eye or tongue; and the glandular sensations are assuredly distinct from those of the muscles.

The following is the classification which seems to me desirable, after what has been said respecting the various forms of consciousness (see p. 53-56).   All those sensations which arise in the organic processes, or which, belonging to the general system, are not localised in any special organ, I call *systemic sensations;* whereas those, on the contrary, which are localised in special organs — the eye, the ear, the nose, the tongue, and the

* On the development of psychical complexity, see the remarkable work by HERBERT SPENCER: *Principles of Psychology.*

hand — I call *sense-sensations*. The former only tell us of our own internal condition — they are the subjective senses.[*] The latter give us conceptions of things external to ourselves — they are the objective senses. Although the food which stimulates the alimentary canal, or the air which stimulates the lungs, are objects not less *external* than the colour or the odour of a rose, we do not habitually refer the sensations they produce to distinct cognisable objects, as in the case of the colour and odour. We have great difficulty in localising the systemic sensations, and never succeed in doing so with any precision; whereas we are in no doubt that the sensation of colour is derived through the eye, and nowhere else.

Systemic sensations may be divided into two classes: *Organic* and *Surface Sensations;* these we will now consider.

I. ORGANIC-SENSATIONS. — That we receive sensations from the varying states of our organs, not less than from the varying impressions of objects on our Senses, is abundantly manifest. The agitation of the heart, the pains or pleasures of the alimentary canal, the feelings of fatigue, sleepiness, hunger, thirst, and the various feelings attendant on maternity, are obviously of organic origin. It would doubtless create some surprise were we to speak of a Respiratory Sense; yet there would be more warrant for such a term than for the Muscular Sense, which has gained general acceptance. Indeed Mr. Bain, who has treated this topic of the organic sensations with great fulness and felicity,[**] properly remarks that we have in respiration all the particulars necessary to constitute a Sense: an *external object* — the air of the atmosphere; an *organ;* and a resulting *state of feeling.* This cannot be said of the Muscular Sense, which has no external object. No one will doubt that we receive distinct sensations from the purity, or closeness, of the atmosphere; we cannot draw breath without exciting a sensation, although in general we are not "aware" of it. In like manner the sensations of the

[*] KANT's classification into *sensus vagus* and *sensus fixus* corresponds pretty nearly with the above.
[**] BAIN: *The Senses and the Intellect.*

alimentary canal generally pass unperceived by us; but they go
to form that stream of Consciousness which I have before noticed.

Referring the reader to Mr Bain's work for further details on
this subject, I will now pass to the very important class of
sensations arising from the condition of the muscles.

1. *The Muscular Sense.*—In his erudite dissertations affixed to
Reid's Works, Sir William Hamilton has sketched the history of
the conception, revived in our own day by Sir Charles Bell, of
a distinct Muscular Sense. Whether it is legitimate or not to
elevate this into the rank of a distinct Sense—a rank denied to
the glands and alimentary canal—may be questionable, and is,
indeed, often questioned; but there has long been general
unanimity as to the fact that the muscles are the sources of peculiar
sensations, such as those of exercise, weariness, cramp, &c.
It has also been admitted that the *adjustments* necessary for all
movements for walking, riding, dancing, sitting upright, and
so forth, are dependent on the sensitiveness of the muscles.
The body is balanced by an incessant shifting of the muscles,
one group antagonising the other. But this would be impossible
unless each muscle were adjusted and co-ordinated by sensation.

"When a blind man, or a man blindfolded, stands upright,
neither leaning upon nor touching aught; by what means does
he maintain his erect position? The symmetry of his body is not
the cause. A statue of the finest proportion must be soldered to
its pedestal, or the wind will cast it down. How is it, then,
that a man sustains the perpendicular posture, or inclines in the
due degree towards the wind that blows upon him? It is obvious
that he has a sense by which he knows the inclination of his body;
and that he has a ready aptitude to adjust the parts of it, so as
to correct any deviation from the perpendicular. What sense is
this? He touches nothing, sees nothing; it can only be by the
adjustment of the muscles that the limbs are stiffened, the body
firmly balanced and kept erect. In truth, we stand by so fine an
exercise of this power, and the muscles from habit are directed
with so much precision, and with an effort so slight, that we do
not know how we stand. But if we attempt to walk on a narrow
ledge, or rest in a situation where we are in danger of falling, or
balance on one foot, we become subject to apprehension: and

the actions of the muscles are then, as it were, magnified, and demonstrative of the degree in which they are excited."*

If we watch an infant learning to walk, or attend to our own sensations when learning some new muscular movement, we shall become aware of the necessity of a very fine sensibility for all these adjustments. It is only by means of guiding sensations that we can perform such actions. All this was admitted by physiologists; but there still remained the question whether the sensations derived in muscular contraction could properly be referred to the muscles. In his admirable treatise on Physiology, Schiff maintains that all the phenomena attributed to the muscular sense are due to the foldings and stretchings of the *skin* when the muscles contract. Spiess and Schröder van der Kolk hold similar views. Indeed when we learn that the posterior, or so-called *sensory* nerves, traverse, but do not terminate in muscles, we are in a dilemma if we grant the muscles to be the channels of sensation; since they are supplied only with anterior, that is, the so-called *motor* nerves. How can these motor-nerves convey sensory stimuli? This difficulty does not seem to have been generally recognised. It is only to be escaped by denying that the muscles are channels of sensation; or by denying that the so-called motor-nerves are not *also* sensory nerves. Schiff rejects the muscular sense, and attributes to the *skin* all the phenomena grouped under this sense. The reader is aware that I deny the so-called motor-nerves to be *exclusively* motor; and one proof on which I rely is the proof of a muscular sense.

In a paper read at the Aberdeen Meeting of the British Association,** I adduced the following decisive experiments, which, if we admit that sensations are necessary to muscular adjustments, leave no doubt that the muscles and muscle-nerves are the sources of such sensations. I etherised a frog, and then carefully removed the whole of its skin, except a very small patch about the end of the back, and another patch over mouth, nose, and eyes. These patches were left for comparison. If Schiff's views were correct, — if all the phenomena assigned to a muscular sense were due to foldings and stretchings of the skin,

* BELL: *On the Hand*, p. 238; 6th edition.
** *A Demonstration of the Muscular Sense.*

it was obvious that this frog could manifest none of these phenomena, having no skin to be folded or stretched. What was the
fact? Why, that no sooner had the frog recovered from the
effects of the ether, than it hopped off the table on to the ground.
I then tested its sensibility. Those patches, where the skin
remained, were as sensitive as ever; a touch there, made the
frog hop, or shrink, or draw up its legs in defence. If its nose
was touched with acetic acid, the fore-legs were used to rub
the acid away; showing that it had the same power of adjusting
its muscles as when the skin was on. But this was no absolute
proof that the frog had any sensation derived through these
muscles; and to obviate all objection I sought for such proof.
It is to be observed that, as regards external impressions, the
frog was utterly insensible. I pinched the limbs, pricked them,
cut them, burnt them with acetic acid, and reduced them to
cinders with the flame of a wax taper — and to all these violent
stimuli the frog remained insensible, motionless,* although a
touch on the skin-patches made it hop or wince. Here then was
an animal which, if it had sensations at all, could only have
them from internal stimuli, except on two minute patches of
skin. Yet when it was placed on its back, it immediately turned
round again, and settled in a comfortable position. Lest this
change of position should be attributed to the "will" of the
animal, whose brain might be thought to have originated the
act, I cut its head off; the headless frog, placed on its back,
always turned round as before. The position was obviously
uncomfortable, and was altered. The hind-legs were then

---

* Whenever I adduce experimental evidence, the reader will be pleased
to remember that, unless the contrary is stated, I am always speaking of facts
repeatedly observed, and controlled by comparative experiments. What is
said in the text respecting the insensibility of the skinned frog is exact; it has
been observed in many cases; but there is one strange exception recorded in
my note-book which deserves notice here. "Found traces of sensibility in
some of the skinless parts. Pinching the joints or the soles of the feet, and
almost anywhere on the fore-leg, made the frog struggle or jump. Acetic
acid had no such effect. Pricking seldom had any. Back quite insensible to
all stimuli. Muscles of the thigh insensible to burns or pricks, but sensitive
to a prolonged pinch with the tweezers." This is wholly inexplicable to me;
but the fact is worth considering.

drawn out: if drawn abruptly, they were abruptly drawn up
again; if drawn very gently, they remained motionless where
they were placed; *but after a few minutes the legs were always
drawn up again.* To what can we attribute this change of position but to a sense of muscular discomfort? Had the muscles
been insensible, the legs would have remained motionless till
the animal was about to spring; but that they were sensitive is
shown in the fact that, after a while, the legs always were drawn
back to the normal position; and this was observed to take place
in a shorter time if the outstretched leg was at right angles to
the body than if it were straight out. That is to say, the more
unusual the position, the swifter was the withdrawal.

We have thus a skinned and headless frog manifesting many
unequivocal signs of those sensations which have been assigned
to the conditions of the muscles; and are justified in considering
this experiment as demonstrating the existence of a muscular
sense. And a striking confirmation of the original conception,
that a muscular sense is necessary for the adjustments on which
combined actions depend, is to be found in a case recorded by
Brown-Séquard.   Sir Charles Bell refers to a woman who,
having lost the muscular sensibility in her arm, could only hold
her infant so long as she *looked* at her arm; directly she averted
her eyes, the loss of this *guiding sensation* made her grasp loosen.
On this Brown-Séquard remarks: "It may be said that the sensibility of the skin being lost in this case, the impossibility of
holding the child arose from this cutaneous anæsthesia.   There
is a decisive reply to this objection: it is, that muscular sensibility alone is sufficient for the direction of voluntary movements.
I have seen a child completely deprived of cutaneous sensibility
(unable to feel contact, pressure, pricking, pinching, tickling,
cold, or heat), yet able to walk well without looking at its feet,
and undoubtedly owing this power to the persistence of guiding
sensations in the muscles. In this case, besides the peculiar
sensibility which guides voluntary movements, the muscles had
the power of giving pain. When they were excited to contract
spasmodically, the patient had the feeling of cramps." *

* BROWN-SÉQUARD: *Lectures in Lancet*, Oct. 16, 1858.

In singing, a wonderful adjustment of the muscles takes place; and although the direction impressed on these is mainly due to the sense of hearing, this is no more than the direction of our locomotive movements impressed by sight. Dr. Kitto, in his interesting autobiographical sketch,[*] narrates how difficult, and even painful, it was for him to speak, on first recovering from the accident which made him deaf. But he subsequently learned to speak, and this was of course entirely due to the muscular sensations in his vocal organs. In the same way, a man blindfolded, or suddenly blinded, finds great difficulty in walking straight ahead; the loss of his eyesight is the loss of the accustomed guiding sensation; yet in a little while his muscular sense suffices to guide his steps. Mr. Mayo's energetic phrase, "We lean upon our eyesight as upon crutches," is inaccurate. We derive no power of walking from sight, we only ascertain our course by it. Eyesight is a finger-post, not a crutch.

Having made clear to ourselves that we have a distinct class of muscular sensations, we shall at once recognise the important element they must form in our general Consciousness, little as they ever emerge into that prominence which causes the mind to attend to them. We shall also recognise the sensory function of the motor-nerves (see Vol. IL p. 22 *et seq.*) And now an interesting problem presents itself, namely, how the contractions of a muscle can awaken sensation. In the ordinary conception of sensation, it is implied that some external object should impress a nerve, and this impression, transmitted to the brain, will produce a sensation. This conception renders internal sensations difficult of explanation. But a more accurate survey of the facts leads to the conclusion that the mere *disturbance of the electrical equilibrium* in an organ is sufficient to excite a sensation.

Let us dissect out the lumbar nerves of a frog (*l*), and, taking the leg of another frog with its nerve dissected out, let us place this nerve (*c*) on the muscles of the first (*m*). When the two poles of a battery are applied to the lumbar nerve (*l*), the legs (*m*) are violently contracted, and this contraction so affects the

---

[*] KITTO: *The Lost Senses: Deafness.*

Fig. 63.

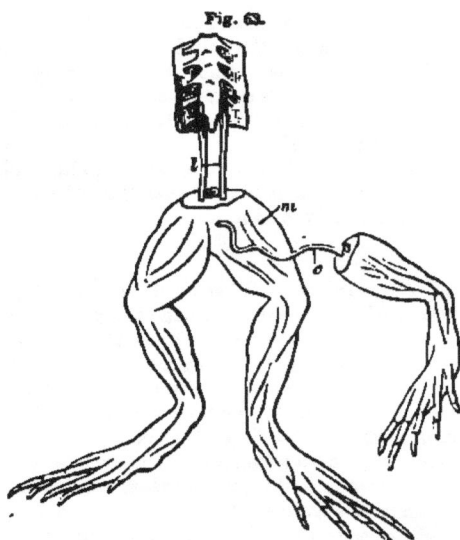

nerve of the leg (c) lying on the contracted muscles, that *this leg also contracts*. Here, then, the mere contraction of a muscle, stimulates another nerve in contact with it. Now, it is indifferent to our present argument what explanation we accept of this fact; the fact that a *change in the state* of the muscle will excite the Neurility of a nerve, is enough for us.* And it is extremely important to bear in mind that not only will a muscle in contraction excite any nerve with which it may be in contact, but it will do so if, without contracting, it even *tends* to contract.

By disturbances of the electrical equilibrium the Neurility of nerves is excited. Hence it is that the manifold chemical changes

---

* Will not this explain the paradox of parts wholly destitute of nerves being nevertheless susceptible of intense pain? The altered *state* of a tendon may propagate an influence to the muscles, and these may excite the sensory nerves in their neighbourhood.

going on — the processes of nutrition and secretion — the oscil-
lations of the circulation and the activities of the muscles, create
those manifold streams of sensation which make up our general
Consciousness. Hence may we deduce the exaltation of sensibility in delicate states of health; and the marked difference in
the nervous excitability of frogs before and after the pairing
time. But we dare not venture into so wide a field. It is enough
to have indicated the existence of a vast class of organic sensations; and we will now pass on to the

II. SURFACE-SENSATIONS. — These are more appreciable than
the Organic sensations, because we can to some extent measure
the effects produced by external objects on the surface. We do
not know what is going on in our organs, we do not know what
agents are at work; but we *can* ascertain what agents are stimulating the surface, with what variations of degree these agents
affect us, and in what places they affect us.

The skin is everywhere sensitive. It is everywhere supplied
with nervous filaments; and these filaments seem more sensitive
in the skin than in the trunks from which they issue. Not only
are they more *variously* sensitive — capable of more distinct sensations — but they are susceptible to a greater *amount* of excitement. For example, it is through the skin, and only through
the skin (and the mucous membrane, which is the internal skin)
that we receive sensations of Temperature. Application of a
hot or cold substance to the nerve-trunk itself, produces no sensation of heat or cold, but one of pain. It is the same with
itching, tickling, and some other surface-sensations. Nevertheless it is not the skin which is sensitive; destroy the nerve-
filaments, or cut off their communication with the nerve-centre,
and the skin is insensible.

Further, the intensity of sensation is much greater in the
skin than in the nerve-trunk. Hence the painfulness of an operation chiefly depends on the division of the filaments at the surface, and not on the division of the nerve-trunks when the
muscles are cut through. Arnold, Volkmann, Weber, and
others, have abundantly illustrated the superior sensitiveness

of the nerve in its distribution through the skin, to that of the same nerve in any other part of its course.

But although everywhere sensitive, the skin is not everywhere equally susceptible to the same kind of impression. A specialisation has taken place. The face is more sensitive than the hand to Temperature; the sole of the foot is more sensitive than the back to Tickling; the tips of the fingers are more sensitive than the palm of the hand to Pain, and less to Tickling. In cold weather we see men beating their hands together, or clapping their sides, to stir a little warmth; but they never think of slapping their faces with this energy. The schoolboy has often to hold out the palm of his hand for a stroke with the cane, which would be intolerable on the back of his hand. It was an easy supposition that this varying sensitiveness might be due to the varying amount of nervous filaments distributed over each part; but the supposition is without the basis of anatomical accuracy. Valentin says that, although the filaments at the apex of the tongue are more numerous than those on the skin of the back, they bear no corresponding proportion to the respective sensibilities of these parts — the sensibility of the tongue being fifty to sixty times greater than that of the back. * Moreover, the part which is eminently sensitive to one kind of stimulus is scarcely at all so to another.

If we bring a portion of this sensitive surface in contact with an external substance, the result will be a sensation of *touch*. On pressing that substance we have the sensation of *pressure*, or of *pain*. If the substance be lower in temperature, the result is *cold*; if higher, *warmth*; if the difference of temperature be considerable, the result is *pain*. Contact will also give the sensation of *smoothness* or *roughness*, if the object moving over the skin be of even or uneven surface.

Here we may notice a cardinal distinction between the skin, and the organs of special Sense. The same portion of skin will respond differently to different stimuli, or degrees of the same stimulus; but each organ of Sense can respond only in *one* way, and produce only one specific group of sensations. Thus, while the skin will give us sensations so distinct, as those of pain,

* Valentin: *Textbook of Physiology* (translated by Brinton), p. 495.

tickling, temperature, or mere touch, the eye will give us only
sensations of light, the ear only sensations of sound, and so
on, no matter how various the stimuli may be.   Hence the pro-
priety of separating these *special* organs of Sense from the general
surface, although, strictly speaking, they also are parts of the
general surface; and indeed the first of these organs, the Hand,
has a very slight degree of specialisation, and shares with the
whole surface its function of Touch.

III. SENSE-SENSATIONS. — These are derived from our Five
Senses.   They have five special organs devoted to them, if we
include, as, for the sake of following popular conceptions, it is
necessary to include, the Hand as a separate organ of Touch.
We must remember, however, that, properly speaking, Touch
is not localised in any one special part of the surface.   We can
touch an object as well with the foot as with the hand, with
the nose as with the finger, with the tongue as with the knee.
The hand, by reason of its flexibility, enables us to feel an
object rapidly in various ways; but this is its sole speciality.   The
sensations it conveys are not different from those conveyed by
any other part of the skin; nor are they superior in intensity
and variety.   The hand is notably inferior in delicacy of tact
to the tip of the tongue.   Had not exact experiments demonstrated this, we should at once admit its truth, on recollecting
how, when touched by the tongue, a cavity in a tooth seems
to be thrice as large as it really is; because, being accustomed
to estimate size by sensations of touch from the hand, we are
misled, by the greater sensitiveness of the tongue, into the
belief that the cavity is as large as it would be if the finger had
given us such sensations.
1. *Touch.* — The organ of Touch, therefore, although really
coextensive with the whole surface, we may, for convenience,
localise in the Hand.   I shall say nothing of this wonderful organ
here, but refer the reader to Bell's delightful and instructive
work, wherein everything that was then known will be found
elucidated.   Nor is it necessary to do more than allude in passing to the so-called "tactile corpuscles" discovered by Meissner,
and too readily admitted as "organs of touch" by many phy-

siologists. These corpuscles are microscopic structures found in the papillæ of the skin on the sole of the foot, palm of the hand, and occasionally in the lips and tongue. There is still great dispute as to the nature of these structures;[*] and my own very limited acquaintance with them does not enable me to express a preference for any one opinion; but I feel quite certain that they are *not* tactile organs, because the sensations of touch are as various and delicate in parts without these organs, as in parts with them.[**]

Instead, therefore, of saying anything about the organ, we will devote our brief space to the sensations of Touch. The first question which meets us is, How we *localise* our separate sensations, since the whole of the surface is sensitive, and sensitive, to nearly all the same stimuli?

Every one knows that we feel an impression in the sensorium, to which the nerve conducts the impression nevertheless, we *refer* this impression to a distinct spot on the skin, and not indiscriminately to any spot. How does this localisation take place? How is it that sensations really felt in the centre should irresistibly be referred to the surface, so that to an uninstructed audience it would sound absurd to tell them their fingers did not feel the object which they touched?

The young infant has no such tendency to localise impressions. It feels the sensation of a pin pricking its legs, or the lancet lancing its gums, or the fire burning its finger; but has not learned to refer these sensations to special localities. It has not yet conceived the idea of externality.

> "The baby new to earth and sky,
> What time his tender palm is prest
> Against the circle of the breast,
> Has never thought that 'this is I.'

---

[*] MEISSNER: *Beitrâge zur Anat. und Physiol. der Haut*; and in Siebold und Kölliker's *Zeitschrift*, vl. 296; KÖLLIKER in the same Journal, iv. 43; and *Gewebelehre*, 1859, p. 106; HUXLEY in *Quarterly Journal of Micros. Science*, Oct. 1853, p. 1; FUNKE: *Lehrbuch der Physiol.* i. 680. LEYDIG in *Müller's Archiv*, 1856, p. 150, and *Lehrbuch der Histologie*, p. 68.

[**] SCHIFF is also of the same opinion. He remarks that the hands of the squirrel are without these corpuscles.

> But as he grows, he gathers much,
> And learns the use of 'I' and 'me,'
> And finds 'I am not what I see,
> And other than the things I touch.
>
> So rounds he to a separate mind,
> From whence clear memory may begin,
> As through the frame that binds him in,
> His isolation grows defined." *

The infant world is wholly subjective. To conceive an external, objective cause of its sensations, would be more difficult for the infant, than it would be in after life to *dissociate* the external object from the sensation, and to conceive sensations as nothing but states of the organism. Only the psychologist can conceive that heat is not in the fire, hardness in stone, or sound in the thunderclap. We begin life with a complete ignorance of the external world; as we advance, the presence of this external world becomes more and more obtrusive, till we need the aid of philosophy to reinstate the vanished conception of our inner life.

The growth of the tendency to refer all sensations from within outwards, and to localise them in particular spots, depends on two causes: First, there is a difference in the sensations excited by impressions on different parts — those on the toe being somewhat unlike those on the finger, and both unlike those on the back or face. These differences the infant soon learns to distinguish, and learns to connect them with its experience of external bodies, — which is the second cause in operation.   The infant incessantly moving its arms and legs, brings them in contact with objects, and learns to connect the two facts — contact and sensation — by which a dim conception of an external is reached. The same object is found to produce different impressions on hands and feet — and in time the recognition of each sensationis inseparable from a recollection of the part affected.

It is because we thus learn to connect sensations with external objects, owing to the incessant contact of the surface with various objects, that even the sensations of our viscera are,

* *In Memoriam.*

so to speak, *projected* from the nervous centres, and conceived as external to the sentient organism. When the optic nerve is pressed, a flash of light appears *before* the eye — that is to say, there where light appears under ordinary circumstances. When the ulnar nerve is pressed — at what is popularly called the "funny bone" — a pricking sensation is felt in the fingers. When the auditory nerve is pressed, sounds are heard which seem to come from without, like other sounds. So indissoluble is the connection of sensation with some distant spot on the surface, that after an arm, or a leg has been amputated, the patient constantly *feels* sensations in the lost fingers and toes. In vain experience contradicts the sensation; in vain he sees that his fingers and toes are not there to feel; he feels them as distinctly as ever he felt them when they were parts of his living body. Nay, so urgent is this conviction at times, that men have actually had the feet cut off because of the pain felt there; and the pain still continuing after the feet were removed, they have had the leg removed from the knee; this not succeeding, they have had the hip joint removed. Here the seat of injury was not in the foot, but the sensation was *referred* to the foot. Schiff tells of a man whose leg had been cut off in childhood, and who felt pains in the toes of that foot during the whole of his subsequent life: at times he would forget his crutch, spring up from the sofa, as if both legs were at command, and only be aware of his lameness when he was prostrate on the ground.

Long after we have learned to refer all sensations to the surface, we have but an indistinct conception of the exact spot on that surface, where the impression is made; and throughout life we are totally unable to refer with any accuracy to the particular portions of the viscera, back, neck, and legs, which are affected; whereas the hands, feet, tongue, and face admit of marvellous nicety in this respect.

Weber measured the relative sensibility of various parts of the surface by means of a pair of compasses the points of which were tipped with cork. He noted the various degrees of distance at which the two points could produce two distinct impressions, when the patient's eyes were bandaged. These measurements show that the tip of the tongue can distinguish two impressions when the compass-points are only half a line* apart; the tip of the finger when they are one line apart. Other spots vary still more widely; for example, the distance of the lips is 2 lines, the tip of the nose 3 lines, the cheek 5 lines, palm of the hand 5 lines, forehead 10 lines, back of the hand 14 lines, chest 20 lines, back and thigh 30 lines.

Sir William Hamilton remarks,** that if this experiment be repeated with a pair of compasses capable by slight pressure of exciting a sensation of pricking or scratching, it will be found that there is no corresponding difference between the parts in their sensibility to pain. On the contrary, in places where the sense of touch is most alive, the sense of pain is in the first instance at least deadened, and the parts most obtuse in discriminating the duplicity of the touching points are by no means the least acute to the sensation excited by their pressure. The tip of the tongue has fifty times the tactile discrimination of the arm; but the arm is more sensitive to a sharp point applied, but not strongly, to the skin, than either the tongue or the finger, and at least as alive to the presence of a very light body, a hair, or feather, drawn along the surface.

How much the degree and kind of sensation in various parts will depend on the nature of the epidermis covering those parts, may be gathered from Weber's experiments on patients who had lost a portion of the epidermis by burns. The sense of *touch* was completely destroyed in those parts; the sense of *temperature* was so imperfect that no discrimination was possible between substances differing so widely in temperature as 48° and 113°: the patient sometimes declared he was touched with the colder substance, when in truth it was the warmer, and *vice versâ*. On another occasion, when the substance was still higher in temperature, no sensation of warmth was felt, but one of pain.

Curiously enough, the right hand, which is more sensitive to Touch than the left, is less sensitive to Temperature. If the two hands be dipped in two basins of water at the same temperature, the left hand will feel the greater sensation of warmth; nay, it

* A line is the 12th of an inch.
** HAMILTON: *Dissertations* in Reid's *Works*, p. 863.

will do this even when thermometers show that the water in the left basin is really somewhat colder than that in the right basin. I suspect that with "left-handed" persons the reverse would be found.

Having established these two points — first, that all sensations are referred to the surface; and, secondly, that various parts of the surface differ in their degrees of Sensibility — we shall now be able to understand how it is that sensations come to be accurately localised. Touch a cold object with the foot, with the hand, with the arm, or with the cheek, and sensations of different quality will be felt, which experience readily recalls as arising from those different parts. That it is experience recalling the past, and enabled to do so by the multiplicity of similar sensations in the past, is evident from this, that only those portions of the body which are habitually employed in such service are capable of rendering *exact* local references. Thus, let an insect sting us on the back, neck, arm, or leg, and we cannot, without the aid of some other guiding sensation, place our fingers on the spot, but only *near* it; whereas on the face, tongue, or hand we can unerringly find out the spot at once. If the reader will rub his finger gently over the surface of his hand, he will find a succession of sensations, all slightly different, arising in each portion of the rubbed surface: let him do the same with his arm, and he will find the sensation is almost continuous. These differences are registered in the mind; and it is because different spots yield different sensations that we can unerringly refer each sensation to its particular spot. And thus we may explain why it is that a sensation of temperature cannot be excited by the application of a hot or cold body to the *trunk* of a nerve, although the same application to the filaments of that nerve, distributed through the skin, excites the sensation: our experience of Temperature is indissolubly connected with the *peculiar* sensations excited in the skin, and *these* cannot of course be excited where there is no skin.

Before quitting this subject, it may not be uninteresting to notice the familiar phenomenon which succeeds pressure on the nerve-trunk of the arm or leg, and is popularly called "pins and needles," or "leg asleep." It arises thus: By pressure, for a

certain length of time, the sensibility of the nerve is greatly
blunted. *   When this pressure is removed suddenly, the sensibility will *gradually* be revived: as each nerve-fibre, composing
the trunk, returns to its *normal* condition of sensibility, a pricking sensation is felt, and the successive prickings from the
successive awakenings of the numerous fibres cause the "pins
and needles."

There are many other points connected with the Sense of
Touch, but they belong properly to the province of psychology,
and we shall not treat of them here, having to consider the other
surface-sensations.

2. *The Sense of Taste.* — This is indubitably a *special* sense.
It has a special apparatus, and only in this appatus can the
sensations known as those of Taste be excited by savoury bodies,
and only *these* sensations can be excited in it by electrical or
mechanical stimuli. Instead, therefore, of seeking for the source
of these sensations in the general surface of the body, we have to
seek it in a particular part of the surface. What is that part?
Ordinary usage has assigned to the tongue alone the function of
Taste; and I think ordinary usage is here physiologically correct, in spite of the disputes which have been, and still are, kept
up by various experimenters.

Müller, for example, maintains that the back part of the
mouth (*fauces*) is the seat of this sense, which is, however, more
especially seated in the tongue. Valentin thinks the whole
lining membrane of the mouth, as well as the upper and under
surfaces of the tongue, are the seat of this sense. And as these
are two of the most eminent names in modern science, a great
weight necessarily attaches itself to their opinions. The subject
is one, however, in which experiment is apt to be delusive, unless
excessive caution be employed, because when a savoury body is
brought in contact with any part of the mouth, the dissolved
particles are diffused by the saliva through the mouth, and
quickly come in contact with the nerves of Taste. If, however,
a sweet or bitter substance be rubbed against the gums, the

* The phrase "sensibility of the nerve" is used in the text in its popular
acceptation. The reader is aware that I admit sensibility only in nerve-
centres.

palate, or the under part of the tongue — care being taken that
the tongue does not touch gums or palate — no sensation of
sweetness or bitterness will *at first* be felt. Soon afterwards a
sensation is felt, but that arises from the diffusion of the savoury
particles. If the tongue be allowed to touch the spot, the sensation will be instantaneous. This experiment is easily performed,
and its results are uniform. *

For a substance to be tasted, it must either be in solution, or
be soluble in the moisture of the tongue. If insoluble, it excites
a sensation of touch, but not of taste. The sensations of Taste
may also be excited by mechanical and electrical stimuli — by
gases, or a stream of cold air; which shows that the quality of
sweetness, sourness, bitterness, or the like, depends on the nerve
affected, even more than on the nature of the substance affecting
it. Thus Henle found that a stream of cold air directed upon the
tongue gave rise to a cool saline taste, like that of saltpetre.
Dr. Baly found "that if the end of the finger be made to strike
quickly but lightly the surface of the tongue at its tip, or its edge
near the tip, so as to affect, not the substance of the tongue, but
merely its papillæ, a taste sometimes acid, sometimes saline, like
the taste produced by electricity, will be distinctly perceived.
The sensation of taste thus induced will sometimes continue
several seconds after the application of the mechanical stimulus."** I have found that active gargling with cold water
often produces a decided sweet taste, which lasts for several
seconds; yet drinking cold water will not produce the slightest sensation of taste. And Stich has recently published researches ***
which prove that gases are tasted no less than solutions. If the
tongue be outstretched, carefully dried, the lips pressing upon it,
and the nose stopped, a stream of carbonic acid gas directed upon
the *edges* of the tongue will instantly produce the acid sweet taste
of carbonic acid; whereas carbonic acid may be directed through
water for a long while without rendering it perceptible to taste.
Chloroform vapour also produces a taste under similar circum-

* The investigations of SCHIRMER, *Nonnullæ de gustu disquisitiones*, 1856,
entirely confirm this view.
** MÜLLER's *Physiology*, II. 1062; Dr. BALY's note.
*** See CARSTATT: *Jahresbericht*, 1857, p. 111.

stances; but if the edges of the tongue be covered, and the vapour
be directed on the upper or under *surface*, no taste is felt. That
electricity produces a sensation of taste, every one knows. Indeed,
it was in this very fact of taste arising from the contact of tow metals
in the mouth, that Volta's discovery originated; and among the
marvels of science we may surely rank this, that an observation,
apparently so trivial, should have been the starting-point of a
series of discoveries which have changed the whole body of
science, and have profoundly altered the whole possibilities of
industrial art. Here, as throughout the study of Nature, we learn
that nothing is trivial except to trivial minds; and to trivial minds
nothing is important unless it directly concerns their interests.

Our senses are the sentinels which guard us against the
approach of danger. The sense of Taste warns us against
swallowing deleterious substances, as that of Smell warns us
against noxious gases, and against some that are not noxious,
while it allows others to pass which are very injurious. Indeed,
the value of this service must not be exaggerated, as by many
writers it is, who seem blind to daily fact, when they have a thesis
to maintain. The Senses are sentinels which sometimes sleep,
and sometimes allow an enemy to pass, if the watchword be
given; and thus children are poisoned by agreeable berries, men
eat with great relish substances which prove very noxious.
"Among the lower animals," says Dr. Carpenter, "the instinctive
perceptions connected with this sense are much more remarkable
than our own" — a statement which is somewhat startling, considering that man's instinct has enabled him to detect so many
eatable substances which prove eminently beneficial; but the
grounds on which the statement is made are questionable:
"Thus," he continues, "an omnivorous monkey will seldom
touch fruits of a poisonous character, although their taste may
be agreeable." * Agreeable to whom? — to the monkey? If
the taste were agreeable to the monkey, the poisonous character
of the fruit would not prevent his eating it; if disagreeable to the
monkey, there is surely small marvel in his leaving it untouched,
however pleasant the flavour may be to *another* animal.

Sensations of Taste are properly only those of flavours. Many

* *Human Physiology*, p. 696.

pungent substances, such as mustard, produce powerful sensations; but although frequently classed among the sensations of Taste, these are really nothing more than irritations, differing in degree, but not in kind, from those produced by the same substances on other parts of the surface.

Taste and Smell act so constantly together that we not unfrequently confound them. Many substances which are considered eminently savorous are tasteless if the sense of Smell be in abeyance — as when the nose is held, or at the early stage of a cold in the head. The *bouquet* of wines intensifies their flavour; and there is no more popular method of taking a black draught than that of holding the nose till all be swallowed.

There is another point in which Taste resembles Smell: a moist surface is absolutely necessary for the organ to become sentient. No substance, however savoury, can be tasted if the tongue be perfectly dry; whereas gases, as we have seen, require that the tongue should *not* be moist if they are to produce a taste.

After-tastes are sometimes observed. They endure long after the substance which excited them has been removed, and modify the taste of other substances. Müller remarks that after he had chewed a piece of the root of sweet-flag (*Acorus calamus*), milk and coffee had a *sourish* taste. The intensely bitter taste of tannin is followed by sweetness. Every one knows how sweets injure the flavour of wines, and how some other substances, such as olives or cheese, improve it. There appears to be something of the same relation existing among tastes which is observed among colours; those which are opposed, or complementary, rendering each other more vivid.

Taste soon becomes blunted, unless varied; as the sensation of colour becomes more and more indistinct the longer the eye dwells on it. In illustration of this there is a familiar experiment: a man's eyes are bandaged, and he is made to drink alternately of port and sherry; at first he readily distinguishes the one wine from the other; but after a few sips it becomes impossible for him to say which is port and which sherry: whereas if he were allowed to eat a bit of biscuit, or to drink a little water from time to time, he could continue distinguishing each wine indefinitely.

"The reaction of the sense of taste seems capable of being excited also through the medium of the blood, in the same way that the sense of vision is affected, so as to produce flickering before the eyes, &c., by the presence of narcotic substances in the circulation.   M. Majendie has observed that dogs, into whose veins milk has been injected, lick their lips with their tongue, as if they tasted.   It is probable that the sense of taste is sometimes modified, and peculiar sensations of taste excited by internal changes in the condition of the nerves; but it is difficult to distinguish such phenomena from the effects of external causes, such as changes in the nature of the secretions from the mouth." *

3. *The Sense of Smell.* — The organ of Smell is situated in the upper part of the interior of the nose.   This much is certain; but the reader will probably be surprised to learn that serious doubts are permissible as to whether the so-called Olfactory nerves (the first pair) are in truth olfactory in function.   Let us first take a general view of the parts supposed to contribute to the sense of smell, as represented in fig. 64, after Sömmering.

Fig. 64.

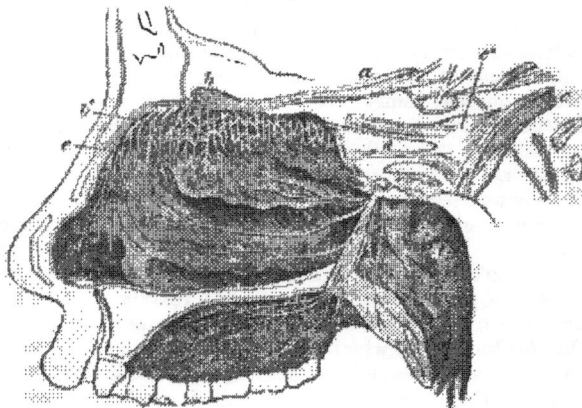

* MÜLLER: *Physiol.*, II. 1324.

From the base of the brain there issues on each side a long process, with a bulb at the end (*a* and *b*). This process is called the Olfactorius. It is now no longer regarded as a nerve, but as a portion of the cerebrum. It was thus also that Galen regarded it, not on very accurate knowledge, we must admit; and till the time of Willis this opinion prevailed. From Willis down to our own day the process was considered to be the olfactory nerve, until microscopic examination showed that it was not a nerve, but a ganglionic mass. The olfactory bulb (*b*) lies upon that part of the skull named the cribriform plate. Through the holes in this plate some five-and-twenty smaller processes, called the olfactory filaments (*b'*), descend, and ramify on the mucous membrane of the nose.

To complete our survey of the organ, let us glance at the other nerves which enter the nose. At *e* we observe a twig of the ophthalmic branch of the fifth nerve, which has nothing to do with the sense of Smell. At *c* is the fifth nerve, and the Gasserian ganglion *c'*; and at *d* its superior maxillary division, sending off filaments which anastomose with the olfactory filaments. At *o* there are the twigs which supply the palate.

All these are nerves; but whether the olfactory filaments are *nerves*, is not, to my mind, absolutely certain; and whether they have any intrinsic relation to the sense of Smell is even more dubious.

If the olfactory filaments are really nerves, they are unlike every other nerve in the body. The bulb is a ganglionic mass, but the filaments which descend from it are unlike all other nerves issuing from ganglia. They are neither formed of tubular fibres, nor sur-

Fig. 65.

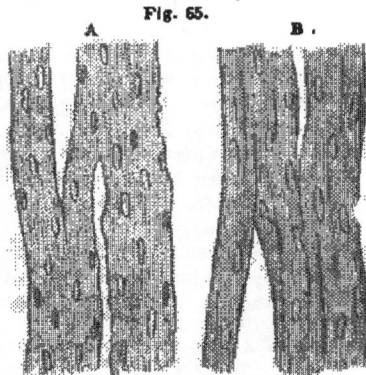

OLFACTORY FILAMENTS OF DOG.
A, in acetic acid; B, in water.

rounded with the investing membrane (neurilemma), such as
is found in other nerves, but with a very different membrane.
They consist of a striped granular mass, not of distinct fibres.
Nuclei are abundantly, but irregularly, scattered through this
mass. Todd and Bowman remark, that if these filaments be compared with the filaments of the fifth nerve, which anastomose
with them, the contrast will be very obvious. Those anatomists
have given a representation of an olfactory filament of the dog,
which is here reproduced.

This peculiarity in the structure of the olfactory filament has
been carefully investigated,* and likened to that of the *grey* or
gelatinous fibres which Remak first discovered intermingled with
true nerve-fibres in the sympathetic system. These grey fibres,
however, are by many recent anatomists pronounced to be peculiar forms of connective tissue, and not nerve-fibres. Be this as it
may,** we must remember that the grey fibres only intermingle
with the ordinary fibres; they do not constitute the whole, or
greater part of a nerve; so that, if the olfactory filaments are
nerves, they are markedly different from all other nerves. Indeed, two recent writers, Seeberg and Erichsen, declare them
to be formed of connective tissue, and not to be nerves. Bidder,
their master, holds the same opinion.

There is one fact which is almost decisive. We know that
all nerves degenerate when the ganglion with which they are in
connection is destroyed. If, therefore, the olfactory filaments
were nerves, they ought to degenerate after destruction of the
bulb; and as they do *not* degenerate after destruction of the
bulb, it is almost certain that they are not nerves.

Having thrown doubts on the nature of the olfactory nerves,
I must now proceed to throw doubts on their olfactory function.
These doubts are by no means new. Majendie thought he had
proved by experiment that Smell persisted after the nerves had
been destroyed; but his experiments have been rejected, as
proving nothing. Majendie said it would be important to ascer-

* TODD and BOWMAN: *Physiol. Anat.*, II. 6; KÖLLIKER: *Gewebelehre;*
LEYDIG: *Histologie*, 215; SHARPEY and ELLIS: *Quain's Anat.* III. 32.
    ** See KÖLLIKER: *Gewebelehre*, p. 343; LEYDIG: *Histologie;* BIDDER und
KUPFFER: *Untersuchungen über die Textur des Rückenmarks*, p. 27.

tain whether the congenital absence of the olfactory nerves was coincident with the absence of Smell. "I do not know," he added, "that any such case has been observed." Hereupon Longet replies with triumph, "In my *Treatise on the Nervous System*, vol. ii. p. 38, may be read cases reported by Schneider, Rolfinck, Magnemus, Falmer, Rosenmüller, Cerutti, Valentin, and Pressat, in which the complete absence of Smell coincided with a congenital absence of the olfactory nerves." *

This answer seemed very conclusive to M. Longet, and may seem so to the reader, until he reflects that the fact of a function being absent at the same time that a particular organ is absent, is no proof of a direct and absolute relation between the two; whereas if one case can be adduced in which the function was present, and this particular organ absent, *that* is categorical proof of the function not being dependent on the organ. One such positive would outweigh a hundred negatives.

Majendie cited one case in which disease had entirely destroyed the olfactory nerves without destroying the sense of Smell. But Bérard, who communicated the case, subsequently came to the conclusion, "that the information respecting the olfactory sensibility of this patient having been collected after the destruction of the nerves was ascertained, it is far from reliable, and, I am convinced, was false." **

In cases of disease we are never certain as to the precise effects, for we can never be certain as to the extent of the organic interference. But in cases of congenital deficiency we sometimes meet with instructive evidence; and on this very subject we can bring forward one which has all the characters demanded by rigorous scrutiny, reported by an authority of the highest eminence, Claude Bernard. When he was Majendie's assistant at the Collège de France, he commenced the dissection of the head of a woman who had died of consumption in the hospital. On opening the skull he was startled to find a complete absence of the olfactory nerves. Closer investigation showed that in all other respects the brain was of the normal structure, its membranes and vessels normal, and the origin of all the other

---

* Longet: *Traité de Physiol.*, II. 278.   ** Ibid.

nerves perfectly regular; but of olfactory nerve, or bulb, there was not a trace. This was not a case of absence from disease, but of congenital malformation. This interesting anatomical specimen is still preserved in the Collège de France; and a figure, representing the brain and the base of the skull, is given by M. Bernard. *

In the presence of such a remarkable fact as this, M. Bernard naturally sought its physiological interpretation. He went to the persons with whom the young woman had lived for the last six months, and without giving them any clue as to the object of his questions, interrogated them minutely respecting her modes of life, and her likes and dislikes, taking especial care to draw the conversation to topics which would elicit details respecting her sense of smell. From them he learned that "Marie found the odour of tobacco insupportable," and that "particularly in the morning, when she came into the room in which any one had been smoking overnight, her first act was to open the window to let out the unpleasant smell of stale tobacco — *la mauvaise odeur de pipe renfermé.*" He learned also that she frequently complained of the fetid smell of a closet which was near her room; and that for six weeks she officiated as cook, tasting sauces, &c., and being rather distinguished for her skill at it.

M. Bernard then went to the man with whom Marie had cohabited during four years. He said that Marie was fond of flowers, and always smelt at them. In fact, she tasted and smelt like every one else. A third person, who had tended Marie during her last illness, mentioned in particular that Marie often complained of unpleasant odours.

It is impossible to escape the conclusion that Marie really did possess the sense of Smell, unless we suppose a conspiracy on the part of all those persons to state what they knew to be false — a conspiracy as incredible as it would have been idle. Even assuming an exaggeration in their statements, the particulars are such as force our belief that some degree of Smell must have been manifested; and the presence of even a feeble function in the complete absence of the olfactory nerves, is enough to prove that the function in question cannot be that of those nerves. For

* CLAUDE BERNARD: *Système Nerveux*, II. 232.

observe, it is not a case of degree we have here; it is not a case
of olfactory nerves partially destroyed, or incompletely developed; it is a case of entire absence of those nerves, ganglion
and all; yet with this entire absence there is unequivocal evidence
of the sense of Smell being present.

M. Bernard remarks, that in no case hitherto recorded has
the absence of olfactory nerves been *predicted* from the imperfection of the sense of smell, and this prediction subsequently
found to be accurate; but that after the anatomical fact has been
discovered, men have sought for proofs of the absence of a sense
of smell in what nurses or relatives could narrate. "If," he says,
"any one case can be shown me in which, during life, the physician has observed absence of the sense, and predicted a corresponding absence of the nerves, which prediction has subsequently been verified, I will willingly hold my case to be insignificant. No such case, however, exists." M. Bernard here seems
to me more ready to concede the insignificance of his case than
philosophy justifies. However great a presumption might be
founded on the successful prediction, it would still be very far
below the value of such a case as that recorded by him.

This inquiry into the organ of Smell has only interest for the
student; the general reader must pardon its introduction — a
pardon he can the more easily grant, since he has probably
skipped the paragraphs devoted to the inquiry. Enough, then,
if we know that the mucous membrane lining the upper cavity of
the nose is the *seat* of smell; and as this part is also furnished
with filaments from the fifth pair of nerves, we may conclude
that these can serve the function of Smell as their fellows can
serve the function of Taste.

The odorous substances are very numerous; but it is indispensable that they should be in a gaseous or volatile condition
before they can excite the sensation of smell. Musk itself, powerful as is its odoriferous property, would produce no sensation on
the olfactory organ, if applied to it in a solid state; nor can
liquids produce odours till they evaporate. * Our distinguished

* "It throws some light on the diversity of taste which prevails in regard
to scents, that the same substance may be agreeable in a diluted which is
offensive in a concentrated state. The volatile oils of neroli, thyme, and

chemist, Mr. Graham, contributes the following valuable note to Mr. Bain's work on the Senses and the Intellect: —

"Odorous substances are in general such as can be readily acted on by oxygen. For example, sulphuretted hydrogen, one of the most intense of odours, is rapidly decomposed in the air by the action of the oxygen of the atmosphere. In like manner, the odorous hydro-carbons are all oxydisable — the ethers, alcohol, and the essential oils that make aromatic perfumes. The gases that have no smell are not acted on by oxygen at ordinary temperatures. The marsh gas, carburetted hydrogen, is a remarkable case in point. This gas has no smell. As a proof of the absence of the oxydisable property, Professor Graham has obtained a quantity of the gas from the deep mines where it had lain for geological ages, and has found it actually mixed up with free oxygen, which would not have been possible if there had been the smallest tendency for the two to combine. Again, hydrogen has no smell, if obtained in the proper circumstances: now this gas, although combining with oxygen at a sufficiently high temperature, does not combine at any temperature endurable by human tissues. It is farther determined, that unless a stream of air containing oxygen pass into the cavities of the nostrils along with the odoriferous effluvium, no smell is produced. Also, if a current of carbonic acid accompanies an odour, the effect is arrested. These facts go to prove that there is a chemical action at work in smell, and that this action consists in the combination of the oxygen of the air with the odorous substance." *

In few things do human beings differ more widely than in their sense of Smell. Not only is the acuteness of this sense markedly different in different men, but of twenty men having average susceptibility, perhaps no two will be found to agree in considering the same odours agreeable. Musk is notoriously very offensive to many persons; others do not like mignonette; some do not recognise any odour at all in a flower considered very

patchouli are in themselves unpleasant, but when diluted with a thousand times their bulk of oil or spirit, their fragrance is delightful." — JOHNSTON'S *Chemistry of Common Life*, II. 244, last edition.
* BAIN: *The Senses and the Intellect*, p. 163.

odorous by others. The *Iris persica* was found by Turner to have
a pleasant odour by forty-one out of fifty-four persons, a disagreeable odour by one, and very little scent by four others. Of
thirty persons, twenty-three held the *Anemone nemorosa* agreeable in its perfume, and the other seven did not think that it
smelled at all." *

The uses of smell are important, and in animals much more
so than in man. It is by smell that they are guided to their food;
by smell they hunt their prey; by smell they recognise each
friend or foe in the dark. That we are not endowed with such
keenness of scent, is probably owing to the comparatively small
exercise of that function in civilised life. Having so many other
avenues of sensation, so many other modes of recognising objects, this one falls into abeyance, and becomes weakened from
disuse. But in men born with one or more of the other senses
defective, Smell is seen to be an important avenue to the mind;
and in savages the keenness of scent notoriously surpasses that
of civilised races. James Mitchell was born blind, deaf, and
dumb; yet by smell he at once perceived the entrance of a
stranger into the room. People who have a strong antipathy to
cats, detect their presence by the odour in circumstances which
would be thought impossible. A lady in my study one day suddenly remarked — "There is a cat in the room;" on my assuring
her there was none, she replied, "Then there is one in the passage." I went out to satisfy her; there was no cat in the passage;
but on the first landing-stairs, looking through the railings,
there, sure enough, was the cat!

Humboldt, whose authority renders credible what might
otherwise seem questionable, declares that the Peruvian Indians
can, in the dark, distinguish by the smell the different races,
European, American-Indian, or Negro.

There is one more point needful to be noted here: it is, that
the animal effluvia are all dense gases (except sulphuretted hydrogen), and are diffused slowly. In course of a little time, they
will mingle with the lighter gases, according to the law of diffu-

* DRAPER: *Human Physiol.*, 427. Comp. also MÜLLER, II. 1317. There is
a valuable collection of facts with regard to smell in CLOQUET, *Osphresiologie*,
1821, a work often cited, but one I have not seen.

sion, but inasmuch as they thereby become diluted, the odour
will best be perceived somewhere near the ground. It is on this
account that the pointer and bloodhound run with the nose to the
ground. The unwholesome effluvia of decaying matter will be
felt in the ground-floor, scarcely perceived by the persons in the
first-floor, and perhaps not at all in the garret. Hence the danger
of lying on the ground in tropical swamps. "Swung on a tree
fifty feet high, one may pass the night safely."

4. *The Sense of Hearing.* — The sensations of sound are quite
special, and are only capable of being excited in a special organ,
the Ear. This organ is very complicated, and as the functions of
its various parts have not yet been all ascertained, it would lead
us into unnecessary detail were we here to examine its structure
minutely. Referring the student to anatomical writers, * we will
endeavour to render the general structure intelligible.

The following figures represent a section of the auditory

Fig. 66.

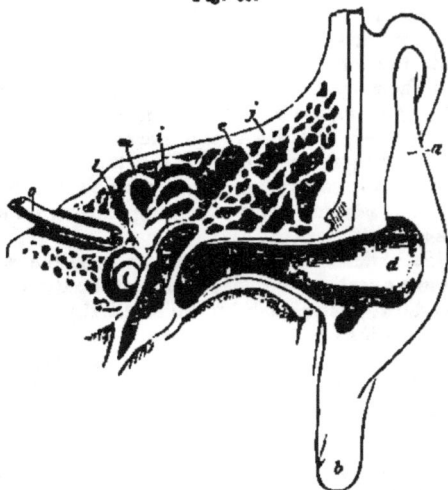

* TOYNBEE: *Philos. Trans.*, 1851; TODD and BOWMAN: *Physiol. Anat.*,

organ, somewhat magnified in respect to the deeper structures.
They are copied, with alterations, from Milne Edwards : —

The ear-bones removed from this figure are exhibited magnified in Fig. 67.

The essential part is, of course, the auditory nerve, numerous minute filaments of which are distributed over the membrane which lines the spiral chambers of the Labyrinth, or internal ear. This membrane is a sac, enclosing liquid. It is also surrounded by liquid, which intervenes between it and the bony walls of the spiral chambers. The impression of the vibrations, produced in this liquid, on the auditory filaments, causes the sensation of sound.

Fig. 67.

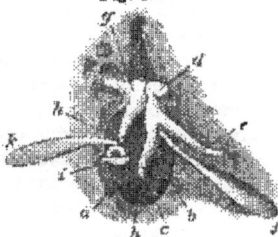

How are these vibrations produced? When bodies are struck, vibrations are communicated to the atmosphere. These reach the external ear. A mechanical contrivance of great simplicity, which has been imitated in the ear-trumpet, collects and concentrates the vibrations on the membrane of the tympanum (or middle ear). The membrane has been likened to the skin stretched across a drum.

According to popular conceptions, the pulsations of air upon this membrane stretched across the tympanum are the causes of the sounds we hear. This is a mistake. A drum is silent if its skin be burst; because the skin is the vibrating surface of the drum. But the ear is not a drum, and the membrane of the tympanum may be burst, not only without destruction of hearing, but in some cases with a terrible *increase* in susceptibility to sounds. Cheselden destroyed both membranes in dogs, and found they were terrified at all loud sounds; and there is a case on record of a man with a hole in his tympanum, to whom the whistling of another man in an adjoining room was intolerable.

ii.; Sharpey and Ellis: *Quain's Anat.*, III.; Kölliker: *Gewebslehre*, 1859; Corti in Siebold u. Kölliker: *Zeitschrift*, 1851, III. In Müller's *Physiology*, the chapter on the Sense of Hearing is very exhaustive. Longet, also, is worth consulting: *Traité de Phys.*, ii.

Nevertheless, we must bear in mind that the vibrations of this membrane are really of great assistance in hearing; and it is found that a thickening, or stiffening of it, or even unusual dryness, will render hearing dull. Many a temporary deafness has passed away after the ear has been well syringed with warm soap-and-water. According to a valuable memoir by Dr. Edward Clarke, an American physician, the membrane plays a more important part than physiologists have been willing to admit. Against the facts cited above may be placed his observations of seventy-five cases of perforated membranes: of these, in five cases, the tick of a watch was not heard; in eleven others it was only heard when the watch was close to the ear; in twenty-three others only at a distance of five inches from the ear; in sixteen others only at a distance varying from six inches to a foot; in fifteen others at a distance of one to two feet; and in four cases at two to four feet; whereas in the ordinary condition of the ear the tick is heard at fourteen or fifteen feet. * These observations are valuable, but I would call attention to a source of fallacy in them. It is forgotten that a man with one perforated tympanum has still the *other* ear unaffected, and with this other ear he ought distinctly to recognise the tick of a watch anywhere within fourteen feet. If he does not, there must be some other cause besides the perforation of one tympanum.

The elastic membrane stretched across the drum of the ear is easily set vibrating by waves of air. These vibrations are communicated to the chain of little bones, called respectively the *malleus*, or hammer (directly attached to the membrane), the *incus*, or anvil, and the *stapes*, or stirrup, which is attached to the oval-shaped membrane stretched across an opening into the labyrinth, and called the *fenestra ovalis*. On the other side of this oval membrane, and filling the cavity of the labyrinth, are, 1st, the liquid, and, 2d, the membranous sac, on which ramify the auditory filaments, previously described. Thus is a communication established between the vibrations of an external body, say a violin string, and the vibrations of the membrane containing auditory filaments. Sonorous waves first agitate the

* CLARKE: *American Journal of Medical Science*, 1858, p. 13; abstracted in BROWN-SÉQUARD's *Journal de la Phys.*, i. 844.

tympanic membrane, which agitates the little bones, which agitate the labyrinthine liquid, which agitates the labyrinthine membrane, and here presses on the nerve-filaments. The process is really *more* complicated than this; but this is a general outline, which must suffice.

The character of the sensation produced will of course greatly depend on the nature of the impression, whether rapid or slow, intense or delicate. There are three physical peculiarities in the sonorous vibrations.

1°. *Intensity*, or loudness and feebleness of sound.

2°. *Pitch*, or the note sounded.

3°. *Quality*, as when the same note is sounded on different instruments, as the piano or the violin, flute or the organ.

An ear may be very susceptible to mere intensity of sound, *noise*, and little so to pitch or quality. The unmusical ear seems almost incapable of discriminating between two sounds differing only in pitch; and there are great individual varieties in the susceptibility even to pitch. Thus the cry of a bat is so acute as to be inaudible to some persons, — passing out of their range. It has been said that the deepest note audible by the human ear is one produced by 32 vibrations in a second; but M. Savart's experiments prove that sounds produced by 14 vibrations in a second are audible. The acutest note audible is one produced by 48,000 vibrations in a second. *

What is the difference between a musical and an unmusical ear? It resides in this: That the musical ear is sensitive to the distinction between a *noise* and a *note*. "A musical note is in itself a harmony, being the equal tuning of successive vibrations or pulses. It is, in a minute or microscopical subdivision, the same effect as equality of intervals, or time, in a musical performance; although the one may be a thousand beats in a second, and the other not more than two in the same time." **

The effect of music on our emotions is an exaltation of the effect which all sounds produce, especially *tones*. The influence

* MÜLLER: *Physiology*, II. 1299.
** BAIN: *The Senses and the Intellect*, p. 207.

exercised by the voice of an actor or an orator, far transcends
that which the mere *meaning* of his words would excite; and if
we disengage the mind from all influence of meaning — as when
a foreigner speaks in a language unintelligible to us — we shall
appreciate this powerful effect of tone. The speech which roused
an audience to extravagant enthusiasm, may be read by people
unacquainted with the speaker, and therefore incapable of even
faintly imagining the *tones*, with complete calmness, and discriminating criticism; nay, even the audience may subsequently
read with calmness the speech which they heard with rapture.
Hence it is that great orators can never be fairly appreciated by
those who have not heard them. And we may also observe that
this personality of the speaker has often gained a reputation in
society for wit, or eloquence, or capacity, which amazes those
who have only the printed wit, or wisdom, on which to found
their judgment.

It is notorious that children and animals are affected by our
voices, when quite incapable of understanding the meaning of
our words. It is notorious also that the meaning of a phrase may
be diametrically changed, by repeating the phrase with a slight
variation in the tone; and it is *this* which constitutes one of the
iniquities of those who repeat to us what has been said behind
our backs. The phrase may have been careless or insignificant,
but the tone in which it is repeated may make it a wound.

What are called *subjective* sounds — *i. e.* those sensations of
sound which have no external cause — depend upon a pressure of
blood-vessels on the auditory nerve. All students know the
singing in the ears which accompanies overwork of the brain;
and all persons who have attended reviews, or made long and
noisy journeys in rattling vehicles, will remember the continuance
of the sounds long after the original cause had ceased.

"A sudden noise excites in persons of excitable nervous
system an unpleasant sensation, like that produced by an electric
shock throughout the body, and sometimes a particular feeling
in the external ear. Various kinds of sounds, such as the friction
of paper or scratching of glass, cause in many people a disagreeable feeling in the teeth, or, indeed, a sensation of cold trickling

through the body. Intense sounds are said to make the saliva collect in the mouth in some people."*

One of the marvels of hearing is the appreciation of the direction from which sounds proceed. Sensations of Touch are referred to particular spots, only after multiform experience of the difference in the degree of the sensations excited in various spots. It is the same with hearing. We judge of the distance and direction of the sound by the kind of impression produced. The rumbling of a waggon in the street is thus often mistaken for distant thunder, or the distant thunder is mistaken for the rumbling of a waggon. The voice is known to proceed from above, or below, or behind us, solely by the *kind* of impression produced. How delicate is the susceptibility to shades of difference, may best be illustrated by the wonderful accuracy with which blind men thread their way along crowded streets: not only do they learn to recognise the different kind of persons — policeman, porter, or gentleman — by the sound of the tread, but they learn, it is said, to recognise the difference between a man standing still, and a lamp-post at a short distance, simply by means of the reverberations of their own footsteps.

5. *The Sense of Sight.* — Although that objective something, whatever it may be, which we call Light, affects the whole general surface, and in some animals excites very appreciable evidences of Sensibility, yet it is only through the Retina that it is capable of causing that specific sensation we call Sight. When rays fall upon the eyeless Polype, or Actinia, they cause it to move towards them, or away from them — they affect it; but not with the sensation of *light;* when they fall upon the optic nerve they produce no sensation of light; but when they fall upon the *retina*, and through it affect the optic nerve, the special sensation of light is produced. That it is not the *object* — undulating ether, or luminous corpuscle — which gives this specific quality to the sensation, but the condition of the optic apparatus itself, is evident from the fact, that pressure or irritation of the optic nerve also produces the sensation of a flash of light.

* MÜLLER, II. 1311.

15*

It is obvious that if the whole of this retina were exposed
directly to the light, the whole surface would be stimulated —
like the photographer's plate — and no images formed.   To produce an image on the retina, or a picture on the plate, an optical
apparatus must be interposed.   The globe of the eye is such an
apparatus.   Let it be briefly described.

Fig. 68.

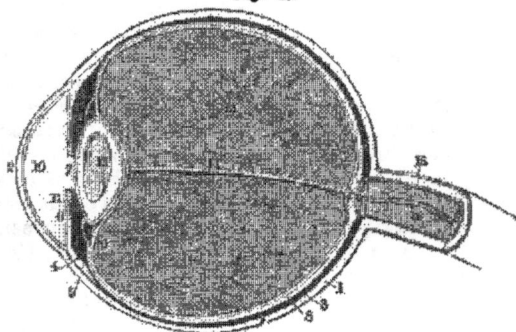

The globe of the eye is composed of three enveloping *coats*,
and three *refracting humours*.   The coats are as follows: —

I. The *Sclerotic*, (1) or outermost, a white, tough, fibrous
membrane, into the front of which the transparent *Cornea* (2) is
let in, like a watch-glass.   In the centre of the *Iris* (6) is the
Pupil (7).

II. The *Choroid*, (3) or middle coat, formed of blood-vessels,
on the inner side of which is a layer of black *pigment*, which is
deserving of particular attention, as will be seen hereafter.

III. The *Retina* (8), or innermost coat, being an expansion of
the optic nerve (15), through which runs the artery (16).

The refracting humours are as follows: —

I. The *Aqueous* (10) is the watery humour contained within
the cornea.

II. The *Crystalline* (12) forms the lens.

III. The *Vitreous* (13), or glassy, fills the bulk of the globe, and is enclosed in a delicate membrane called the *hyaloid*.

In these parts, only the Retina and the Choroid coat are concerned in producing the *sensation* of Sight. The rest of the apparatus is entirely optical, and subserves the purpose of throwing images on this sensitive apparatus. If we suppose an animal to possess an eye destitute of this optical apparatus, and having only a layer of pigment and a layer of nervous matter, we shall conclude it to have luminous sensations, but no images; it can distinguish light from darkness, but has none of the wondrous vision of higher animals. *

Two questions present themselves, What are visual images, and, Where are they formed? The old philosophers, following Democritus, believed that objects were continually throwing off attenuated images — *eidola* — of themselves; these entered the soul through the avenues of sense. This naïve material conception was in time replaced by one less material, but less intelligible, namely, that the mind perceived objects through the medium of *ideas*, which were exact *copies* of objects. This conception was displaced, and the direct perception of the things themselves, without any medium of ideas, was substituted for it. Throughout the course of metaphysical speculation, no one hesitated to believe that images of some kind were formed in the eye, as in a mirror, and thence "transmitted to the mind." The fact, now familiar, that images can be *seen* upon the retina of an animal, as in a mirror, seemed to place this belief beyond dispute.

How many physiologists and philosophers of the present day really entertain this notion of images being transmitted to the brain, it is difficult to say, because ordinary language is so impregnated with the old conception, that men who have long rejected it as an hypothesis may still use it as a metaphor. We must be on our guard against such metaphors. Even on the supposition that images are formed on the retina, as the final condition of the sensitive stimulus — as the *cause* of the sensation — these images cannot be transmitted *as* images to the brain. That which is transmitted is an excitation of the Neurility of the optic

* Compare *Sea-Side Studies*, p. 342.

nerve, which will excite the Sensibility of its centre; or in more untechnical language, it is the sensation which is transmitted, not the image.   The optical apparatus which converges the rays of light into definite images may be, and is, indispensable for the proper excitation of definite sensations; as the acoustic apparatus of a pianoforte is indispensable for the production of those tones which in the ear will excite musical sounds: a succession of waves of light will produce no images without such an apparatus, any more than a succession of waves of air will produce musical chords.

The formation of an image on the retina is the precursor of a visual sensation; but this image is not transmitted to the brain. The oxidation of a volatile substance is the precursor to an olfactory sensation; but this oxidation is not transmitted to the brain.   The destruction of tissue which is the precursor of a sensation of a burn is not transmitted to the brain.   That which is in each case transmitted is the excited sensation.

For centuries metaphysicians have been misled by the notion that the idea of an object is a *copy* of that object — an image. The source of the fallacy is their having taken vision as their standard.   If it seemed plausible to say that the image seen of the fire is an accurate copy of the fire, the plausibility vanished when the pain of a burn was the sensation spoken of.   When I see a rose, my eye is affected; when I smell it, my nose is affected; when I touch it, my fingers are affected: these three sensations are entirely different; yet how can I be entitled to assume that the eye gives me a more accurate copy of the rose, than the hand or nose gives me?

Moreover, as regards the formation of images on the retina, it is necessary to be borne in mind, that wherever the image is formed, it has to be *decomposed* before it becomes a sensation. And this leads us to the second inquiry, Where are images formed?   The usual answer is, On the retina.   But there is every reason for believing that the retina is not the sensitive surface — not the analogue of the photographer's iodised plate.   As this will probably surprise the reader, we may pause a while to consider the evidence.

The retina is not simply an expansion of the optic nerve; it is that, and something else; it has a very complex structure.   The optic nerve, on entering the globe of the eye, expands, and forms a layer of fibres; underneath this layer, and forming part of the retina, there is a layer of matter generally supposed to be nervous, but declared by some recent histologists to be nothing of the kind. The accompanying figure, copied from Kölliker, represents the appearance of the retina in a transverse section, as seen under the microscope.*

Fig. 69.

TRANSVERSE SECTION OF THE HUMAN RETINA.

a, hyaloid membrane; b, limitary membrane; c, bright globules (nature unknown); d, layer of optic fibres; c, large cells; f, granules; g, radial fibres; h, granules; i, k, rods and cones.

Here we perceive a layer of fibres (d), beneath this a layer of large cells (e), beneath this layers of granules (f, h), united by *radial* fibres to the cells; and beneath this again a layer of perpendicular rods and cones (i, k), formerly known as Jacob's membrane. All these layers are radially connected; so that the nerve-fibre is said to pass downwards from the inner surface of the retina to the pigment layer of the choroid. It is generally held by modern anatomists that these rods and cones are the real percipients of light: from these the impression is transmitted to the cells, and thence to the fibres of the optic nerve.

It was hinted just now that the nervous character of the retina was under question, only the fibres of the optic nerve being admitted by some writers to have that character. The doubt came from the Dorpat school, and was at first hotly disputed.**

* It may save some trouble and vexation to the student who desires to investigate this structure, if he learn that the appearance thus figured will probably never be seen by him in any one section. After making at least fifty attempts in vain, I learned, in Germany, that Müller himself, who first described it, professed never to have seen the whole in any one preparation; his picture was made up by combination of various sections.

** See BLESSIG: *De retinæ structura*, 1855; CANSTATT: *Jahresbericht*, 1855; BIDDER und KUPFFER: *Textur des Rückenmarks*, p. 87; FUNKE: *Physiologie*, I. 711; KÖLLIKER: *Gewebelehre*; LEYDIG: *Histologie*.

The question is too abstruse to be argued here, but there is one experiment, which, if confirmed, I should consider decisive. The reader knows that when a nerve is separated from all connection with ganglionic substance, it degenerates; but so long as any fibres are united with ganglionic substance, they survive. Now the cells found in the retina are held to be ganglionic, and indeed resemble those of the brain. If they were ganglionic, they would preserve the fibres of the optic nerve with which they were connected. Here, then, experiment may pronounce, and has pronounced. Lehmann divided the optic nerve of a dog, and twenty days afterwards examined the retina — he found *only* the layer of optic fibres degenerated; and as these were not protected by the cells, the conclusion is that the cells are not ganglionic. Thus the whole of the retina, except the optic fibres, is held to be connective tissue.[*]

Let this question be decided as it may, the point for our present consideration is this, that the surface of the retina which is sensitive to light, is *not* the surface on which the rays first impinge — *not* the layer of optic fibres — but the inner surface, which is in immediate contact with the pigment layer. A moment's consideration will now make it evident that images cannot be formed on the retina, as they are on the receiving-screen of a camera lucida. In the first place, we must remember that during life the retina is transparent as glass. The rays of light will consequently pass *through* it, as through glass, and will be arrested by the black pigment on which they impinge. In the second place, it is certain that the optic fibres are insensible to light. There is a blind spot in every eye, which may be proved by the following experiment: Fix a red wafer against the wall, close one eye, and slowly retreat from the wall, looking steadfastly at the wafer: on reaching a certain distance, the wafer will suddenly vanish from sight. If you now take a step backward, or a step forward, the wafer then becomes visible; but always at that particular distance where the rays converge so as to throw the image on one spot of the retina, the wafer is invisible. Now this blind spot is none other than the spot where the optic

* LEHMANN: *Experimenta quædam de nervi optici dissecti ad retinæ texturam vi et effectu*, 1857. Cited by HENLE: *Bericht über Anat.* 1858, p. 162.

nerve enters the eye, and where, consequently, nothing but nerve-fibres exist.

If, therefore, the retina is directly insensible to light, the rays of which necessarily pass through it to be absorbed by the pigment layer, we have to inquire how the retina becomes affected by the light after impinging on the pigment.   That the pigment is really the part first affected, and that the retina is secondarily affected through this pigment, seems to me demonstrable from the fact that in the invertebrate animals the pigment layer is in *front* of the retina, not *behind* it, as in vertebrates, consequently the rays of light must first affect the pigment;* and no one will suppose that images can be formed on a transparent substance, if the light first falls on a black surface covering the transparent substance.

But what is the nature of the effect on the pigment when the light has traversed the retina?   Here Professor Draper comes to our aid.   Franklin, he reminds us, placed variously-coloured pieces of cloth in the sunlight on the snow.   They were so arranged that the rays should fall on them equally.   After a certain period he examined them, and found that the black cloth had melted its way deeply into the snow, the yellow to a less extent, and the white not at all.   The conclusion Franklin drew has since been abundantly confirmed, namely, that surfaces become warm in exact proportion to the depth of their tint, because the darker surface absorbs the greater amount of rays.   Applying this to the eye, Professor Draper maintains that the black pigment layer is the real optical screen.   Its perfect opacity causes it to absorb the rays of *light*, turning them into *heat*.   An image is thus burnt in upon the retina.   "The primary effect of rays of light upon the black pigment is to raise its temperature, and this to a degree which is in relation to their intensity and intrinsic colour.   In this local disturbance of temperature the act of vision commences."**   In the blind Crustacea there is no pigment, and in Albinos, whose vision is very imperfect, the pigment is of a lighter colour than ordinary.

The conclusion at which we have arrived is, that the optical

* The point is argued in *Sea-Side Studies*, p. 347-52.
** DRAPER: *Human Physiology*, p. 367.

apparatus of the eye is necessary for the formation of definite images on a sensitive surface, which would otherwise be indefinitely stimulated. These images, or rays of light, pass through the retina, and impinge on the black pigment, in which they cause a change of temperature exactly proportionate to the intensity and intrinsic colour of each ray. This change of temperature acts upon the inner layer of the retina, the rods and cones; which in turn stimulates the Neurility of the outer layer, the fibres of the optic nerve; and this Neurility awakens the Sensibility of the optic ganglion, which may or may not awaken that of the brain. How far this is from the doctrine of "images transmitted to the brain" need not be pointed out.

Our conclusion further elucidates the *subjective* nature of vision. We can no longer suppose that we see the objects themselves. Our visual sensations are simply excited states of our sentient organism. Hence it is not more wonderful that a man whose eye was extirpated should perceive, when the other eye was closed, different images, such as lights, circles of fire, dancing figures, &c., floating in front of the eyeless orbit, than that a man whose leg had been amputated should feel distinct prickings in the absent toes. The fact that luminous sensations are excited ordinarily by the action of the retina, but also, exceptionally, by internal causes irritating the optic centre, enables us to understand *spectral* illusions. It is well known that persons suffering from brain disease, or disturbance of cerebral circulation, have seen spectral objects with a vividness equal to that of actual vision. A black cat is seen to run up the wall; a person is seen to enter the room; and no assurance of the bystanders to the contrary will persuade the patient that what he sees so vividly is not actually present.

At the Leeds Meeting of the British Association, Professor Stevelly narrated the following anecdotes: —

At the close of the last college session he had been in weak health, and had gone out to his brother-in-law's seat in the country for a few weeks. While there, he had become greatly interested in the economy and habits of the bees. "One morning, soon after breakfast, the servant came in to say that one of the hives was just beginning to swarm. The morning was a beautifully clear, sunny one, and I stood gazing at the insects, as they appeared projected against the bright sky, rapidly and uneasily coursing hither and thither in most curious yet regular confusion, the drones making a humming noise much louder and sharper than the workers, from whom also they were easily distinguished by their size; but all appearing much larger in their rapid flights than their true size. In the evening, as it grew dark, I again went out to see the bee-hive, into which the swarm had been collected, removed to its stand; soon after I was much surprised to see, as I thought, multitudes of large flies coursing about in the air. I mentioned it to my sister-in-law, who said I must be mistaken, as she had never seen an evening on which so few flies were abroad. Soon after, when I retired to my chamber, and knelt to my prayers before going to rest, I was surprised to see coursing back and forward, between me and the wall, what I now recognised as the swarm of bees, the drones quite easily distinguishable from the workers, and all in rapid whirling motion as in the morning. This scene continued to be present to me as long as I remained awake, and occasionally when I awoke in the night, nor had it entirely faded away by next night, although much less vivid. This was the first instance I had ever heard of moving impressions having become permanently impressed on the retina, nor can I give the slightest guess at the *modus operandi* of the nerve. Notices of fixed impressions, particularly after having been dazzled, are now common enough. The Rev. Dr. Scoresby, at the late meeting at Liverpool, had given a detailed account of some which had presented themselves to him; and a very curious one had occurred to me some years since. I was walking down the streets of Belfast with Sir John Macneill, the eminent engineer, when he said to me — 'What has become of my old friend Green who kept that shop? I see new people have got it.' Turning suddenly to look at the shop indicated, I was completely dazzled by the bright reflection of the sun shining on the new brass-plate under the window of the shop, so that for some seconds I could see nothing. As we walked on, I soon observed before me in the air the words 'J. Johnstone & Co.,' in blood-red characters, which soon, however, changed to other colours. With an exclamation of surprise

I stated the fact, and we turned back to see whether or not this
was really the inscription on the brass-plate, and found that it
was. The optical account of this was simple enough. The retina
had been partially paralysed from the intense light reflected
from the plate, but as I had turned with pain from it instantly,
the part corresponding to the black letters on the plate had escaped; and as I walked on, the red strong light reflected from
surrounding objects on this part became contrasted with the
darkness, as yet showing itself on all the surrounding parts of
the disordered retina: as the retina recovered its tone, other
colours in succession took possession of the place which at first
had been red. Sir J. Macneill then told me that when first he
had gone to reside in London, a murder had been found out by a
similar circumstance. The murderer, then unknown, had been
dazzled by the reflection of the sun from a bucket of water which
another man was carrying before him; and soon after seeing in
the air what he took for a bucketful of blood going before him,
he was seized with such horror that he declared himself the
murderer, and disclosed such facts as brought the crime home to
him, so that he was convicted and executed."

These curious cases are doubtless referable to different causes. In the first and third, we have the effect of *suggestion*
acting on an over-excited brain, and producing a spectral illu-
sion, similar to that of mania, or dreaming. In the second,
we have simply the effect of the *duration* of a sensation. It is
well known that a sensation endures some time after the cessation of the actual impression. According to Plateau, the sensation endures about 1-35th of a second after the impression has
ceased. But this duration must of course vary with the intensity
of the impression. If we look at the moon and close our eyes,
the image will vanish much more rapidly than the image of the
sun under similar circumstances. If we fix our eyes on the
panes of a window through which the sunlight is streaming, the
image of the panes will continue some seconds after closure of
the eyes.

It would be pleasant and profitable to enlarge on this subject of ocular spectra, were there space at disposal; but we
have still more pressing topics to which we must address our-

selves. There is, for instance, the interesting and often-mooted problem of how, with two eyes directed to a single object, we have only one image, and not two. Both eyes are equally capable of seeing; both retinas are certainly affected by the object; both eyes can alternately be directed towards it, and see it; yet when both are simultaneously directed towards it, only one image is seen, only one sensation is perceived. Many explanations have been offered of this paradox; but I think they have all failed, because they have all been sought in a wrong direction. A few years ago I proposed an explanation, which still seems to me the only one consistent with what is known of the other senses. Instead of seeking an anatomical or optical cause, it seemed to me that we ought to seek a psychological cause. Instead of trying to explain single vision as the result of the decussation of the optic nerves, or of those optical principles which Professor Wheatstone has made familiar by his stereoscope, let us first ascertain whether the fact to be explained is *peculiar* to the sense of sight? To ask this question is to answer it. If we have two eyes and single vision, we have also two ears and single hearing, two nostrils and single smelling. The mere citation of such facts suffices to overthrow all the anatomical and optical explanations. The cause must lie elsewhere; and must be common to all sensations.

Inasmuch as the object affects both eyes *simultaneously*, and with *equal intensity*, it cannot produce two sensations, but only one sensation. Simultaneouaness of two impressions renders them indistinguishable from each other. Let two sounds of precisely similar pitch and intensity *succeed* each other, and, however slight the interval, the two will be heard as two — provided the interval be appreciable, and the sensation of the first have diminished before the second be excited; but if, instead of this appreciable interval, the sounds are simultaneous, the two will be heard as one; they can only be distinguished as two when some difference in quality exists. It is the same with vision. Only when the images are successive, or different, can they be successively or differently recognised: two identical impressions must produce one sensation.

There are, indeed, occasions when single objects produce

double images.   The drunken man sees objects double.   I think
this perfectly explicable on the principles just laid down.   The
effect of alcohol has been shown by Ecker * to be a considerable
interruption to the circulation in the brain; this irregularity
in the circulation will produce an irregularity, or want of simultaneous co-ordination, of the muscles, and consequently a want
of simultaneity in the action of the senses.   Again, there is the
popular experiment of crossing the second finger over the first,
and with the surfaces of both, feeling the tip of the nose, which
gives two very distinct sensations, so that we seem to feel two
noses.   The explanation I take to be this: by the pressure on
the nerve of the second finger, the impression is slightly retarded
and deadened, so that the two fingers convey the same impression successively and differently.   If the two fingers, uncrossed,
touch the nose, the two impressions will be simultaneous, and
only one sensation will be felt.

Another interesting question is, Why objects are not seen
inverted?   It is demonstrable, on optical principles, that the
image of an object formed on the retina must be inverted.   Why
then do we not see it so?   Here again the question is psychological, not optical.   If *all* objects are inverted, the relative
position of each will be unchanged; when all are inverted there
can be no perception of their inversion: it is as if none were so.
It is in our own sensations we must seek for top and bottom.
We learn to associate certain sensations with certain relative
positions.   "An object seems to us to be up or down according
as we raise or lower the pupil of the eye in order to see it; the
very notion of up and down is derived from our feelings of
movement, and not at all from the optical image formed at the
back of the eye.   Wherever this image was formed, and however it lay, we should consider that to be the top of the object
which we had to raise our eyes or our body to reach." **

Among the remarkable phenomena connected with vision is
that of an inability to distinguish certain colours and shades of
colour, which recent investigations have proved to be much more

---

* ECKER in SCHMIDT's *Jahrbücher der Medicin*, LXXIX. 154.
** BAIN: *The Senses and the Intellect*, p. 255.

frequent than was suspected.* Dalton, the celebrated chemist, published an account of his own infirmity in this respect, and the name of "Daltonism" was for a long period given to it. Dr. Wilson not only shows that it is of very frequent occurrence, but that in some cases it is the source of ludicrous, and in others of lamentable results. We learn with surprise that there are a great many people, apparently in possession of eyes as good and true as our own, and who have never suspected any defect in their appreciation of colours, yet who, on the examination, turn out to be totally incapable of distinguishing red from green, or black, when substances of these three colours are placed side by side. Out of 1154 cases in Edinburgh alone, it was found that 1 in every 18 was more or less afflicted with colour-blindness. Of these, 1 in every 55 confounded red with green; 1 in 60 confounded brown with green; and 1 in 46 confounded blue with green.

Dr. Wilson tells of a tailor who, having been raised from the position of "cutter-out" to that of foreman, put green strings on a scarlet livery, and assured a customer that a red and blue stripe was all blue. Another tailor sewed a black coat with red thread. A Quaker shocked his wife by purchasing a bottle-green coat for himself, and scarlet merino for her, thinking he had secured a lovely drab. One gentleman, meeting a lady dressed in vivid green, mistook this for mourning, and began condoling with her. It is obvious that a sailor or a railway guard — to whom the colours are the alphabet in signals — would be dangerously misplaced if he were troubled with this colour-blindness. It appears from Dr. Wilson's researches, that women are seldomer colour-blind than men. It also appears — and this is remarkable — that those colours which to ordinary vision are most strongly contrasted, are more frequently confounded by the colour-blind than the intermediate tints.

In closing here our necessarily imperfect survey of the great subject of our Senses and Sensations, the chief points of which have alone been noticed, it will be needless to indicate the deep psychological interest which attaches to such inquiries, since every one is aware of the strange blending of Thought in the

* WILSON: *Researches on Colour-Blindness*

act of Perception. We fancy that we *see* the solidity of an object, when in truth we *infer* it; we say "we heard thunder," when all that we heard was a sound, which we *inferred* to be the sound of thunder. The other day, during a country walk with a friend, the sound of horses' hoofs behind us reached our ears, unaccompanied by any voices. Presently the riders passed us, and I remarked to my companion: "It's very odd, but I was convinced that there were two women and a man on horseback behind us, and, sure enough, there they are." My companion declared he had formed the same conjecture. This conjunction of our inferences made it improbable that it should have been mere vague fancy — a guess without justifiable grounds; and I began to consider what could have been the indications which led us both to form it. All that we had to infer from was the sound of horses. In what could that suggest the sex of the several riders? Do women ride differently from men? Yes: they canter, men trot. The sound of two cantering horses accompanying the sound of a trotting horse, suggested that two women were riding with one man. I may further remark that neither of us had, to our knowledge, ever *noticed* the fact, as distinctive of women's riding; we must have noticed it, and silently registered it in our minds, otherwise the sound would not have suggested the sex of the riders: but we had never taken distinct cognisance of it; and had we been asked if there was any peculiarity by which the sound of a horsewoman could be distinguished from that of a horseman, it is most probable that we should have been unable to specify it.

Finally, I would call attention to the psychological importance of that vast class of sensations which has been termed Systemic-consciousness, and which psychologists and physiologists have so strangely neglected. They have given to the Sense-Sensations an almost exclusive part in the formation of our sensational activity, and often spoken of the mind as a mere educt of the Five Senses. The most striking example of this is seen in Condillac's famous statue, which is endowed successively with each óf the five senses, and with each endowment developes gradually a complete mind. Monstrous as this hypothetical statue is, it is only a logical development of the conception that mind is the combination of the five senses. In these pages an attempt has been made to show that Mind is the psychical aspect of Life — that it is as much the sum total of the whole sensitive organism, as Life is the sum total of the whole vital organism — that various organs may be set apart for the performance of various special functions, mental as well as vital, but that no one exclusive organ of Mind can be said to exist, any more than one exclusive organ of Life can be said to exist. The reader may reject this view, which is submitted to him as the result of many years' meditation, and with that hesitation which naturally belongs to an opinion incapable of proof; but he is not at liberty to reject the fact that, over and above the sensations derived through our five Senses, there is a vast class of sensations derived through the Muscles and Viscera, sensations not less specific, not less important, than those of eye or ear: he is not at liberty to reject this, because it is capable of proof, as rigorous as the proof of the existence of Sight or Taste.

CHAPTER XI.

SLEEP AND DREAMS.

What is sleep? — Sleep and Death — Characteristics of sleep — Irresistible nature of the demand for sleep — Story of Dr. Solander — Sleep under control — Heat and cold predisposing causes — Duration of sleep — Instances of refreshment from "forty winks" — Sleep of children and old people — Is sleep the period of repair? — Error of the ordinary opinion — Influence of sleep on the organism — A new theory of dreaming.

"Our little life is rounded with a sleep." The toils and anxieties, the schemings and excitements of the day, all merge in Sleep, which brings peace and renovation to mind and body. The fretful child cries itself asleep; in sleep the weary man loosens his overstrung faculties; the wretched man forgets his misery. Nearly a third part of our lives is passed in sleep, which for all the active purposes of life, is a blank.

I. Sleep. — What is Sleep? We do not know. We can only say that it is a condition belonging to almost every animal organism (at any rate, to every organism possessing a high nervous development), which seems naturally brought about by the activities of that organum, and which, in some unexplained manner, helps to reinstate exhausted energy of brain and muscle. What is called the sleep of plants has, I conceive, only a superficial analogy with the sleep of animals, and is altogether dependent on totally dissimilar processes. The phenomena of sleep are restricted to the brain and higher senses; there can be no sleep where these are absent.

It is not difficult to decide whether a man is asleep, or dead, or swooning, or in a state of coma, or in a profound reverie. Artfully as he may feign to be asleep, observers will soon detect the feint; not because we know what sleep is, but because we know the many invariable signs of sleep. This is very much the position in which Physiology stands with reference to the problem of sleep. Certain phenomena have been well observed, but the organic condition, or sum of conditions, on which these depend, remains so entire a mystery, that we cannot even venture on a tolerable definition of Sleep. Let us, therefore, leave it undefined, and be content with noticing some of its leading characteristics.

Look at that child: wearied with play, he has thrown himself upon the ground, and, resting a flushed cheek upon one arm, he lies there breathing equably, with motionless limbs, eyes closed, brain shut out from the lights and noises around him. If you touch his hand, he will withdraw it; if you tickle his cheek, he will impatiently turn his head aside; but even should he turn his whole body round, he will not, perhaps, open his eyes — will not *know* who it is, or what it is, that molests him; he will not awake. His mind, engaged in dreams, is disengaged from external things: they may make impressions on him, excite sensations in him, but these sensations are not wrought up into knowledge.

His senses are dormant, or but feebly active, and his brain is occupied with dreams; his limbs are motionless, his fingers relax their grasp, and the muscles of his neck no longer support his head. But the heart beats vigorously, and pumps the blood incessantly all over the body, the chest expands and contracts, the stomach and intestines digest, all the secretions are going on.

We thus perceive how very superficial is the analogy of Sleep and Death, supposed by the ancient mythology to be brothers, and even by moderns supposed to resemble each other so closely that Death is called an eternal sleep. But, strictly speaking, there is not only no true antagonism between Sleep and Life, there is not even an antagonism between Sleep and Waking. In Death, *all* the activities peculiar to the vital organism cease; in Sleep they *all* continue: and if some of them are more languid and intermittent than during the waking hours, and if, in consequence of this languor, their mutual action and reaction are modified, this will constitute a difference, but not an antagonism. Sleep is a form of life, not a cessation of life. Indeed, Grimaud, Brandis, Fessel, Buffon, Burdach, and probably other physiologists, have declared Sleep to be the normal condition of

16*

Life, out of which it periodically passes into the waking condition; and certainly the whole of the life of the embryo is passed in sleep: nor does the infant, during the first months after birth, keep awake for more than brief periods; sleep is to it the rule, and waking the exception.

It would perhaps be more consistent with all our ideas to consider both Sleep and Waking as normal conditions of the vital organism, which periodically succeed each other.

After this survey, can we decide on any one characteristic which would serve as the sign of Sleep? The motionlessness of the limbs will not serve us, for limbs are motionless in coma; in repose, or in feigned sleep, and they are active in somnambulism. Nor will the stillness of the mind and senses serve us, for the mind is indubitably active during dreams, and quiet during coma; while the senses are almost as heedless of impressions during reverie. As we think, walk, and talk during sleep, it is clear that sleep must be some condition which permits all forms of vital activity, though not all the ordinary combinations.

The impossibility of specifying any one characteristic, disposes us to adopt Sir Henry Holland's view, that "sleep is not a unity of state, but a *series of fluctuating conditions*, of which no two moments are perhaps strictly alike." * This renders it intelligible that men are known to sleep on horseback, soldiers to sleep while marching, and village minstrels while playing to indefatigable dancers. It is a rapid oscillation between sleeping and waking. The muscles are in constant activity, and the Sensibility is sufficiently active to respond to delicate stimuli. I can see no reason for adopting the ordinary explanation of these actions during sleep, namely, that they are "automatic," or "secondarily automatic," if by these terms sensation is meant to be excluded (as it always is meant). On the contrary, it seems clear that in each case a suspension of the Sensibility would be followed by a cessation of the actions. The muscular sensibility must be excited, otherwise the reins would fall from the relaxed grasp of the rider, the musket would fall from the hands of the soldier, and the fiddle from the hands of the minstrel. This would at once cause them to wake up in alarm; or, if the stupor

* HOLLAND, *Chapters on Mental Physiology*, p. 81.

had become too intense, the men themselves would fall. The better explanation is that of Sir Henry Holland: "At every moment, the mind lapses into a dozing state, from which the loss of the balance of the body as frequently and suddenly arouses it. Neither the sleep nor the waking consciousness is perfect, but the mind is kept close to an intermediate line, to each side of which it alternately passes. No such line, however, really exists; and it is merely a rapid shifting to and fro of conditions of imperfect sleep and imperfect waking, giving curious proof of the manner in which these states graduate into one another."

"Watch again," he continues, "the loss of voluntary power in a person sinking quietly into sleep — how gradual it is — how exact a measure of the state coming on. An object is grasped by the hand, while yet awake; it is seen to be held less and less firmly, till at last all power is gone, and it falls away. The head of a person in a sitting posture gradually loses the support of the muscles which sustain it upright; it droops by degrees, and in the end falls upon the chest. Here again we have proof of the rapidity with which the loss of recovery of voluntary power may alternate on the confines of sleep. The head falls by withdrawal of power from particular muscles. The slight shock thence ensuing partially awakens and restores this power, which again raises the head.

"The gradual changes which occur in the perceptions from the senses, while sleep is coming on, afford the same curious notices of the condition of the mind in its relations to the world without. The sight, the hearing, the touch, all show the progressive lessening of sensibility through every stage of change, with the same fluctuations which attend those of voluntary power; and giving similar proof that the state of sleep is ever varying in degree as respects these several functions. We find, for example, one condition of sleep so light that a question asked restores consciousness enough for momentary understanding and reply; and it is an old trick to bring sleepers into this state, by putting the hand into cold water, or producing some other sensation not so active as to awaken, but sufficient to draw the mind from a more profound to a lighter slumber. This may

often be repeated, sleep still going on; but make the sound
louder and more sudden, and complete waking at once ensues.
The same with other sensations. Let the sleeper be gently
touched, and he shows sensibility, if at all, by some slight
muscular movement. A ruder touch excites more disturbance,
and probably changes the current of dreaming; yet sleep will
go on, and it often requires a rough shaking, particularly in
young persons, before full wakefulness can be obtained." *

The series of fluctuating conditions which we name sleep —
and which passes by insensible gradations from waking to
dozing, from dozing to dreaming sleep, and from that (perhaps)
even to dreamless sleep — is determined by the state of our
organs. It cannot be brought on by any effort of our will, unless
other predisposing causes co-operate. Every one knows the
wretchedness of a sleepless night. On the other hand, no effort
of ours will can prevent sleep under certain conditions of the exhausted organism. Neither pain nor fear of death will suffice.
Damiens slept on the rack, exhausted by torture; and many a
victim to chronic pains knows the temporary refuge of sleep.
Gunners fall asleep beside the booming cannon. An engineer
has been known to fall asleep within a boiler which his comrades
were beating outside with their ponderous hammers. Men sleep
soundly the night before their execution; and they will rather
brave death by sleep, than escape death by keeping awake.
A curious example is recorded in the first volume of *Cook's
Voyages*. Mr. Banks and Dr. Solander had been botanising
among the hills of Terra del Fuego. On their return towards
the ships, after travelling through considerable swamps, the
weather became bitterly cold, accompanied by sudden blasts of
piercing wind, and heavy snow. Finding it impossible to get
back to the ships before morning, they resolved to push on
through another swamp that lay in their way into the shelter of
a wood, where they might build a wigwam and kindle a fire.
Dr. Solander, who had more than once crossed the mountains
dividing Sweden from Norway, and who well knew that extreme
cold, especially when joined with fatigue, produces a torpor
and sleepiness which are almost irresistible, conjured his com-

* HOLLAND: *Chapters on Mental Physiology*, p. 84.

panions to keep moving, whatever pain it might cost them, and whatever relief they might be promised by an inclination to rest. "Whoever sits down," said he, "will *sleep;* and whoever sleeps, will *wake no more.*" Thus at once admonished and alarmed, they set forwards; but they had not gone far before the cold became so intense as to produce the effects that had been most dreaded. Dr. Solander was the first who found the inclination, against which he had warned the others, invincible, and he insisted on being suffered to lie down. Mr. Banks entreated and remonstrated with him to no effect. Down the Doctor lay upon the ground, and it was with difficulty he was kept from sleeping. One of the black servants, named Richmond, did the same; when he was told that if he did not go on he would soon be frozen to death, he replied that he desired nothing more than to lie down and die. The Doctor said he was willing to go on, but he must first take some sleep; although he had only recently told them that to sleep was fatal. After an angry altercation, the two were propped up against some bushes, and in a few minutes were profoundly asleep. Five minutes after, some of the men returned to say a fire was kindled a quarter of a mile farther on. Mr. Banks then roused Dr. Solander; but although he had only slept five minutes, he had almost lost the use of his limbs, and the flesh was so shrunk that his shoes fell from his feet. He consented to go forward with such assistance as could be given him, but no attempts to relieve poor Richmond were successful. He, together with another black left with him, died.

Although we can neither fall asleep by willing it, nor keep from falling asleep under particular states of exhaustion, we have a certain power over the predisposing circumstances, and can thus help to bring on or ward off sleep. Nay more, we can induce a habit of going to sleep at any time, or of awaking at any time. Seamen and soldiers on duty soon learn this habit. They fall asleep almost immediately their "spell" comes. Napoleon could take "forty winks" at almost any hour of the day. Captain Barclay, during the performance of his famous feat of walking 1000 miles in 1000 hours, learned to fall asleep the instant he lay down. We all awake at the usual hour every morning, no

matter what time we go to bed; and every one knows that, going
to bed with a strong desire to wake at a certain unusual hour in
the morning, we are tolerably certain to awake at that hour, or
even before it.

Heat is one of the predisposing causes of sleep. "We often
witness this in the summer season, sometimes in the open air,
but more frequently at home, and above all in a crowded church.
An intolerable lassitude falls over the spirit; we are unable to
walk, or move, or think; our eyes become heavy and languid;
we are seized with yawning, and, resting upon the first suitable
object which presents itself, drop into a profound slumber. This
is perhaps the most rapid of all sleep, excepting that from apoplexy or narcotics. The mind seems in a few minutes to glide
away, and sinks into a state of overpowering and almost instantaneous oblivion. The slumber, however, not being a natural
one, and not occurring at the usual period, is seldom long: it
rarely exceeds an hour, and when the person awakes from it, so
far from being refreshed, he is usually dull, thirsty, and feverish, and finds more than common difficulty in getting his
mental powers into their usual activity. A heated church and a
dull sermon are almost sure to provoke sleep. There are few
men whose powers are equal to the task of opposing the joint
operation of two such potent influences. They act on the spirit
like narcotics, and the person seems as if involved in a cloud of
aconite or belladonna. The heat of the church might be resisted, but the sermon is irresistible. Its monotony falls in
leaden accents upon the ear, and soon subdues the most powerful attention. Variety, whether of sight or of sound, prevents
sleep, while monotony of all kinds is apt to induce it. The
murmuring of a river, the sound of the Eolian harp, the echo of
a distant cascade, the ticking of a clock, the hum of bees under
a burning sun, and the pealing of a remote bell, all exercise the
same influence. So conscious was Boerhaave of the power of
monotony, that in order to procure sleep for a patient, he
directed water to be placed in such a situation as to drop continually on a brass pan. When there is no excitement, sleep is
sure to follow. We are all kept awake by some mental or bodily
stimulus, and when that is removed our wakefulness is at an end.

Want of stimulus, especially in a heated atmosphere, produces powerful effects; but where sufficient stimulus exists, we overcome the effects of the heat, and keep awake in spite of it."[*]

Cold prevents sleep, unless it be of sufficient intensity to produce internal congestion of the blood, in which case, as all readers of arctic travels well know, cold produces a stupor which is fatal. Heavy meals predispose to sleep, especially when the digestion is feeble.

Whatever tends to quiet the brain, tends to produce sleep; whatever tends to keep the brain in excitement, tends to prevent sleep; and that is why maniacs often remain sleepless for weeks.

II. DURATION OF SLEEP. — There are great varieties among individuals, both in the lightness of the slumber and the extent of its duration.   There are heavy sleepers and light sleepers; there are those who require several hours, and those who require but few. It is unnecessary here to repeat the statements which uncritical writers have accepted respecting extraordinary achievements both as to extreme length and extreme shortness of sleep; but there is no doubt that many persons have been satisfied with five hours in the twenty-four, which is the amount attributed to John Hunter and Frederick the Great; while on particular emergencies a much shorter sleep seems to have sufficed.   It is difficult to assign the degree of credit due to such statements as those of Pichegru, that during a year's campaign he had not slept more than one hour in every twenty-four.   People make great mistakes respecting their own experience in such matters, and very seriously declare they have not slept many minutes, when we know them to have slept a couple of hours.   It must, however, be admitted that even "forty winks" is an extraordinary refreshment, so much so as to render Pichegru's statement not wholly incredible.   I have on several occasions, during nights of hard study, fallen asleep over a book, remained thus for some five minutes, and have awaked to find myself so reinvigorated that drowsiness did not recur during the next two or three hours; and every student, or watcher by the bedside of sickness, can doubtless recall similar cases.   The following is the most remarkable example of this in my own experience.   I had

* MACNISH: *Philosophy of Sleep*, p. 15.

spent an exciting and fatiguing day in company with several
distinguished artists and men of letters, rehearsing for private
theatricals, and filling up the intervals with merriment, discussion, and excitement of various kinds. At one o'clock in the
morning, after having performed in three pieces, I sat down with
the rest to supper, which was not the least exciting part of
the day. In the midst of the noise, the quips and cranks, the
laughter and the jingling of glasses, I suddenly fell asleep.
How many seconds this sleep lasted I cannot say; but they could
have been but very few, since no one at the table, or on either
side of me, was aware of the fact. It was a flash of unconscious-
ness. Suddenly I awoke, and felt as ready for fresh excitement
as ever; nor did any sense of fatigue make me shorten our pleasant
sitting. If sleep be caused, as seems most probable, by a temporary congestion, the foregoing case may be understood as a
momentary congestion; the re-established circulation brought
back with it mental activity.

Children sleep much. In old age sleep is generally slight and
brief; but in extreme old age there is a sort of return to the
sleepiness of infancy. It is well to bear these facts in view, although we are at present quite unable to explain them. Writers
who find phrases as satisfactory as they are facile, and who
care little about clearly understanding the processes they describe,
will tell you that in infancy sleep is enormous in amount, because in infancy the processes of growth are so enormous, and
it is during sleep that Nutrition goes on. They will further tell
you that in extreme old age likewise sleep is excessive, because
then the Nutritive processes are slower and feebler, and require
this long repose for their accomplishment. But every inquirer
who is really anxious to have some distinct understanding of the
process, will feel, I think, very considerable difficulty in re-
alising to his mind any such conception. There is, I am aware,
a general belief, which is almost accepted as an axiom, that
Nutrition takes place mainly, if not solely, during sleep, and
that the purpose of sleep is to permit the waste of tissue to be
repaired. But without venturing to speak decisively on a subject so very obscure as the process of Nutrition, I feel impelled
to say that this general belief seems to me wholly unwarranted by

any facts hitherto ascertained. On the contrary, as far as present knowledge enables us to pronounce, the truth seems to be that Nutrition goes on *incessantly*, in conjunction with destruction of tissue; and that during sleep a very considerable waste of tissue takes place. Only a false analogy could suggest that sleep was the period for the building up of the fabric, which had been worn out in waking activity. Physiology knows of no such definite periods for destruction and reconstruction.

Assimilation (or Nutrition) is a molecular process. Molecule by molecule the tissue is destroyed, and molecule by molecule it is repaired. These processes depend on chemical affinities, the one bringing about conditions which favour the other. No one really imagines the organism to be like a machine, which wears out in action, and is repaired when at rest. No one imagines that the tissues are only worn out during the hours of waking activity, and not at all worn out during the hours of sleep. Many *say* this, but do not picture it to their own minds. They do not imagine, for example, that the Duke of Wellington repaired in two or four hours of sleep the waste of twenty-two or twenty hours of anxiety and activity; and was the next day ready for the same amount of exertion and the same waste. Nor do they picture to themselves the condition of those who have remained sleepless for weeks, and even months—a condition which, as it must have been produced by all waste and no repair, would have made the tissues present very much the aspect of a moth-eaten coat. Above all, they do not consider the contradiction which exists between this position of theirs respecting Nutrition during sleep, and their other position that sleep is caused by a slight congestion of the brain, or by the slower and feebler circulation: since they are fully aware that congestion, or feeble circulation, is the very worst condition for active nutrition; and they must either give up the idea of sleep being the period of most active nutrition, or else give up the idea of sleep being caused by congestion, or feeble circulation.

What we know leads us to affirm that Assimilation is a continuous process; new material is incessantly being formed; old material is incessantly, but with varying intensity, being destroyed. The waste and repair of the scarf-skin may furnish an

example. Incessantly new cells are in process of formation and
development, which take the place of the outermost layer of
cells as these fall off, dead. Should there be a greater waste
than the repairing process can immediately supply, the skin is
rubbed *bare;* and if the bare spot be rubbed, it becomes a *sore*,
but if left undisturbed, it soon becomes covered with a fresh layer
of protecting cells. It is thus with all the tissues: they grow,
particle by particle; they act; they die particle by particle, and
are replaced. The growth is not more rapid during sleep than
during any other period; rather less, if anything. And that
the destruction is not arrested during sleep, is positively proved
by many striking facts — for example, by the amount of carbonic
acid and excretory matters, and by the very obvious loss of substance in all the tissues which Valentin has shown to occur in the
winter sleep of the hybernating animals. If, therefore, it can
be shown that Assimilation goes on during all periods, and that
waste of tissue goes on during all periods, the idea of sleep being
a period specially allotted for the repair of the tissues must be
given up.

And yet the fact remains that sleep *is* "tired Nature's sweet
restorer." The fatigues of the day are vanquished during this
repose. We awake reinvigorated. What has been the change?
Müller speaks with caution on this point. "The excitement of
the organic processes in the brain," he says, "which attends an
active state of mind, gradually renders that organ incapable of
maintaining the mental action, and thus induces sleep, which is
to the brain what bodily fatigue is to the other parts of the nervous system. The cessation or remission of mental activity
during sleep, in its turn, however, affords an opportunity for
the restoration of *integrity to the organic conditions* of the cerebrum, by which they regain their excitability." But what are
these organic conditions, and how is their integrity restored?
Light seems to fall upon this question from the fact already recorded — namely, that the nerve of a frog's leg, separated from
the body, becomes exhausted by stimulus, and will no longer
cause the muscle to contract. If this nerve be allowed repose, it
will gradually *regain* its lost power, and on the application of a
stimulus it will cause a contraction. According to the vague

conceptions of Nutrition which prevail, this looks as if the functions of a nerve could be restored without any influence of Nutrition; and it has been cited to prove that position, even by so eminent a physiologist as Virchow.* But I would suggest that Nutrition, being essentially the process of molecular Assimilation, will continue as long as there is any material to be assimilated; the circulation may be necessary for the conveyance of material to the tissues; but the material, once conveyed, is under the laws of Assimilation. The case of the over-stimulated nerve is probably not unlike that of an overstretched piece of elastic substance. If India-rubber be in a state of continued tension, its elasticity is destroyed; but alternate relaxations preserve its elasticity. Is not this the analogue of those alternate tensions and relaxations which the nerves and muscles of the heart, lungs, and alimentary canal exhibit and the reason why these, although always in activity, are never fatigued? The action is not greater than the repose. The heart and chest expand, but they also contract: the muscles are as long in repose as they are in action. If our senses and voluntary muscles require longer intervals of repose, it is because their tension is longer; but even with them there is a kind of alternation; and we all know the unusual amount of fatigue which is produced by a very slight tension of the muscles, provided that tension be continuous. To hold the arm out straight for five minutes will produce more fatigue than to employ that arm in various movements for two hours. The same principle may be seen in intellectual or emotional excitement. Every student knows that diversity of work is a sort of relaxation, and that nothing is so exhausting as concentration of thought.

The conclusion to which the foregoing arguments point is, that Sleep, strictly considered, is a condition of repose of the brain and senses, produced by a slight congestion in their blood-vessels; and during this repose they recover that molecular integrity, or that molecular polarity, on which their vigorous action depends, and which has been disturbed during prolonged activity.

Sleep is caused by fatigue, but not because fatigue has

* VIRCHOW: *Die Cellularpathologie*, p. 263.

wasted a large amount of tissue which needs repose for its restoration. It is caused by fatigue, because one of the natural consequences of continued action is a slight congestion; and it is the *congestion* which produces sleep. Of this there are many proofs. The causes which tend to produce sleep at unaccustomed hours, before fatigue is felt, are all causes which lower the action of the heart, or which tend to a retardation of the circulation in the brain; the causes which tend to wakefulness are all causes which accelerate this circulation, or which diminish the pressure of the blood on the brain. If fatigue were in itself the cause of sleep, we could not be awakened until repose had restored the integrity of the nervous system; whereas it is notorious that just as we are dropping off, or only a short time after we have been asleep, an alarm of fire or thieves, a dash of cold water, a sudden pain, or even a strong light, will at once arouse us into energetic activity. This is a consequence of the relieved congestion and accelerated circulation — not a consequence of the few minutes' repose. The fatigue remains; it is the congestion which disappears. On the other hand, while fatigue causes sleep, by causing congestion, fatigue, if carried beyond a certain point, prevents sleep, by causing a feverish exaltation of the circulation. Every student and every sorrower knows what it is to be rendered sleepless by over-excitement of the brain. Let a man, wearied with bodily and mental labour, unable to keep from drowsiness, suddenly hear thrilling news, or alight on an illuminating track of thought, and the drowsiness will vanish as by enchantment — the wearied brain will have energy for hours of activity.

We conclude, therefore, that it is not *as* fatigue, but as producing congestion, that fatigue causes sleep; and the hybernating animal, which in full activity can be thrown into a state of sleep merely by a sudden fall in external temperature, and will continue thus until warmth accelerates its circulation, presents us with a striking illustration of such a conclusion. We conclude, moreover, that sleep is not produced by the necessity of repairing the waste tissue, since that repair goes on irrespective of sleep. Finally, we conclude that sleep is not dependent on any need of repose, since it is exhibited in greatest intensity by those who least need repose, having least actively exerted themselves. It is not persons of active and excitable temperaments who are the greatest sleepers; it is infants, very old people, people of sluggish, indolent, lymphatic temperaments. And men, no less than animals, fall asleep when perfectly quiet, perfectly free from external or mental stimulus to excitement.

III. DREAMS. — It was my intention to have treated the subject of Dreaming in some detail, but the length to which the chapters on the nervous system have extended, forces me to be very brief, and to abstain altogether from illustrating the subject with the numerous stories which might have given it interest. It naturally encroaches on Psychology at almost every point; but the explanations hitherto offered, at least those which I have seen, have the initial defect of not being based on a proper understanding of the physiological process. Only a true philosophy of nervous action can give us the clue to the mystery of Dreaming. For the sake of brevity, I shall venture to assume that the exposition of nervous action given in the foregoing pages is the true one, and endeavour by its aid to explain Dreaming.

Dreams are mental processes carried on during sleep, and are closely allied to the Reveries carried on during waking hours. In sleep the external senses are almost entirely closed against their ordinary stimuli, and the active organs are in repose. The consequence is that all, or nearly all, those multifarious sensations which, through the Five Senses and the Muscles, stimulate the activity of the Brain during the waking hours, have no longer any influence in swelling the stream of Consciousness, or in determining the direction of the thoughts. We do not see objects, smell odours, hear sounds, or taste flavours; even the sense of Touch has no distinctness, such as would create the perception of objects, but is confined to a general feeling of contact with the bed-clothes. Now, whoever for a moment reflects on the immense influx of sensation which is incessantly stimulating the brain through the senses, during waking hours, and reflects on their influence in determining the direction of the thoughts and in furnishing the mind with materials, will see at

once that the removal of such a source of excitation must very
considerably *alter* the mental conditions. Instead, therefore, of
marvelling that dreams should be incongruous with waking
thoughts, our marvel must be to find so much congruity as we
often find between them.

To understand Dreaming, we must try and discover what the
action of the brain would be under such conditions as are present
in sleep; and we can only do so by analogies drawn from our
waking experience, coupled with a correct interpretation of
nervous action in general. For example, in our waking condition, we are familiar with what has been styled *subjective* sensations: that is to say, we *see* objects very vividly, where no such
objects exist; we *hear* sounds of many kinds, where none of their
external causes exist; we *taste* flavours in an empty mouth; we
smell odours, where no volatile substance is present; and we *feel*
prickings or pains in limbs which have been amputated. These
are actual, not imaginary, sensations. They are indistinguishable from the sensations caused by actual contact of the objects
with our organs. They are sometimes so intense, or accompanied
by a cerebral excitement which so completely domineers over the
controlling suggestions of other senses, that they produce Hallucinations. And as it is the inevitable tendency of our nature
to connect every sensation with an external cause — to project it
outside of us, so to speak, — we should never think of doubting
that every one of these subjective sensations had a corresponding object, did not the suggestions of some *other* sense control
this idea. A man feels prickings in his amputated fingers, but
he sees that the fingers are not there, and, consequently, he
knows that his sensation is deceptive. He smells the horrible
stench of a sewer long after he has passed out of the reach of its
volatile gases. He tastes the bitter flavour long after the bitter
substance has been removed. But the sensations require constant confrontation with the reports of other senses, otherwise
they would be credited as sensations produced by actual objects.
In the state of cerebral excitement named Hallucination, this
confrontation is *disregarded;* in the state of cerebral isolation
named Dreaming, this confrontation is *impossible:* the first condition is one in which the cerebral activity completely domineers

over the excitations from without; the second condition is one in
which the cerebral activity, though feeble, is entirely isolated
from external excitations — thus, in both cases, the cerebral
reflexes are undisturbed, uncontrolled by reflexes from Sense.

It is the fact that sensations may be subjective — in other
words, that they may arise from internal stimuli no less than
from external stimuli, and *must* arise whenever the centres are
excited: it is this fact which gives us the clue to Dreaming. The
avenues of Sense are closed in Sleep, but the sensational centres
may be reached from within. That Law of Sensibility, which
has been so fully expounded in previous pages, whereby every
sensation discharges itself either in a reflex-action or a reflex-
feeling (or in both together), and whereby every centre, once
stimulated, must inevitably stimulate some other, gives us the
explanation why subjective sensations may arise in sleep, or
waking, and why they must stimulate cerebral action. Moreover, the external senses have not their avenues completely
closed in sleep; and a sound will be heard by the sleeper, though
dimly; a light will be seen, or a touch felt. These dim sensations are reflected in his dreams. The coldness of a touch
will cause him perhaps to dream that he has grasped a corpse;
the rattling of the windows will suggest a storm, or a battle.
There is a story told of a lady who dreamt that her servant was
coming to murder her; she opened her eyes in terror, and saw
the servant at her bedside, knife in hand! The explanation of
this is, probably, that she heard in sleep the creaking of the
footsteps on the stairs, or the opening of the door; and this sensation, which might have suggested any one of a thousand
different trains of thought, happened to suggest (perhaps because the idea was not unfamiliar to her mind) the idea of the
servant's intention to murder her. All our experience, both of
our own dreams and those of others, ratifies the position, that
the train of thought may be, and must be, determined by any
sensation felt during sleep; but inasmuch as this sensation cannot be confronted with the actual cause, inasmuch as the other
sources of verification are closed, which in waking hours enable
us to connect any particular sensation with a particular cause,
the perceptions and ideas it will give rise to are usually in-

accurate and incoherent. If, when awake, we perceive an odour of something burning, we at once look about to discover the cause. If, when asleep, we perceive this odour, we cannot thus confront the sensation with its external cause; but the sensation suggests a train of thought, and we dream that the house is on fire, or that we are at work in a manufactory. If, when awake, we feel a cold draught of air blowing upon us, we look at the door or window to see whence it comes; but asleep, the sensation of cold will suggest a dream that we are in the street in our night-shirt, or riding outside a coach; the sensation starts a train of ideas — and that is a dream.

If we reflect that the nervous centres must be incessantly called into activity, either through the imperfectly-closed channels of the Five Senses, or through the Systemic Senses, and that these centres, once excited, must necessarily play on each other — and if we reflect farther, that the sensational and ideational activities thus stimulated operate under very different conditions, and in very different conjunctions, during sleep, we shall be at no loss to understand both the incoherence and the coherence of dreams — the perfect congruity of certain trains of thought amid the most absurd incongruities. The coherence of dreams results from the succession of associated ideas; the train of thought follows very much the course it would follow in waking moments, at least when uncontrolled by reference to external things — as in Reverie. The incoherence results from this train being interrupted or diverted from its course by the suggestion of some other train, either arising by the laws of association, or from the stimulus of some new sensation. And because in Dreams, as in Reverie, we do not pause on certain suggestions, do not recur to them, and reflect on them, but let one rapidly succeed another, like shadows chasing each other over a cornfield, we take little or no heed of any incongruities. It is constantly said that in dreams nothing surprises us. I think this is a mistake. Nothing *arrests* us; but every incongruity surprises us, at least as much in dreams as in reveries. I am distinctly conscious of this in my own experience. If when I dream that I am in a certain place, conversing with a certain person, I am also aware that the place suddenly becomes another place, and the person has a very different appearance, a slight surprise is felt as the difference is noted, but my dream is not arrested; I accept the new facts, and go on quite content with them, just as in reverie the mind passes instantaneously from London to India, and the persons vanish to give place to very different persons, without once interrupting the imaginary story. In dreams no perception is confronted with actual objects; no ideas are confronted with present existences. The waves of sensation and of thought succeed each other, and are interrupted, broken, diverted by the fresh streams of sensation constantly pouring in from the changing states of the system. This interruption is to some extent controlled in waking moments by the presence of objects both to the senses and the mind; yet even the presence of objects, and the energetic resolution which a strong motive will give, will not prevent the most steadfast mind from continually wandering, although the mind may be recalled from its wanderings to the subject originally occupying it. If I sit in my study, and my thoughts wander to Bagdad or Bassora, the continual presence of my books, chairs, a microscope, engravings, &c., infallibly bring me back again before long, and prevent my believing myself to be in the East. If when I am working out some plan, or thinking of some problem, the thoughts wander away, lured by some accidental association, they are soon recalled again by the suggestions of the paper, portfolio, desk, or even by the very attitude in which I am sitting, and I recommence. But asleep, this recall would never take place. The objects are not there to suggest the requisite thoughts. The sensations I receive are carried along with my dream, each succeeding sensation or idea having a diverging influence; and thus a dream is never long, never very coherent. If the reader wishes to understand this operation of the mind, let him attend to the fluctuating stream of thought which passes through his brain as he lies awake in bed, with his eyes closed, and in perfect stillness; he will soon be aware of the influence which must be exercised by the presence of external objects in determining the direction of his thoughts.

That our dreams are greatly influenced by the Systemic Sensations, will be evident to every one who reflects on the notorious effects of indigestion. The state of the secretions also manifestly determines many dreams. The wretched sufferers in the shipwreck of the Medusa, dying from thirst, had perpetual dreams of shady woods and running streams. The nursing mother is made to dream of her child by the flow of milk to her breasts.

If, therefore, it is certain that Systemic Sensations produce dreams, and certain also that, in spite of the inactivity of the Five Senses, they can, one and all, furnish their accustomed sensations, if excited by external objects, and also if their centres are excited by internal stimuli; and if, farther, it is admitted that sensations determine trains of thought, we shall find little difficulty in assenting to the proposition, which many psychologists deny, that even in the deepest slumber dreams occur. The physiological reasons for supposing that the brain is active during sleep, though not perhaps so active, nor having all its various parts in such perfect co-ordination, as during waking hours, seem to me very strong, although the point scarcely admits of proof. Whereas the only strong argument against it is that we have seldom any consciousness of having dreamed, some persons, indeed, declaring that they never dream. This argument is, however, weakened by the fact that somnambulists, who not only dream, but *act* their dreams, and often in a very surprising manner, never remember these dreams when awake. It thus appears that our forgetfulness of dreams is no proof of dreamless sleep; and Sir William Hamilton declares that, having experimented on his own person, and caused himself to be roused at different hours of the night, he was always able to observe that he was in the middle of a dream. "The recollection of this dream was not always equally vivid. On some occasions I was able to trace it back until the train was gradually lost at a remote distance; on others, I was hardly aware of more than one or two of the latter links of the chain; and sometimes was scarcely certain of more than the fact that I was not awakened from an unconscious state." *

---

* Hamilton: *Lectures on Metaphysics*, I. 323.

In describing Sleep we had occasion to notice the partial though oscillating congestion which characterises it. In proportion as this congestion is extensive will the sleep be profound, and the dreams necessarily imperfect and fragmentary: for the effect of congestion will be to prevent certain parts of the nervous mechanism from being stimulated by the others; and thus, instead of consecutive trains of thought, there will only be irregular and imperfect trains called up by the various sensations.

CHAPTER XII.

THE QUALITIES WE INHERIT FROM OUR PARENTS.

The contradictory statements current — Mr. Buckle's rejection of the Law of Inheritance examined — The general characteristics which are inherited — Differences in families — Peculiarities inherited — Are the effects of accident transmitted? — Habits and tricks inherited — Influence of the second parent — Vices, Diseases, Idiosyncrasies inherited — Longevity inherited — Predisposition to Insanity — The respective influences of father and mother — Refutation of the notion that the father gives the animal organs, and the mother the vegetal organs — Curious examples — Children of great men — Necessary fusion of the parental influences — Perturbing causes: Atavism; Potency of the individual; Age; Sex — Summary of the evidence — Is marriage justifiable where the hereditary "taint" exists.

"THAT boy is the very image of his mother!" is the exclamation frequently heard; and not less frequently, "That boy is remarkably unlike his parents!" We also hear it said, "He has his father's talent, or his mother's sharpness;" and conversely, "He has none of the family talent." That the sons of remarkable men are generally dunces, and that men of genius have remarkable mothers, are two very questionable statements which have become proverbial.

Such contradictory statements seem to indicate that qualities are, and are not, inherited from parents; that inheritance is very much a matter of chance, and that what we usually suppose to be evidence of hereditary transmission, is really nothing more than coincidence. This seems to be the view taken by Mr. Buckle; in his remarkable work there is the following passage, which must excite the physiologist's astonishment: "We often hear of hereditary talents, hereditary vices, and hereditary virtues; but whoever will critically examine the evidence, will find that we have no proof of their existence. The way in which they are commonly proved is in the highest degree illogical, the usual course being for writers to collect instances of some mental peculiarity found

in a parent and in his child, and then to infer that the peculiarity
was bequeathed. By this mode of reasoning we might demon-
strate any proposition, since in all large fields of inquiry there
are a sufficient number of empirical coincidences to make a plausible case in favour of whatever view a man chooses to advocate."*

It must be admitted that many of the cases collected to prove
hereditary transmission have been allowed to pass unchallenged
by criticism, and many of them are worthless as evidence; but is
Mr. Buckle prepared to deny that the tendencies and peculiarities of men depend on their organisations? If he is not prepared
to deny this, his scepticism is illogical, since there can be no
shadow of doubt that organisations are inherited. He will not
say that it is a mere coincidence which preserves intact the
various "breeds" of animals: which makes the bull-dog resemble
the bull-dog, and the bull-terrier resemble the bull-dog and the
terrier; which make the Jews all over the world resemble Jews,
because they keep their race free from admixture, by never mar-
rying into other races; which gives us short-horned cattle, and
fan-tailed pigeons; and which makes the pedigree of a horse, or
dog, a value estimable in hard cash. Unless parents transmitted
to offspring their organisations, their peculiarities and excellen-
cies, there would be no such thing as a breed, or a race. The cur
would run the same chance as the best-bred dog of turning out
valuable. The greyhound might point, and the cart-horse win
the Derby. Daily experience tells us that this is impossible.
Science tells us that there is no such thing as chance. Physiology
tells us that the offspring always, and necessarily, inherits its
organisation from the parents; and if the organisation is inherited, then with it must be inherited its tendencies and aptitudes. Mr. Buckle seems to have been misled by that which
conceals the fact of transmission from ordinary apprehension,
namely, the very great number of instances in which the offspring does *not* closely resemble either parent; or rather, in
which the resemblance is not *discernible* by us. If the law of
transmission is not a figment, these seeming contradictions are
susceptible of explanation; and in the course of the brief survey

* BUCKLE: *Civilisation in England*, I. 61.

which will here be given, I hope to be able to convince the reader that an explanation is possible.*

We must first note the indubitable fact that the organisation of the offspring always and necessarily resembles that of the parents in its *general* characters. So uniform is our experience of this constancy, that nothing would be more incredible than that negro parents should give birth to a child, with the straight hair, aquiline nose, small heels, &c. of an European; or that two sheep should produce a goat. But while there is this constancy in the transmission of *general* characters, there is considerable variation in the transmission of *individual* peculiarities. One of the negro parents may be tall, robust, joyous, stupid; the other short, feeble, querulous, clever: now.as the child cannot be at once short and tall, clever and stupid, feeble and robust, in inheriting its parents' organisations it may either resemble one of the parents more than the other, or may apparently resemble neither, by being a mingling of the two. It is this fact of double parentage, and double inheritance, with an inequality in the amount of influence exercised by each parent, which complicates the question, and produces the seeming contradictions to the law of transmission. Let two Jews produce offspring, and inasmuch as both parents have the Jewish physiognomy, the offspring will be unmistakably Jewish; but let a Jew and a Saxon produce offspring, and the mingling of these two different organisations will be as visible in the offspring as it is in a Mulatto, or in any other cross breed.

People often express surprise at observing the strange differences in aspect and disposition between brothers bred up together in the same nursery, and under similar influences. From Cain and Abel, to the brothers Buonaparte, the diversity in families has been a standing marvel. Nay, such diversities are observed not only between brothers, but between twins; and it was noticed in the striking case of the celebrated Rita and Christina,

* The materials for this chapter are drawn from the extensive but uncritical work of PROSPER LUCAS: *Traité de l'hérédité naturelle*, 1847-1850; the lectures *On the Physiology of Breeding*, by Mr. ORTON, 1855; the *Traité de la Génération*, by GIROU DE BAZARINGUES, 1828; the work by M. MOREAU: *La Psychologie Morbide*, 1859; and an article, by the present writer, on *Hereditary Influence*, in the July number of the *Westminster Review*, 1856.

twins who were so *fused together* that they had only one body and one pair of legs between them, with two heads and four arms, yet they manifested very different dispositions and tempers.[*] The same was observed of the Presburg twins, the Siamese twins; and of the African twins, recently exhibited in London. The cause of these diversities is the inequality with which the parental organisations were inherited; both parents contributed their elements, but these elements were differently compounded.

It is to this inequality in the influence of a particular parent that we must attribute the fact that, while certain peculiarities, trifling and even whimsical, are sometimes seen to be transmitted, they are not uniformly transmitted. I am disposed to receive with great scepticism many of the cases which have been advanced, without in the least swerving from my position that even trifling peculiarities are inherited. Plutarch speaks of a family in Thebes, every member of which was born with the mark of a spear-head on his body: Plutarch is not a good authority for such a fact; yet we need not summarily reject it. An Italian family had the same sort of mark, and hence bore the name of *Lansada*. Haller cites the case of the Bentivoglio family, in whom a slight external tumour was transmitted from father to son, which always swelled when the atmosphere was moist. Again, the Roman families *Nasones* and *Buccones* indicate analogous peculiarities; to which may be added the well-known "Austrian lip" and "Bourbon nose." All the Barons de Vessins were said to have a peculiar mark between their shoulders; and by means of such a mark, La Tour Landry discovered the posthumous legitimate son of the Baron de Vessins in a London shoemaker's apprentice. If these cases be received with an incredulous smile, we must remember the series of indisputable facts noticed in the breeding of animals. Every breeder knows that the colours of the parents are inherited; that the spots are repeated, such as the patch over the bull-terrier's eye, and the white legs of a horse or cow; and Chambon [**] lays it down as a principle derived from experience, that by choosing the parents

---

[*] GEOFFROY ST. HILAIRE: *Philosophie Anatomique,* II.; and SERRES: *Recherches d'Anatomie transcendante.*

[**] *Traité de l'Education des Moutons,* I. 116.

you can produce *any* spots you please.   Giron noticed that his
Swiss cow, white, spotted with red, gave five calves, four of which
repeated exactly the spots of their mother; the fifth, a cow-calf,
resembling the bull.   Do we not all know how successful our
cattle-breeders have been in directing the fat to those parts of
the organism where gourmandise desires it? and have not sheep
become moving cylinders of fat and wool, merely because fat and
wool were needed?

More questionable are the facts of *accidents* becoming hereditary.   A superb stallion, son of *Le Glorieux*, who came from the
Pompadour stables, became blind from disease: all his children
became blind before they were three years old.   Burdach cites
the case of a woman who nearly died from hæmorrhage after
blood-letting; her daughter was so sensitive that a violent
hæmorrhage would follow even a trifling scratch; she, in turn,
transmitted this peculiarity to her son.   Horses marked during
successive generations with red-hot iron in the same place, are
said to transmit the visible traces of such marks to their colts.   A
dog had her hinder parts paralysed for several days by a blow;
six of her seven pups were deformed or excessively weak in their
hinder parts, and were drowned as useless.* Treviranus ** cites
Blumenbach's case of a man whose little finger was crushed and
twisted, by an accident to his right hand: his sons inherited
right-hands with the little finger distorted.

These latter cases, I confess, have an air of suspicion, which
almost justifies Mr. Buckle's assertion that the evidence for hereditary transmission is founded on mere empirical coincidences.
It is not only physiologically unintelligible how the effect of an
accident could be thus transmitted; but it is incredible that, were
such transmission within the course of nature, men should for
centuries have lost arms and legs without becoming the progeni-
tors of armless and legless babies; or how for generations the
terrier's ears and tails should be cut short, yet terrier pups never
come into the world ready cropped.   The savages who tattoo
their bodies, and bore holes through their noses, do not bring tat-
tooed babies into the world.   The truth of the matter seems to
be this: The organisation of the parent is transmitted, and with

* GIROU, p. 127.   ** *Biologie*, iii. 458.

that organisation all those characters and tendencies which the organisation in activity would naturally manifest. A habit, or trick, which has been acquired, and so long established that it may be said to be *organised* in the individual — whose mechanism has *grown* to its performance — will stand the same chance of being inherited, as the bulk of bone and muscle, or the sensibility of the nervous system. An idiosyncrasy which results from some organic disposition — say, for example, the repugnance to animal food — may as easily be inherited as a good constitution, or a scrofulous tendency. Explain it as we may, there is no fact more certain than that a habit once firmly fixed, once "organised" in the individual, becomes almost as susceptible of transmission as any normal tendency. Pointer pups inherit the aptitude, *i. e.* the organisation, fitting them for easily learning to "point;" and this aptitude is sometimes so strong that they will point before they have been taught. It is the same with dogs that have been taught to "beg." I had a pup, taken from its mother at six weeks old, and before, therefore, it could have learned to beg from her, which spontaneously took to begging for everything it wanted; and one day I found it opposite a rabbit-hutch, begging, apparently, the rabbits to come and play. Girou relates that he knew a man who had the habit of sleeping on his back, with his right leg crossed over his left. One of his daughters showed the same peculiarity from her birth upwards, and constantly assumed the attitude in her cradle. Venette knew a woman who, without being lame, had a sort of limp in her right leg; her daughter had the same defect in her right leg. Every one's experience will furnish examples of trifling peculiarities of manner — too individual to be mistaken — which are manifested by children who have never seen the parents they imitate. Nor is there anything surprising in this. The habit or manner, the attitude or trick, results from some peculiarity in the bodily framework, congenital or acquired, and this peculiarity is transmitted in the framework. It would *always* be transmitted were there not the counter-influence of a second parent, whose organisation is also inherited. This second parent has not the peculiarity, and the peculiarity may therefore be counteracted by her influence. Two pointers will produce pups that

easily learn to point, or even do so spontaneously; but if a
pointer be crossed with a setter, it is very likely that some of the
pups will not point at all, although some may inherit the parental
tendency. If a man of great musical aptitude marry a woman
with none, it is probable that of two children one will inherit the
musical aptitude, and the other be as insensible as the mother;
but it is also probable that both will inherit the aptitude, or that
neither will. Whenever we observe rigorous constancy in the
transmission of qualities — as in the breeds of animals — the
secret is that both parents had more or less of these qualities.
Whenever we observe inconstancy in the transmission, the secret
is, that only one parent had the qualities; and inasmuch as both
parents transmit their organisations, the double influence determines the product.

Instead, therefore, of feeling any surprise at a quality not
being inherited when only one parent had that quality, we must
anticipate such a result being very frequent; and our attention
should be rather fixed on the numerous cases in which the quality
is transmitted in spite of the influence of the other parent. Two
consumptive parents will inevitably bring forth consumptive, or
scrofulous, children; but one consumptive and one vigorous
parent will bring forth children, *none* of whom may be consumptive or scrofulous, or only *some* of them, or *all* of them. These
variations throw no doubt on the law of inheritance, but are in
strict conformity with it; because no sooner are the disturbing
influences removed than the law acts with unvarying uniformity. The evidence of direct transmission is ample, not
only in the case of "breeds," but in the case of individual
peculiarities. Thus Girou relates the case of a sporting-dog,
taken young from its mother and father, who was singularly
obstinate, and exhibited the greatest terror at every explosion of
the gun, which always excites the ardour of the species. On the
owner expressing his surprise to the gentleman from whom he
received the dog, he was told that nothing was more likely, for
the dog's father had the same peculiarity. How the vicious
disposition of horses is transmitted, all breeders know. Again,
we know that the vice of drunkenness is very apt to be inherited
and that the passion for gambling is little less so. "A lady with

whom I was very intimate," relates Da Gama Machado, "and
who possessed great wealth, passed her nights in gaming: she
died young, from pulmonary disease. Her eldest son was equally
addicted to play, and he also died of consumption at the same
age as his mother. His daughter inherited the same passion and
the same disease."[*] Tendencies to particular vices are inherited,
and are exhibited in cases where the early death of the parents,
or the removal of the children in infancy, prevents the idea of any
imitation or effect of education being the cause. That the
organisation of a thief is transmitted from father to son through
generations, seems tolerably certain. Gall[**] has cited some
striking examples. And murder, like talent, seems occasionally
to run in families. Parents with an unconquerable aversion to
animal food have transmitted that aversion; and parents, with
the horrible propensity for human flesh, have transmitted the
propensity to children brought up away from them under all
social restraints. Zimmermann cites the case of a whole family
upon whom coffee acted as opium acts on others, while opium
had no sensible effect whatever on them; and Dr. Lucas knows a
family upon whom the slightest dose of calomel produces violent
nervous tremblings. Every physician knows how both predisposition to, and absolute protection against, certain specific
diseases are transmitted. In many families the teeth and hair
fall out before the ordinary time, no matter what hygiène be
followed. Sir Henry Holland remarks, "The frequency of blind-
ness as an hereditary affection is well known, whether occurring
from cataract or other diseases of the parts concerned in vision.
The most remarkable of the many examples known to me, is that
of a family where four out of five children, otherwise healthy,
became totally blind from amaurosis about the age of twelve;
the vision having been gradually impaired up to this time. What
adds to the singularity of this case is the existence of some family
monument long prior in date, where a female ancestor is represented with several children around her, the inscription recording
that all the number were blind."[***] Unless we are to suppose all

* *Théorie des Ressemblances*, p. 154, quoted by LUCAS.
** *Fonctions du Cerveau*, t. 207.
*** *Medical Notes and Reflections*, p. 29. Compare also a striking passage
in Dr. INMAN's *Foundation for a New Theory of Medicine*, p. 5.

these cases simple coincidences, we must admit individual heritage; but the doctrine of probabilities will not permit us to suppose them coincident. Let us take the idiosyncrasy of cannibalism, which may be safely said not to appear more than once in ten thousand human beings: if, therefore, we take one in ten thousand as the ratio, the chances against any man manifesting the propensity will be ten thousand to one, but the chances against his son also manifesting it will be — what some more learned calculator must declare.

We can even produce a race having any peculiarities we will, provided we have parents possessing the germs of these qualities. M. Danney made experiments during ten years with rabbits, a hundred couples being selected by him with a view to the creation of peculiarities. By always choosing the parents, he succeeded in obtaining a number of malformations according to his preconceived plan. And such experiments have been repeated on dogs, pigeons, and poultry with like success. It is on this fact of individual heritage that longevity depends. There is no term of life for the "species," only a term for the individual — a fact which sets the speculations of Cornaro, Hufeland, and Flourens at nought. There are limits which neither the "species" nor the individual can be said to pass: no man has been known to live two hundred years; but the number of years which each individual will reach, without accident, is a term depending neither on the "species," nor on his own mode of life, but on the organisation inherited from his parents. Temperance, sobriety, and chastity, however desirable, both in themselves and in their effects, will not insure long life; intemperance, hardship, and irregularity will not prevent a man living for a century and a half. The facts are there to prove both propositions. Longevity is an inheritance. Like talent, it may be cultivated; like talent, it may be perverted; but it exists independently of all cultivation, and no cultivation will create it. Some men have a talent for long life.

M. Charles Lejoncourt published, in 1842, his *Galerie des Centenaires*, in which may be read a curious list of examples proving the hereditary nature of longevity. In one page we have a day-labourer dying at the age of 106; his father lived to

104, his grandfather to 108, and his daughter, then living, had reached 80. In another we have a saddler whose grandfather died at 112, his father at 113, and he himself at 115. This man, aged 113, was asked by Louis XIV. what he had done to so prolong life; his answer was—"Sire, since I was 50, I have acted upon two principles: I have shut my heart and opened my wine-cellar." M. Lejoncourt also mentions a woman then living, aged 150, whose father died at 124, and whose uncle at 113. But the most surprising of the cases cited by Lucas is that of Jean Golembiewski, a Pole, who in 1846 was still living, aged 102, having been eighty years as common soldier, in thirty-five campaigns under Napoleon, and having even survived the terrible Russian campaign, in spite of five wounds and a soldier's reckless-ness of life. His father died aged 121, and his grandfather 130. Indeed, the practice of every annuity and insurance office suffices to convince us of ordinary experience having discovered that length of life is somehow dependent on hereditary influence. That the predisposition to insanity and nervous diseases is inherited, every one knows.

M. Moreau has cited the following examples from his notes: — At Bicêtre there is now a monomaniac, whose paternal grand-mother died mad; his father died mad; his maternal aunt is epileptic; his eldest brother had melancholy madness, which terminated in suicide; his sister is subject to attacks of hysterical epilepsy. Another inmate of the same asylum is subject to dan-gerous hallucinations; his father, although not precisely insane, is eccentric almost to a degree of insanity; his eldest brother is excessively irritable and violent, and becomes almost maniacal under the smallest excess of alcoholic stimulants; four of his paternal uncles committed suicide. A third case is of an epileptic woman, who has given birth to eight children; three died early from convulsions; one of the remaining five is hysterical, and another epileptic. This woman's sister died *of grief*, aged twenty-five. Her father died mad in an asylum. Her grandfather was insane. Her mother died of consumption, and was slightly epileptic. *

* MOREAU: *La Psychologie Morbide*, p. 139.

If these cases stood alone , we should suspect something more than coincidence underlying them; but every physician knows that such cases are frequent. No one expects that two hacks will produce a racehorse; two mongrels a pure hound; two scrofulous parents a strong healthy child; two irascible, excitable parents, a gentle, placid child; two semi-idiots a child of genius. Every one expects that the qualities of the parents will be inherited by the child, and when they are not inherited, we assume that there has been some disturbing influence.

But now comes the difficult part of our inquiry. Which is the predominating influence, the male or the female? If both parents join to form the child, does one parent give one group of organs, and another parent another group, or do both give all?

Speaking of mules, Vicq-d'-Azyr says, with proper caution, "It seems as if the exterior and the extremities were modified by the father, and that the viscera emanate from the mother." The reserve with which the great anatomist expresses himself has not been imitated by his successors. Indeed, it is noticeable that men in general dislike uncertainties and qualified statements; they prefer decisive opinions, distinct formulas. On this subject they have preferred the distinct formula, which has been also adopted by Mr. Orton, in his Lectures, namely, "that the male gives the external configuration — or, in other words, the locomotive organs; while the female gives the internal — or, in other words, the vital organs." This is the theory generally adopted; but although it has the countenance of authority, an extensive survey of the facts, and a more accurate study of embryology, seem to me wholly adverse to it.

Linnæus said that the *internal* plant (that is to say, the organs of fructification) is in all hybrids like the female; the *external* organs, on the contrary, resemble those of the male. This statement is diametrically opposed by de Candolle, who announces it as a law that the organs of vegetation are given by the female, those of fructification by the male. When two doctors of such eminence differ on a point like this, we may reasonably suspect that both are right, and both are wrong; and here our suspicion is supported by the mass of facts adduced in the experiments of M. Sagaret, which refute the hypothesis of Linnæus, and the hypothesis of de Candolle. What we have just indicated with regard to plants, has been the course pursued with regard to animals: one class of observations has seemed to prove that the father bestows the "animal system;" another class of observations has seemed to prove that the mother bestows it; and a third class has proved both theories inadequate. Quite recently General Daumas published the result of his long experience with Arab horses,* arguing that, according to the testimony of the Arabs, the stallion was the most valuable for purposes of breeding. Upon this, the *Inspecteur des Haras*, who had traversed Asia for the express purpose of collecting evidence on the subject, published his diametrically opposite conclusion, declaring that it was the mare whose influence preponderated in the foal. General Daumas replied, and cited a letter addressed to him by Abd-el-Kader, who may certainly be said to understand Arab horses better than Europeans. The letter is worth reading for its own sake; we can, however, only quote its testimony on the particular point now under discussion. "The experience of centuries has established," he says, "that the essential parts of the organisation, such as the bones, the tendons, the nerves, and the veins, are always derived from the stallion. The mare may give the colour and some resemblance to her structure, but the principal qualities are due to the stallion." This is very weighty testimony, on which we will only for the present remark, that it merely asserts the *preponderance* of the male influence as respects the locomotive system; it does not assert that absolute independence of any female influence maintained in the formula which we are now combating. Abd-el-Kader's statement is tantamount to that made by Mr. Orton, — "I do not mean it to be inferred that either parent gives either set of organs uninfluenced by the other parent; but merely that the leading characteristics and qualities of both sets of qualities are due to the male on the one side, and to the female on the other, the opposite parent modifying them only."

This is a much more acceptable theory than the other, but it is only an approximation to the truth. Mr. Orton's first illustra-

* *Les Chevaux de Sahara;* see also an article in the *Revue des Deux Mondes,* May 1855, on "Le Cheval de Guerre."

tion is the hybrid of the horse and ass: "It is known that the produce of the male ass and the mare is a mule; but I do not think it is equally well known that the produce of the stallion and the female ass is what has been denominated a hinny — yet such is the case. . . . . The mule, the produce of the ass and mare, is essentially a modified ass — the ears are those of an ass somewhat shortened — the mane is that of an ass — the tail is that of an ass — the skin and colour are those of an ass somewhat modified — the legs are slender, the hoofs high, narrow, and contracted, like those of an ass. The body and barrel are round and full, in which it differs from the ass and resembles the mare."

This description is accurate, but — we put it interrogatively — is it *always* the description of a mule, and *never* that also of a hinny? This latter, the produce of the stallion and the female ass, "is essentially a modified horse — the ears like those of a horse somewhat lengthened — the mane flowing — the tail bushy like that of a horse — the skin is fine like that of a horse — the legs are stronger, and the hoofs broad and expanded like those of a horse. The body and barrel are flat and narrow, in which it differs from the horse, and resembles its mother the ass." From these facts Mr. Orton deduces the conclusion, that the offspring of a cross is not simply a mixture of the two parents, nor is it an animal that has accidentally a similitude to one or other of its parents, inasmuch as we can produce at will either the hinny or the mule. The reader will presently see why such a conclusion cannot be accepted; and we may at once anticipate what will hereafter be more fully explained, by saying that the differences Mr. Orton signalises are easily interpreted by another theory. In point of fact, both mule and hinny are modified asses: in each the structure and disposition of the ass predominates; and it does so in virtue of that greater "potency of race" which belongs to the ass — a potency which is less effective on the hinny, because the superior vigour of the stallion modifies it, according to ascertained laws.

"I would call your consideration," Mr. Orton continues, "to a very curious circumstance pertaining to the voice of the mule and the hinny; to which my attention was called by Mr. Lort.

The mule *brays*, the hinny *neighs*. The why and wherefore of this is a perfect mystery, until we come to apply the knowledge afforded us by the law I have given. The male gives the loco-motive organs, and the muscles are amongst these; the muscles are the organs which modulate the voice of the animal: the mule has the muscular structure of its sire the ass, and brays; the hinny has the muscular structure of its sire the horse, and neighs."

This seems decisive, until we extend our observations, and then we find the law altogether at fault. The produce of a dog and a she-wolf sometimes bark and sometimes only howl, accord-ing to Buffon; and the produce of a bitch-fox and a dog, ac-cording to Burdach, barked like a dog, though somewhat hoarsely, and howled like a wolf when it was hurt. A similar remark has been made by all who have attended to cross-breeding in birds: the hybrid of the goldfinch and the canary has the song of the goldfinch mingled with occasional notes of the canary, which seem perpetually about to gain the pre-dominance.

These illustrations, apart from their interest, teach us to be cautious in generalising from a few facts, however striking, in questions so complex as all biological questions are. Let us, however, continue to call on Mr. Orton for facts. He quotes a letter from Dr. George Wilson to Dr. Harvey, respecting the produce of the Manx cat and the common cat. The Manx cat has no tail, and is particularly long in the hinder legs. "You will see," says Dr. Wilson, "from the facts communicated, that where the Manx cat was the mother, the kittens had tails of a sort; where the Manx cat was the father, three-fourths of the kittens had no tail." Mr. Orton also quotes a communication made to him by Mr. Garnett, of Clitheroe: — "From these I select those pertaining to the Muscovy duck and some hybrids produced between it and the common duck. You are aware that the Muscovy drake exceeds in a striking degree the duck in size; the drake weighing from 8 to 9½ lb., while the duck weighs only from 3 to 4 lb. Hybrids produced from the Muscovy drake and common duck followed this peculiarity of the male parent as to the relative size of the male and female hybrids; the male weigh-

ing from 5 to 6 lb., the females not half as much. On the other
hand, the difference in the size of the sexes when the hybrids
were the produce of the common drake and the Muscovy duck,
was not apparent."

A valuable observation, certainly. Mr. Orton adds the
following of his own. He placed a Cochin cock with his common
hens, "reasoning that if the vital organs were due to the female,
then the cross between these birds (being externally Cochins and
internally common hens) should lay white eggs, the secretion of
the egg being a vital function. You know that the Cochin lays a
chocolate-coloured egg. The half-breed did what theory said
they should do — laid white eggs; and not only white eggs, but
eggs also which, on the evidence of myself and family, were
very inferior in taste, having lost the mellow, buttery taste of the
Cochin egg."

But he has recorded another curious fact respecting this same
experiment, which might have made him aware of the proble-
matical nature of his theory, had not his sagacity been hood-
winked by the theory: — "These same half-bred birds afforded
another and a very unlooked-for illustration of the position we
have taken. They were all, when first hatched, like the Cochin
cock, profusely feathered on the legs and feet — so much so, that
they had to be marked to distinguish them from the pure-bred
birds. We see here that, according to the law, the male parent
implanted his characteristics; but what was curious, in a few
weeks, in some of the half-breeds all, and in many most of the
leg feathers were shed. Two out of some twenty birds only
retained them in any very conspicuous degree. Now, why was
this? The cock had implanted his external characteristics, the
hen had given her vital organs. The feathers of the male were
there; but the vital organs necessary to their growth were not
there; and consequently, after a time, for want of nutriment,
these feathers were shed."

We will not here enter on the question of the growth of
feathers (a very complex matter), but, accepting his own pre-
mises, ask him, if the external characteristics are thus dependent
on the vital organs for their growth and development, and these
vital organs are given by the female, how does the child ever

exhibit the characteristics of the male, after infancy? Of what use is it for the male to implant his characteristics, when the female influence is thus certain to annihilate them?

Mr. Orton further cites the practice of Bakewell with respect to his celebrated Dishley sheep. His rams might be bought or hired, for a good price; but his best ewes were sacred. These he would neither sell nor let. As a counter-statement, let it be noted that, according to Girou, the farmers are more particular about the bull than about the cow when they want a good milking cow, for it is observed that the property of abundant secretion of milk is more certain to be transmitted from a bull than from a cow. We question the fact of the bull having greater influence than the cow, believing that in each case the property is transmitted according to direct heritage; but that the bull should be known to have any importance in this respect, is an evidence that the "vital organs" are not solely given by the female.

The result of Mr. Orton's researches proves that the male *does* transmit his qualities to his descendants; as a matter of fact this must be always distinctly remembered; but neither his researches nor those of his predecessors suffice to prove this transmission to be *absolute*, in the sense required by those who maintain that the male gives the *animal* and the female the *vegetative* organs; as well as by those who maintain that the male influence necessarily and invariably predominates in the animal, the female in the vegetative organs. Still it is important to know that by the pollen of flowers we can modify the tints, and produce any varieties of tulip, violet, or dahlia; important to know that we can also modify the plumage of birds and the colour of animals: it is important to know that the male qualities *are* transmissible. But for scientific rigour this is not enough. Before we can establish a law of this kind, we must be sure that the fact is constant and admits of no exceptions, or only of such apparent exceptions as may be classed under unexplained perturbations. Now daily observations, no less than recorded cases, assure us that the law is very far from being constant, that the female as unmistakably transmits her qualities as the male transmits his, and that any theorist who should reverse the

current theory, and declare the mother bestowed the animal
system, leaving the vegetative to the father, would be able
to make a formidable array of facts. Let us glance a while at
the evidence.

The male is said to give the colour; but the female does so
likewise. A black cat and a white cat will have kittens which
may be all black, all white, or black spotted with white, and
white spotted with black. Every street will furnish examples.
Isidore Geoffroy St. Hilaire speaks of a case under his observation, of a black buck and a white doe: the first produce was a
black and white fawn; the second a fawn entirely black, except
a white spot above the hoof.* Burdach mentions the case of a
raven and a grey crow, who had a brood of five — two black like
the father, two grey like the mother, and one mixed. The ass
has only five lumbar vertebræ, the horse six; but the mule has
sometimes five like its mother, and six like its father; the hinny
also shows the same inconstancy. The same result is observed
with respect to all other qualities. But perhaps the most decisive
example we could quote of the twofold influence of parents is in
the singular instance recorded by Buffon. The Marquis Spontin-
Beaufort had a she-wolf living in his stables with a setter dog,
by whom she had two cubs, a male and a female. The male
resembled externally his father the dog, except that his ears
were pointed and his tail was like that of the wolf; the female,
on the contrary, resembled her mother, the wolf, in all external
characteristics *except* the tail, which was the same as her
father's. Here, in one case, the father gave the external characteristics, in the other the mother; while the tail was in each
case, as it were, transposed. But the marvel of this case does
not stop here: the cubs manifested a striking difference in disposition, in each case *resembling in character* the parent it did
not resemble in appearance and in sex: thus the male cub, which
had all the appearance of a dog, was fierce and untamable as the
wolf; the female cub, which had all the appearance of a wolf,
was familiar, gentle, and caressing even to importunity. Lucas
records an analogous case. These hybrids are very instructive,
because the wide differences in the aspect and nature of the

* *Dict. Classique d'Histoire Naturelle*, x. 131.

parents enable us to separate, as it were, the influence of each. The wolf and the dog often breed together; and the following observations, interesting in themselves, will suffice to show the reader how much caution is necessary before drawing absolute conclusions from single illustrations.   Valmont Bomare observed in the various hybrids of wolf and dog which came under his notice at Chantilly, a striking preponderance of the wolf over the dog; Marsch, on the contrary, observed in his experience a preponderance of the dog over the wolf; Geoffroy St. Hilaire and Pallas found the wolf to predominate; whereas, Marolle found the cubs remarkable for their gentleness and doglike instincts, only recalling the wolf in their voracity and fondness for flesh. Girou found the preponderance to vary: sometimes the father, sometimes the mother reappeared in the offspring. If there were no other evidence, this would suffice to disprove the hypothesis of either parent contributing one group of organs to the absolute exclusion of the other parent.

The same fact of twofold influence is shown in the transmission of deformities, such as extra toes, extra fingers, &c.: sometimes the male and sometimes the female, is shown to preponderate, by the offspring inheriting the deformity of the male or the female. It is well said by Girou,* that "if the organisation of the male was the only one which passed to the child, the child would resemble the father, as the fruit of a graft resembles the tree from which the graft was taken, and not at all the tree on which it was grafted." And what is here said of the whole organisation, applies with equal force to any one system, such as the nervous or the nutritive.

Moreover, if the hypothesis we are combating be admitted — if the father bestows the nervous system — how are we to explain the notorious inferiority of the children of great men? There is considerable exaggeration afloat on this matter, and able men have been called nullities because they have not manifested the great talents of their fathers; but allowing for all overstatement, the palpable fact of the inferiority of some sons to their fathers is beyond dispute, and has helped to foster the idea of all great men owing their genius to their mothers: an idea which will not

* *De la Génération*, p. 113.

bear confrontation with the facts. Many men of genius have had remarkable mothers; and that one such instance could be cited is sufficient to prove the error both of the hypothesis which refers the nervous system to paternal influence, and of the hypothesis which only refers the *preponderance* to the paternal influence. If the male preponderates, how is it that Pericles, who "carried the weapons of Zeus upon his tongue," produced nothing better than a Paralus and a Xanthippus? How came the infamous Lysimachus from the austere Aristides? How was the weighty intellect of Thucydides left to be represented by an idiotic Milesias, and a stupid Stephanus? Where was the great soul of Oliver Cromwell in his son Richard? Who were the inheritors of Henry IV. and Peter the Great? What were Shakespeare's children, and Milton's daughters? What was Addison's only son? an idiot. Unless the mother preponderated in these and similar instances, we are without an explanation; for it being proved as a law of heritage, that the individual does transmit his qualities to his offspring, it is only on the supposition of *both* individuals transmitting their organisations, and the one modifying the other, that such anomalies are conceivable. When the paternal influence is not counteracted, we see it transmitted. Hence the common remark, "talent runs in families." The proverbial phrases, "l'esprit des Mortemarts," and the "wit of the Sheridans," imply the transmission from father to son. Bernardo Tasso was a considerable poet, and his son Torquato inherited his faculties heightened by the influence of the mother. The two Herschels, the two Colemans, the Kemble family, and the Coleridges, will at once occur to the reader; but the most striking example known to us is that of the family which boasted Johann Sebastian Bach as the culminating illustration of a musical genius, which, more or less, was distributed over three hundred Bachs, the children of very various mothers.

Here a sceptical reader may be tempted to ask, how a man of genius is ever produced, if the child is always the repetition of his parents? How can two parents of ordinary capacity produce a child of extraordinary power? The answer must be postponed until we come to treat of secondary influences. For the present, we content ourselves with insisting on the conclusion to which the foregoing survey of facts has led, namely, that *both* parents are *always* represented in the offspring; and although the male influence is sometimes seen to preponderate in one direction, and the female influence in another, yet this direction is by no means constant, is often reversed, and admits of no absolute reduction to a known formula. We cannot say absolutely, "the male gives such organs;" we cannot even say, "the male always preponderates in such or such a direction." Both give all organs; sometimes one preponderates, sometimes the other. In one family we see children resembling the father, children resembling the mother, and children resembling both.

This is the conclusion inevitable on a wide survey of the facts. It is equally inevitable *a priori*, if we take our stand upon the evidence of embryology; and as some readers prefer logical 'deductions to any massive accumulation of facts, we will ask them to consider the question from this point of view. Reproduction, in the vegetable and animal kingdoms, is known to naturalists under three forms. In the first a single cell spontaneously divides itself into two cells. Here it is quite clear that the child reproduces the totality of the parent. In the second form, the process called "budding" takes place: the child here grows out of the substance of the parent, until its development is completed, and then it separates itself from the parent to live a free life. Here also the parent is reproduced in its totality. In the third form, a higher complexity of organisation has led to a more complex and more special mode of reproduction: the parent gives off from its own substance, by what may be also considered a "budding process," a mass of cells, which as pollen and ovule, as sperm-cells and germ-cells, unite to develop into plants or animals. Here, again, there ought to be no doubt that the parents are reproduced; their offspring truly may be called "their own flesh and blood." Nor would the doubt have ever arisen, had not the great complexity of the organisms admitted the intervention of the Law of Variations, to which all dissemblances are due. But however such interventions may baffle our inquiries, the mind recognises at once the truth of the proposition that sperm-cell and germ-cell are as much to be regarded in the light of re-productions of the parents, as the cells produced by spontaneous

division are to be regarded in the light of repetitions of the
parent-cell.

It is now time that we should direct our attention to some of
the perturbing causes which mask the laws of transmission from
our perfect apprehension.   While proclaiming as absolute the
law of individual transmission, while proclaiming that the parents
are always reproduced in the offspring, we are met by the obvious fact of the offspring often exhibiting so marked a departure from their parents, being so different in form and disposition,
that the law seems at fault.   We may point to the fact of a genius suddenly starting up in an ordinary family, or to a thousand
illustrative examples in which the law of individual transmission
seems at fault.   To explain these would be to have mastered the
whole mystery of heritage; all that we can do is to mention some
of the known perturbing influences.

Sir Everard Home mentions a striking case, which has become celebrated, of a thorough-bred English mare, who, in the
year 1816, had a mule by a quagga — the mule bearing the
unmistakable quagga marks.   In the years 1817, 1818, and
1823, this mare again foaled, and although she had not
seen the quagga since 1816, her three foals were all marked
with the curious quagga marks.   Nor is this by any means an isolated case.   Meckel observed similar results in the crossing of a
wild boar with a domestic sow; in the first litter several had the
brown bristles of the father; and in each of the sow's subsequent
litters by domestic boars, some of the young ones were easily distinguished by their resemblance to the wild boar.   Mr. Orton
verified this fact in the cases of dogs, pigs, and poultry.

Besides this very remarkable perturbing influence, we must
also consider the phenomenon of *atavism*, or ancestral influence,
in which the child manifests striking resemblance to the grandfather or grandmother, and not to the father or mother.   The
fact is familiar enough to dispense with our citing examples.
How is it to be explained?   It is to be explained on the supposition that the qualities were transmitted from the grandfather to
the father, in whom they were *masked* by the presence of some
antagonistic or controlling influence, and thence transmitted to
the son, in whom, the antagonistic influence being withdrawn,

they manifested themselves. A man has a remarkable aptitude for music; but the influence of his wife is such that their children, inheriting her imperfect ear, manifest no musical talent whatever. These children, however, have inherited the disposition of their father, in spite of its non-manifestation; and if, when they transmit what in them is latent, the influence of their wives is favourable, the grandchildren may turn out to be musically-gifted. In the same way Consumption or Insanity seems to lie dormant for a generation, and in the next flashes out with the same fury as of old. Atavism is thus a phenomenon always to be borne in mind as one of the many complications of the complex problem.

A third cause of complication is one which we propose to call "the potency of the individual." Both father and mother transmit their organisations, but they do so in unequal degrees: the more potent predominates; just as if you mix brandy with equal amounts of water, soda-water, and ginger-beer, the taste of the brandy will predominate more in the water than in the soda-water, more in the soda-water than in the ginger-beer.

According to Rush (quoted by Lucas), the Danes, intermarrying with women of the East, always produce children resembling the European type; but the converse does not hold good when Danish women intermarry with the men of the East. Klaproth observes the same in the mingling of the Caucasian and Mongolian races. Girou, after five-and-twenty years' experience in the breeding of sheep, found this "potency" destroy his calculations. He fancied that, by means of his Roussillon sheep and the Merino rams, he could sooner arrive at the fineness of wool which distinguishes the Merino, than if he coupled the Aveyron sheep with the Merino rams; but he found that the Roussillon type resisted the Merino so energetically that, after a quarter of a century of successive crossings, it still reappeared, whereas the Aveyron sheep had long ceased to be distinguishable from the Merinos. The same potency of particular species is noticeable in plants. Koelreuter is quoted by Burdach as having fecundated the *Nicotiana paniculata* with the pollen of *N. rustica;* and the hybrids thus produced were fecundated with the pollen of *N. paniculata*, but the plants resembled the *N. rustica.* On re-

versing this experiment, he still found the female *N. rustica* to
have the preponderance; so that, cross the species how he would,
the *N. rustica* showed most potency.

But although we thus see that Race has a marked preponderance, we must also remember that it is subject to the individual variations of vigour, health, age, &c. Girou sums up his
observations with this general remark: the offspring of an old
male and a young female resembles the father less than the mother in proportion as the mother is more vigorous and the father
more decrepit; the reverse is true of the offspring of an old female and a young male. In fact, if we consider that the offspring
reproduces the organisation of its parents, and, consequently,
the organisation of *that particular period*, we see at once that
age, health, and general potency of organisation, must be
taken into the account of complicating causes. This also will
help to explain — but not wholly explain — the great differences
observable in the same family: differences of sex, of strength,
and appearance. At present, however, science can only take
note of it as a "perturbing influence."

Reviewing the evidence which has been adduced, we find it
establishing the following important positions. We inherit from
our parents the general form and features, the bony, muscular,
nervous, and glandular structures: there is no absolute constancy in the transmission of any one part of the organisation;
but just as the features may be curiously compounded of the features of both parents, or the eyes and mouth may resemble those
of the mother, while the chin, nose, and brow resemble those
of the father; so may the various parts of the body be a *compound*
of the organs of both parents, or a *distribution* of the organs of
both parents. With this inheritance of the general organisation,
we necessarily inherit its tendencies. We inherit the tempera-
ment, the longevity, the strength, the susceptibility of one or
both parents. We inherit the tendency to scrofula, epilepsy, or
mania. We inherit the nervous system, no less than the muscular
and bony; and with the nervous system, we inherit its general
and particular characters — that is to say, the general sensibility
of the system, and the conformation of the brain and sensory

ganglia, are as much subject to the law of transmission as the size and conformation of the bony and muscular structures are. This being so, it is evident that all those tendencies which depend on the nervous system will likewise be inherited; and even special aptitudes, such as those for music, mathematics, wit, and so on, will be inherited; nay, even acquired tendencies, and tricks of gesture, will be inherited. But this inheritance is in each case subject to the influence exercised by the other parent; and very often this influence is such as to modify, to mask, or even to entirely suppress the manifestation. A man of highly susceptible nervous organisation, a man of genius, marries a woman of powerful organisation, but of rather inferior brain: the influence of the mother is such, that the child turns out perhaps irritable, nervous, but intellectually feeble; or healthy, vigorous, and commonplace; or even stupid, and, it may be, idiotic. Or both parents may be remarkable for intellect, yet because their nervous systems have been developed at the expense of their nutritive systems, their child may be susceptible, but puny and feeble.

Without presuming to fix the limits of inheritance, I must confess that I cannot extend them so far as some writers seem disposed to extend them. F. Cuvier, for instance, says that young foxes, in countries where traps are laid, are less easily caught than young foxes elsewhere! this may be strictly true, but I cannot regard this as evidence that the foxes have inherited greater wariness in regard to traps. It is possible that they may inherit a greater susceptibility to fear of *all* objects, if fear has been more active in their ancestors; because this will depend upon the general susceptibility of the nervous system having been heightened; but to suppose that young foxes inherit any particular fear of traps, is to believe in the existence of innate ideas. It is conceivable that a devout tendency may be inherited from parents in whom devotion was a very eminent quality; because it is conceivable that a peculiarity of organisation may have been inherited, which would impress this *tendency* on the mind of the child; but we cannot conceive anything so specific as the worship of the Virgin to be inherited, even after centuries of devotion.

There are many other topics connected with this subject of inheritance,* but our space will only admit of one more being touched on, and that is the question of whether it is morally justifiable to consent to a marriage when one of the lovers has the "taint" of insanity or consumption, — either directly manifested, or only suspected to exist because it has been manifested in the family. I believe it to be as certain that the tendency to insanity, scrofula, or consumption is transmitted from parent to child as that any other peculiarity is transmitted: if we expect a Roman-nosed father to transmit that form of feature to his son, we must also expect him to transmit the "taint" of insanity, or scrofula. If this were the whole case, the moral rule would be clear, and marriage would be imperiously forbidden. But certain as the law is, it is not single. There is another law equally valid. The child of the Roman-nosed father is just as likely to be born with a nose not at all or very slightly aquiline, inheriting from his mother *as well* as from his father; the child of the tainted father is just as likely to be born with a very slight taint, or none that is appreciable. We see this constantly in families: one parent is carried off by consumption; two or three of the children likewise perish; one or two are merely delicate; the rest seem as vigorous as other people. If this is true in cases where one parent is manifestly and fatally affected, how much more must it be so in cases where the parent is only liable to the *possibility* of being affected, because the disease is in the family? All that we can say is that there is a great risk. Much will depend on the constitution of the untainted parent. A man with tubercles already formed may marry a woman who shall bear him numerous children, all perfectly healthy; whereas the same man may marry another woman whose children would all be doomed. Each individual case would require a deliberate survey of all the conditions before a reasonable judgment could be offered; no absolute rule can be laid down, because none will fit the complexity of the cases.

* In HERBERT SPENCER's *Principles of Psychology* will be found numerous applications of the law of inheritance, especially as regards the Moral Sense and intellectual progress.

CHAPTER XIII.

LIFE AND DEATH.

The mystery of Life — Suspended animation — Is there a Vital Principle? — Examination of the arguments in favour of it — Does Life control chemical affinities? — Does Life precede Organisation? — Life an aggregate unity — What is Life? — Definitions which have been attempted — Cell-life — Life of the parts and life of the whole — The three laws of Life — Vegetal and Animal Life — Criticism of Bichât: Vegetal organs, double and symmetrical; the law of intermittence not confined to animal functions — Life in relation to the external medium — Duration of life — The four Ages — Longevity — Old Age — Death the inevitable residue of Life — Death of the parts — Death of the organism — Apparent Death — Signs of Death.

Life and Death are familiar mysteries. Nothing can be more familiar to our minds; of nothing do we know less. The man whom we loved and honoured, who an hour ago was full of energy, affection, hope, and endeavour, is now lying an inert mass before us, insensible, inanimate. What has made this difference? The form remains, and, but for the paleness of the face, we might suppose him sleeping placidly. Yet Life has vanished, and

"All that mighty heart is lying still."

What is it that has vanished? Whence comes this terrible stillness?

The grains of wheat found in Egyptian tombs, on being planted in the soil of France, grew into waving corn. For three thousand years these grains had been without Life, yet we cannot say they were *dead;* they were organic seeds, products of Life, and had themselves once *lived:* they were developed from cells into seeds, and at this point in their development their vital activity was arrested, because the necessary heat, light, and soil were wanting; but no sooner were these supplied, than the arrested activity was once more set free — the seed became a plant.

The microscopic animals known as Rotifers become, to all appearance, dead, when the water of the moss in which they live is evaporated; and in this state of suspended animation they may remain for years, recovering their energy on the addition of a little water; they may be dried and revived fifteen times in succession; but they are not dead in these cases, and they do not decompose. Frogs and toads, especially the latter, when subjected to the action of intense cold, may be perfectly *frozen*, all their fluids becoming congealed, all their tissues rigid. Yet these animals are not dead. Let heat be cautiously applied, and the congelation ceases: in eight minutes, life is once more in full activity.[*]

In all these cases it is clear that the various phenomena grouped under the term Life are entirely absent; they would *never* manifest themselves, unless the peculiar *conditions* necessary for their manifestation were supplied. The three thousand years would, for the Egyptian grain, stretch to an eternity. The organism in this state of suspended animation is not destroyed; it is like a watch that has run down; until it be again wound up, its delicate mechanism will remain silent and inactive. But once set one part of this mechanism going, and all are set going. Death is not the unwound watch, but the watch with its mainspring broken.

These analogies naturally raise the question, Is there in organic beings anything strictly analogous to the mainspring of a watch? Can we suppose the existence of some vital centre from which all vital actions issue?

Nothing was easier for the early physiologists than to answer this important question. They assumed the existence of two distinct things — dead matter, and a living entity. Life, they said, was an entity, a principle essentially distinct from matter, inhabiting the body, which was composed of dead matter, as living men inhabit dead houses. If this principle quitted the body, the result was Death. If it remained in the body, but

---

[*] The authorities for these statements are GEOFFROY ST. HILAIRE, LEEUWENHOEK, SPALLANZANI, ISIDORE ST. HILAIRE, and DUMÉRIL. For that relating to the toads, see *Comptes Rendus*, vi. 538, and *Annales des Sciences*, 1852, xvii. 10. Compare also the same work, 1858, x. 305.

wholly inactive, as in swooning, it was said to be "suspended."
The Vital Principle animated, directed, formed the body, preserved it from the effects of chemical action, and on quitting it,
left it a prey to this destructive action, which was manifested
by dissolution.

This is, in brief, the hypothesis of a Vital Principle, which
was dominant for many centuries, and is now rejected by all,
except a few metaphysicians and metaphysiologists. It has
fallen into complete discredit, since men have learned that,
besides being in opposition with all the teachings of Science,
it is really nothing more than a substitution of words for ideas,
and while seeming to explain the phenomena, it only gives a
verbal explanation which leaves the problem unsolved. The
same remark is true, although to a less extent, of the modern
doctrine of a Vital Force, or Vital Forces. So long as vital
force merely indicates the dynamical condition of the organism,
the phrase is unobjectionable; and if the vital forces are taken
as the abstract, of which the vital phenomena are the concrete, we
may use the term as freely as we use the terms "mechanical
force," "locomotive power," and the like. But when the abstract term misleads us into a belief in there being a concrete
existence corresponding with the abstraction — when we suppose
that there are vital *forces* independent of, and controlling, the
sum of material conditions present — it is as if we imagined a
watch-principle turning the hands on the dial-plate, or a
moving-principle driving the engine, irrespective of coal burned
and water expanded. To conceive the organism in action, and
to call its activities by the name of vital forces, is one thing; to
conceive that these activities are anything more than dynamic
states of the organism is another. The one conception is physiological, the other is *meta*physiological.

Chemists have analysed organic substances, taken them to
pieces, and in some cases have been able to *make* organic substances — putting together the sort of pieces they have found
in such substances. They have not, indeed, been able to make
any of the higher organic substances, such as albumen; but they
can very accurately unmake them. In all their researches no
one has ever discovered anything which could be called spe-

cially organic — that is to say, formed of elements not found
in inorganic bodies. No one has ever found that the elements
of organic bodies differed, when separated, from those same
elements in inorganic bodies; and the inevitable conclusion has
been, that since organic bodies do not differ from the inorganic
in their *elements*, but only in the *arrangement and combination* of
these elements, the phenomena specially manifested by organic
bodies must be due to this speciality of arrangement. There
can be no such thing as matter essentially dead; there can be no
such thing as matter essentially living. That which to-day we
class as dead, will to-morrow be classed as living, and that
which is living to-day will be dead to-morrow. Living and dead
are terms which indicate certain groups of *phenomena*; and these
phenomena are dependent on certain groups of *conditions*. The
phenomena manifested by sulphuric acid are exceedingly unlike
those manifested by the sulphur and the oxygen of which it is
composed; in like manner, the phenomena manifested by the excessively complex structures, named organic, are exceedingly
unlike the phenomena manifested by the separate substances
composing them.

It is true that if there *were* a Vital Principle, or an independent Vital Force, its presence might be the cause of this very
difference in the conditions which, we have said, determines the
peculiarity of vital phenomena. But we must never gratuitously
multiply existences, we must never assume that which is incapable of proof. A Vital Principle is incapable of proof; if it
exist, we cannot know it; and unless its existence can be proved,
it is to us a mere phrase concealing our ignorance. Phrases
serve to build systems, but they hamper the progress of knowledge.

There are only three arguments, in favour of a Vital Principle
which we need consider here: these are, first, that Life controls chemical affinities; second, that Life *precedes* Organisation, and cannot therefore be a *result* of Organisation; third,
that Life is a presiding unity.

Does Life control Chemical Affinities? — The obvious fact, that
no sooner is life extinct than the body passes into corruption, its
particles yielding to the action of chemical affinities, whereas,

as long as vitality remains, the body retains its form, and does not seem to yield to the destructive action of chemical agencies, early led men to conceive that there was some mysterious principle *controlling* chemical action in the vital organism. And a striking confirmation of this idea seemed furnished by the fact that the gastric juice eats away the coats of the dead stomach, but leaves the living stomach unaffected. When, however, we examine closely these two points, we find that an entire misconception lies at the bottom of the hypothesis. Instead of chemical affinities being controlled by vitality, there is no vital action possible *without* the incessant and complicated action of chemical affinities — all the molecular changes of composition and decomposition occurring in the living body — all nutrition, secretion, and motion, depend on chemical actions. If the oxygen of the atmosphere destroys the dead tissues, not less energetically does it destroy the living tissues; but the destruction of the dead tissue is not *replaced* by the reproduction of fresh tissue, as in the living organism. I have already had occasion to explain why the living stomach is not destroyed by the gastric juice.* No sooner do we admit that *all* chemical affinities are not controlled by vital laws, no sooner are we aware that chemical actions incessantly take place in the living organism, and these actions are dependent on precisely the *same* affinities as those exhibited out of the organism, than it becomes clear that if *any* chemical actions are prevented from taking place in the organism, it is because the *proper conditions* for such actions are not present. No phenomenon, chemical or vital, can take place unless it be under the conditions which permit its manifestation. Wet gunpowder will not explode. Water will not solidify above a temperature of 32°. Chlorine will not unite with Hydrogen in the dark; yet in the sunlight their affinity is so strong that they unite with an explosion. A certain range of temperature is

* See the chapter on DIGESTION and INDIGESTION, vol. I. p. 148 *et seq.* Doubts have been thrown on the explanation there given. It is urged that the presence of mucus is the cause of the gastric juice being inoperative. If this be so, my argument remains just as strong — since the mucus, and not a vital principle, preserves the stomach.

necessary for all chemical actions; and those combinations which take place at the ordinary temperatures of the air may be entirely prevented by cold. If, therefore, many chemical phenomena take place in the living organism which are observable elsewhere, it is because the *conditions* are different. And as for the oft-cited *resistance* to decomposition which the Vital Principle is said to effect, not only is the fact quite otherwise, not only is decomposition incessantly going on in the living organism; but if the fact were as stated, it could be met by the fact that an infinitely better preservative against decomposition is found in Alcohol, Glycerine, or Chromic acid.

Does Life precede Organisation? — There is an unfortunate ambiguity in the word Organisation, which renders it very plausible to say that Organisation is produced by Life, and does not produce it. Men point to the fact of the living germ, which is only a cell, or a mass of cells, and they say, Here is Life, but the organs are not yet formed. They point also to a dead body, and say, Here is Organisation; no lesion has taken place; every organ, every tissue remains intact, yet Life is gone. There was a time when this reasoning seemed to me conclusive; and so long as we understand by an organism a collection of organs, the knowledge of the existence of many plants and animals, and of all embryos in their earliest state, which have no "organs" at all, makes it impossible to reject the conclusion; equally impossible is it, when we conceive the organism as meaning solely the solid fabric, and not also the *whole sum of conditions necessary for its activity.* If I tie an artery, I do not destroy the structure of the limb to which it is distributed, but I destroy the organic relations of the several elements — I destroy the *conditions* necessary to the vitality of that limb. If I prevent the access of oxygen to the blood, I do not destroy the fabric of the body, but I disturb the conditions necessary to the vital activity of the body, as completely as I destroy the conditions necessary to an explosion when I throw water on gunpowder. Recurring to the old analogy of a watch, when the chain has run down, the mechanism is as perfect as ever, but the mechanical relations of the parts are disturbed, and the watch is still: to set it in action once more, we have only to wind it up; that is to say, we have to restore the necessary conditions of mechanical relation.

With regard to Life not resulting from Organisation, this position rests on vague conceptions of both terms. Let us remember that Organisation means the *whole sum of necessary conditions*, no less than the organic fabric, and it will not be difficult to understand that *Life is proportional to Organisation*. The life of a single cell is the *sum-total of the activities of that cell*, and is simple in proportion as the Organisation is simple. The Life of a highly-organised animal is the *sum-total of the activities of all the forces at work*, and is complex in proportion to the complexity of the organism. Take a single cell which is manifesting all its vital activity, spread it out into a layer, and although all the material of which it was composed remains as before, the properties which belonged to it *as a cell* — its Life — can no more be manifested.

And this leads us to the third argument in favour of a Vital Principle, namely, that Life is a presiding unity. "The body is one; all its parts are subordinate; all are bound together in a higher unity. Our consciousness assures us that our Life is a unity." There is an important fact indicated in this argument, but it is misinterpreted. There *is* unity — there is a consensus of the whole organism. But this is not, I conceive, attributable to a Vital Principle, existing independently of the organism; it is due to organic subordination: all the parts are related; all act together by means of the nervous system, as all the parts of an army act together by means of officers and discipline. Where there is no such connection of parts, there can be no such subordination of organs. We may divide a Polype or a worm into several pieces, each piece continuing to live and grow; but we cannot suppose that in such cases we have cut the Vital Principle into several Principles. There is, as we shall see presently, a life of the parts, and a life of the whole organism; each microscopic cell has its independent existence, runs its own career from birth to death; and the *sum-total of such lives* forms what we call the Life of the animal: the unity is an aggregate of forces, not one presiding force.

I have dwelt the longer on this topic, because, although the hypothesis of a Vital Principle has fallen into general discredit, the metaphysical attitude of mind which is implied in the hypothesis, is still unhappily too common among physiologists; and as it is the purpose of this work to consider Physiology even more with reference to general culture than as a branch of special science, the discussion became necessary.   Having lingered thus to refute the hypothesis of a Vital Principle, I may be asked what is the hypothesis to replace it? Instead of an hypothesis, I shall propose a description of vital phenomena.

It is surely more philosophical to consider Life as an ultimate fact; one of the great revelations of the Unknowable; one of the many mysteries surrounding us.   Having made up our minds on this point, having resigned ourselves to the complete relinquishment of all hypothesis, of all endeavours to penetrate into the inscrutable, we cease vexing ourselves with the arcana of Nature, and try to ascertain the *order* of Nature. We no longer set up fictions of our imagination in the place of a reverent observation.   There are minds, indeed, which feel distrust at such resignation.   They seem to dread lest Life should be robbed of its solemn significance, in the attempt to associate it, even remotely, with inorganic phenomena. But this fear arises from narrow views of Nature. It is because reverence for Nature has not been duly cultivated; because familiarity with inorganic phenomena has blunted our sense of their unspeakable mystery. Men who are thrilled at the tokens of the past life of man, when they see, or read of, buried cities, Palmyra, Nineveh, or Yucatan, tremble with no delicious awe at the tokens of the past life of this earth, when they stand in a quarry, or ramble through a geological museum. Yet surely the crystal is not less mysterious than the plant; the ebb and flow of the tides not less solemn than the beating of the human heart? And if patient observation and induction have enabled us to trace something of the order of Nature in crystallisation and the tides, without aid from the metaphysicians, they may also enable us to understand something of the laws of Life.

The general consent of mankind has consecrated the identity

of the words Life and Existence. By the life of an animal is meant the existence of the animal. The particles of which the animal is composed continue to exist after its death — that is, after its existence *as an animal* has ceased. If, then, we accept this general meaning, and say that Life, in its abstract sense, is Existence, we shall have to consider all the various *forms of life* presented to our contemplation, as so many *modes of existence*. These forms often closely resemble each other; they often profoundly differ. According to these resemblances and differences, we group them under two general heads: Organic Existence, and Inorganic Existence. The mystery which underlies all Existence cannot be unveiled by us; but it is not less in the one case than in another; and although custom has affixed the term "living" to one great group of existences, this new term does not introduce a new mystery, nor warrant a new attitude of mind in studying the group. All we are entitled to say is this — there is a *speciality* about vital phenomena, arising from the peculiarity and complexity of the conditions which determine them; and this speciality must warn us against reasoning about them as if they were *not* special, but were in all respects like inorganic phenomena; this speciality, in short, suggests the necessity of studying them in themselves, and not as if they belonged to the general phenomena of physics and chemistry; invaluable as the knowledge of these latter must always be as a means of exploration.

II. DEFINITION OF LIFE. — It would certainly be a great assistance in our efforts to describe vital phenomena, if we could fix clearly in our minds the chief characteristics which distinguish living from non-living bodies; and a definition of Life would be peculiarly acceptable. The attempt has been repeatedly made, but never with entire success.

Aristotle supposed that vital actions were under the dominion of several Vital Principles (*souls*, ψυχαι, he calls them), each distinct, but all subordinate to one supreme Principle. This idea reigned many centuries, and was revived a few years ago by Prout. Kant defines Life "an internal principle of action;" an organism is "that in which every part is at once means and end." This may be said with equal truth of fermentation. Treviranus calls life "the constant uniformity of phenomena under diversity of external influences," which may be equally said of a watch, since if the external influences in any way disturb the organism or the mechanism, the phenomena cease to be uniform. Bichât's celebrated definition, "Life is the sum of the functions by which death is resisted," is only another form of the definition proposed by Stahl, and is every way objectionable; for, on the one hand, it is a paraphrase of the truism that life is the means by which we live; and, on the other hand, it declares that there is a fatal antagonism in external agencies; whereas nothing is more certain than that external agencies are *essential* to vital phenomena: as we saw in the opening paragraphs of this chapter. Dugés calls Life "the special activity of organised beings;" and Béclard says, "Life is the sum of the phenomena proper to organised beings. It consists essentially in this, that organised beings are all during a certain time the centres to which foreign substances penetrate and are appropriated, and from which others issue." De Blainville's definition, adopted by Auguste Comte and Charles Robin, runs thus: "Life is the twofold internal movement of composition and decomposition at once general and continuous;" but this only applies to Nutrition, and does not embrace all the cardinal phenomena: while the definition proposed by Herbert Spencer, namely, "Life is the definite combination of heterogeneous changes, both simultaneous and successive in correspondence with external co-existences and sequences," has the disadvantage of not being perfectly intelligible apart from his explanation of it in detail.*

Perhaps the most intelligible and easily remembered definition would be this: "*Life is the dynamical condition of the Organism.*" This embraces every form of life, from that of the simple cell to that of the complex mammal. It expresses every

* Aristotle: *De Animâ*, L. 2; Kant: *Kritik der Urtheilskraft*, Werke, iv. 260; Treviranus: *Biologie;* Bichat: *Recherches sur la Vie et la Mort;* Stahl: *Theoria Medica vera*, l. 228; Dugés: *Physiol. Comparée*, l. 3; Béclard: *Anat. Générale*, p. 4; Auguste Comte: *Cours de Philos. Positive*, III. 295; Spencer: *Principles of Psychology*, p. 354.

variation in the intensity or complexity of the phenomena, according to the activity or complexity of the organism; and their dependence on all agencies, external and internal. And when we add the three cardinal characteristics which the organism everywhere manifests, Growth, Reproduction, and Decay, we have briefly indicated all that specially distinguishes living from non-living things.

III. CELL-LIFE. — Since the researches of Schwann in 1839, who applied to animals the doctrine of Schleiden with respect to plants, Biology has undergone a renovation almost as great as that which Chemistry underwent after the labours of Lavoisier. The last twenty years, indeed, will be known in history as the cell-epoch, so manifold have been the researches, and so striking the results, with respect to the part played by cells. That in these twenty years the orginal positions have been much modified will surprise no one; nor have we any security that greater changes are not still awaiting the investigator.

A cell is regarded as the true biological atom. Nothing is living but cells, or what can be directly traced back to cells. However great a departure from the cell-form may be disclosed in an anatomical investigation — as in fibres, vessels, bones, membranes — a *morphological* investigation detects that all these were cells in their origin. As a cell the organism commences; all through its career, a large part of the organism is made of cells, and the rest is of transformed cells, or cell-products.

What is a cell? It is usually a microscopic sac, or vesicle, containing a smaller vesicle, called the *nucleus*. In many mature cells this nucleus contains a minute round body, probably solid, called the *nucleolus;* this is, I believe, never found in young cells. Even the nucleus is not always present: it is absent in cells about to perish, — such as the cells of the outermost layer of the skin; or in cells which have only a transitory existence — such as the blood-cells of mammals. Besides the nucleus we must take into account the *cell-contents.* The delicate enveloping membrane, or cell-wall, which forms the sac, contains a liquid and granules, the special nature of which determines the special properties of the cell. Thus the muscle-cell contains a *contractile* substance; a pigment-cell contains colouring matter; a mucus-cell contains mucus, and so on.

Every cell in the organism is independent: it is born, it grows, it reproduces, and it dies, as if it were a single-celled plant, or animal. The growth and decay of an organ, is like the growth and decay of a nation, or of a tree: the individual cells composing the organ grow and perish, as the individual men, or the individual leaves, grow and perish. There is a certain aggregate unity, but it is made up of distinct units. Just as the life of a nation, or a tree, is the sum total of the lives of all its individual parts, so is the life of an organism the sum total of the lives of its individual cells.

This is one of the great revelations of modern science. We no longer speak of a centre of vital activity, for we know that there are myriads of centres. It is therefore no longer surprising to us to know that a part of an organ may be destroyed without the function of that organ disappearing, for this is no more than a regiment's continuing the battle when its ranks are thinned. If the officers are shot down, the regiment will be dispersed, and each soldier will then have to shift for himself; in like manner, if certain regulating parts in the mechanism of the organ be destroyed, the function of that mechanism will disappear, and the individual cells be left to themselves. Thus a man may have an abscess in his liver, which will not prevent the cells of the other unaffected parts of the liver from secreting bile, and pouring it through the gall-duct; but an abscess in the gall-duct would prevent the *function* of the liver, though it would not interfere with the *property* of the liver-cells to secrete bile. A man with half a lung will continue to breathe by means of the half which is unaffected: he will not breathe so vigorously as he did when his lungs were sound; the amount of oxygen he can respire will be of course diminished in proportion to the diminution of the air-cells; but so long as the air-cells remain, and the respiratory mechanism is in action, the breathing function will continue. The student will do well to familiarise his mind with the distinction between the life of the parts and the life of the whole; and to discriminate between those phenomena which depend upon the individual parts, and those which depend upon the mutual *relations* of the parts — in other words, upon the vital structures, and their mechanism.

We have previously stated that there are three cardinal characteristics distinguishing organic from inorganic beings. 1°, *The Law of Nutrition*, the most fundamental of all vital laws since in virtue of it the animal continues to exist as an *active* organism, and increases from infancy to maturity. 2°, *The Law of Development, or Differentiation*, which causes the organism to pass through the *definite cycles of change*, constituting what we call Ages, and leading inevitably to the final change, which we call Death. 3°, *The Law of Reproduction*, another aspect of the first law, in virtue of which the organism gives birth to similar organisms, and thus the lamp of life is handed on from generation to generation.

To no inorganic existences can these three cardinal characteristics be assigned. When inorganic bodies are said to grow ("*mineralia crescunt*," Linnæus), their growth is that of mere aggregation, one part adhering to another similar part. The growth arises from no internal necessity, as in organic bodies. The bulk is not increased by a process of assimilation, which converts the unlike into the like, which makes foreign substances homogeneous — minerals do not *feed*, they *cohere*. Nor have they any Development: they pass through no definite cycles of change: they have no stages of growth, no Ages. Reproduction is equally impossible to them.

Thus, by exclusion, we arrive at a description of the three great *special* characters of living beings: Growth, Development, and Reproduction. It is obvious that the phenomena of beings so markedly distinct from all other beings, must have a corresponding speciality, and must be studied in themselves. Without calling in the delusive aid of a Vital Principle, we may insist on the fact that vital phenomena are peculiar, special, unlike the phenomena of inorganic beings, and must be studied with constant recollection of this peculiarity.

IV. VEGETAL AND ANIMAL LIFE. — Since the time of Bichât,

physiologists have universally accepted the classification proposed by that brilliant thinker, ranging all vital phenomena under two heads: 1⁰, Organic, or vegetative life; *2⁰, Animal, or relative life. The first is common to Plants and Animals; the second is peculiar to Animals. The vegetal phenomena of growth, development, and decay, comprise the whole vitality of the Plant; but over and above these the Animal manifests the phenomena of *relative* life, so called because the animal is brought into active relation with the external world. "Cast your eyes," says Bichât, "on individuals of the two kingdoms, vegetable and animal; you will see that the one has only an internal life, its relations with the exterior being only those of nutrition — it is born, grows, and perishes, fixed to the spot where the seed was deposited; the other unites, to this internal life, an external life which establishes manifold relations with surrounding objects — the animal is thus led to approach or avoid objects according to its desires or its fears."

Although open to criticism, this classification is so convenient that it has been adopted; and we may therefore speak of vegetal functions, and animal functions, of vegetal and animal life, without fear of equivoque. But some of Bichât's other systematic views are less acceptable. For example, I think he was singularly unfortunate in his anatomical generalisation, that all the vegetal organs are single and unsymmetrical, while all the animal organs are double and symmetrical: a very slight examination of this point will disclose its inaccuracy. The parotid and sublingual glands, the lungs and breasts, the kidneys and testes, are all vegetal, and all double and symmetrical — and if the heart and the uterus seem to be single, every anatomist knows that they are as truly double as the cerebrum, or the spinal chord; and although there are certain irregularities, which Bichât has pointed out — in the disposition of the bronchi, for example — there are irregularities

* To avoid the equivocalness and awkwardness of vegetable and vegetative, Mr. Spencer has suggested to me the term *vegetal* as being at once distinctive, and correlative with *animal*; we may thus say vegetal, and vegetality, as well as animal, and animality. I am the more disposed to adopt this suggestion because vegetal is a true English word, not unfrequently used by our old writers, especially the Elizabethan dramatists

as great in the disposition of nerves; and even the brain itself, so confidently relied on by Bichât, is far from perfect in its symmetry — nay, Bichât's own brain was remarkable for the difference in its two halves.

Not less unfortunate is the physiological generalisation Bichât propounded in the celebrated *Law of intermittence*, characterising animal life, and the *Law of continuity*, characterising vegetal life. This generalisation has been accepted as indisputable; let us subject it to a brief scrutiny. All the relative, external functions are intermittent — all the vegetal, internal functions are continuous: that is Bichât's position. In contradiction to this, I affirm that the vegetal functions are intermittent, as well as the animal functions; and that the only processes which can be called strictly continuous are those processes of molecular change — of composition and decomposition — on which existence depends. Let us see which position best covers the facts. It is true that animals require rest after exertion, and sleep, after some hours' waking; this intermittence is caused by an exhaustion of the bodily energy, as we have already endeavoured to indicate. * But that this intermittence is not exclusively animal, may be seen in the equally familiar facts that the vegetal function of digestion is not less periodical; that the vegetal functions of generation and lactation are equally intermittent. A certain time is required to form the gastric juice, and during this interval the function of digestion is impossible. It is the same with all other functions. Nay, even secretion itself is not wholly continuous: the glands are not constantly in action; as we now know from Bernard's discovery respecting the colour of the venous blood flowing from them.** The function of respiration may perhaps be said to be continuous, because its intermittence is so brief and regular; the same also may be said of the circulation; the rapidly intermittent propulsions of the heart, and the continuous processes of molecular change — in the capillaries — on wich circulation depends, give it a certain continuity. But if we except these, all the vegetal functions are obviously intermittent: on the other hand, the

* See p. 253.   ** See vol. i. p. 186.

animal functions have scarcely more claim to intermittence;
since even if we suppose that the brain is ever wholly at rest,
in sleep — of which there is neither evidence nor probability
(see p. 260) — absolute repose for the nervo-muscular apparatus
is impossible, so many of the vital functions being dependent
on this apparatus. The only approach to a generalisation
which seems to me warranted is this: that the vegetal functions are more uniform and rhythmic in their activity, because
the conditions and stimuli are more uniform than is the case
with the animal functions. The conditions of secretion, and
the stimuli to the functions of breathing, &c., are more uniformly present than the conditions of thinking or moving; and
the stimulus is less exhausting, therefore less time is required
for the reintegration of the molecular condition necessary to
activity.

V. Life in relation to the External Medium. — The error,
long dominant, and not even yet entirely effaced, which made
men conceive Life in itself as something unrelated to, and
wholly independent of, the external medium, was consecrated
by the doctrine of a Vital Principle; and yet the facts which
plainly spoke against such a conception were familiar facts,
although their bearing was misunderstood. Every hour men
must have been aware that very slight changes in the external
conditions rendered the manifestation of life impossible; a little
more carbonic acid, or a little less oxygen, a little more heat
or cold, a little less pressure of the atmosphere, a deficiency
of water or food, sufficed to extinguish life, as a lamp is
extinguished when the oil disappears. Every one knew that,
ascending a mountain, certain classes of animals and plants
gradually disappear, a new fauna and flora occupying the higher
districts; so that, all the world over, the same species of plant
will be found at the same heights above the sea-level, and
only these. As we walk down upon the shore at low tide,
we find different species inhabiting distinct zones: those which
live in deep water being unable to bear the temporary exposure which is daily borne by those which live nearer the
tide-mark.

And yet in spite of this knowledge of the constant influence of surrounding conditions on the vital manifestations — in spite of the knowledge that vital phenomena are exalted or depressed, called into existence or entirely destroyed by the influences of light, heat, pressure, moisture, gases, &c., men have gone on asserting that Life is independent of external influences, and that it has the power of controlling physical and chemical laws. In the present state of science such a conception is inadmissible; yet in a widely circulated work we read that "Life resists the effect of mechanical friction," and we find this amazing proposition resting on no firmer basis than an example which will be read with surprise. "The friction," it is said, "which will thin and wear away a dead body, is actually the cause of thickening a living. The skin on the labourer's hand is thickened, to save it from contact with hard substances." Now the fact is, that the friction which wears away a dead body has precisely the same effect on the labourer's hand: so far is Life from resisting this mechanical friction, that in a much shorter time than would suffice to wear away a layer of wood, the living skin would be rubbed bare. When with unaccustomed hands we ply an oar, which is the first to show the effects of friction — the oar or the hand? The peculiarity in the case of a living body is this, that whereas the dead body, when its particles are rubbed off, has no power of *replacing* them, the living body *has* this power, and by its means not only is the loss repaired, but there may be even an increase of the original size. If a labourer's skin is thickened, it is because the growth of its cells has been stimulated, and more are reproduced than are wasted.

We must constantly bear in mind that Life is possible only under the necessary conditions of an *organism*, on the one hand, and an external *medium* on the other. It is the mutual relations of organism and medium which determine the manifestations we name Life; and the error is as great when men attempt to solve vital problems without duly taking all external conditions into account, as when they attempt to solve them without taking the organic conditions into account — that is, when they attempt to explain vital phenomena as if they were simply physical and chemical. The metaphysician, with his "vital forces," is as one-sided as the chemist with his "affinities."

VI. DURATION OF LIFE. — Every organism has its limits of duration which are definite and inevitable; we cannot assign these limits with precision, any more than we can assign the precise stature which an animal will attain; we can only fix boundary-marks within which the duration is possible; for the rest, "the great areas of life cannot be expressed in terms of strict measurement."* These areas mark the accomplishment of a series of organic changes; and such changes, although definite in their order of succession, are so dependent on a variety of influences, "that they do not admit of being weighed in the balance, nor can the vital maturity which they develop be measured by the vibrations of the pendulum."

These great areas of which Simon speaks are the four ages:

1°. *The Fœtal Epoch*, or that in which the egg passes through its successive changes, from a single cell to a multiple of cells, and thence into a complex structure capable of independent existence when separated from the parent organism, at Birth. This epoch is normally of nine months' duration in the human being; thirty days in the rabbit; sixty days in the guinea-pig; fifty-six days in the cat; sixty-four in the dog; one hundred and eight days in the lion; twenty months in the elephant; and so on, varying in the different groups. Nevertheless, although this epoch is one of which the limits are less variable in each group than any of the other epochs, we must remember that Time is only *our* conventional means of measurement; and that the phenomena measured are in no sense regulated by Time. The epoch is really determined by organic conditions, not by Time, and it may therefore be prolonged or shortened by those conditions; the fœtal epoch in human life may last seven months, or eleven.

2°. *Infancy* extends from Birth to Puberty. In this epoch bodily and mental development pass rapidly and strikingly through their phases; but its limits are very variable, puberty

* JOHN SIMON: *Essay on the Thymus Gland*, p. 30.

being much earlier in some organisms than in others, and always earlier in the female than in the male.

3ª. *Manhood* is a sort of table-land of life, but its limits are very variable. In it the body does not increase, except in solidity and vigour. The balance of waste and repair is tolerably even.

4ª. *Old Age.* — The balance begins to lean; the movement of Assimilation slackens, and Death slowly advances. The limits of this epoch are the most variable of all.

These Ages are the Cycles of Change through which every organism must inevitably pass, if it be not earlier destroyed, and they are therefore inseparable from our conception of Life. We have seen how each epoch varies in durátiou, and we can understand, therefore, how the whole of each life will vary one from the other; so that although it is possible to assign the limits for the race, this can only be done as an *average*, — we can never know what will be the duration of an individual life.

And here it may be well to point out a common error in works which treat of Longevity, and one which is explicitly stated by Flourens, the latest writer on that subject.* It is that of supposing the duration of Life to be measurable by beats of the pendulum. We are told that the normal length of life for a human being is one hundred years; and that if the majority of men die earlier, it is because accident, disease, or imprudent habits, have shortened the term. The argument rests on the fallacy that, because some men reach the age of one hundred, all men would reach it were there not disturbing causes (*des causes troublantes*); but inasmuch as these disturbing causes are part of the conditions of human life, inasmuch as man is dependent on the atmosphere, on climate, and on food, and cannot escape their variations — to say that he would live a century were it not for the disturbing influences, is to say that he would enjoy a longer life, if life itself were otherwise ordained. One man lives "faster" than another; he lives more in the same period. If he live imprudently at the same time, he may hasten the changes which will bring about Death. But the utmost prudence will not shield him entirely against external conditions; nor will the wisest care do more than modify the hereditary disposition, which he brought

* Flourens's *De la Longévité Humaine.* 1855.

with him into the world, and which will make him short-lived or long-lived.

What is it which terminates Life, in the natural course of things? Seeing that the organism, like the single cell, has within it the power of Assimilation — the power of repairing its substance wasted in functional activity; and seeing also that this power continues for a long period, a century and upwards, in some cases, why should it not be indefinitely prolonged? The prolongation of human life has been one of the dreams of the speculative, and its essential error has been seldom perceived. Hufeland, who wrote a book on the art of prolonging life, refers to the fact (questionable fact) of men having lived to the age of 150 and even 180 years; and he declares that he can see no reason why others should not live to 200. But I can see no reason why he should modestly stop there. Two centuries is not a magical period, beyond which Life *must* be impossible. There is, indeed, the disturbing fact of no man having yet reached the age of 200; but if we are to argue that, because 150 and 180 have been reached, therefore 200 may be reached — we are surely entitled to argue that, if 200 can be reached, then 300, then 400, and so on, until some *necessity* be shown for the termination.

And here we bring the question to the test. What is the inherent necessity for a termination of that process of repair which we know the organism for a long period possesses? Let us first see what are the phenomena of old age; they may help us to an answer. A French physician graphically says: "Man begins in a *gelatinous*, and terminates in an *osseous* condition." The processes of Life induce changes in the structure which gradually impede its functions. "The great characteristic of all the changes," says Dr. Van Oven, * which gradually occur from early to extreme old age, is *consolidation*, a diminished plasticity and mobility of parts, increased firmness of structure, and diminished bulk: interstitial fat is then absorbed; the muscles become stringy and fibrous, and at their terminations ligamentous; cartilages become bony; bones lose their cancellous structure, and become merely solid masses, whilst the blood-vessels are diminished or obliterated. The coats of the arteries become

* VAN OVEN: *On the Decline of Life.*

harder, and lose their tonicity; many of the smaller trunks are
obliterated, whilst, however, the veins have become larger and
more dilatable than they were in early life; perspiration is nearly
at an end, for the skin has become harsh and dry, wrinkled and
discoloured; and even, as in the vegetable world plants as they
grow older become more and more woody, and the sap traverses
only the larger vessels, so too in the old man the circulation is
carried on only by the larger trunks, and hence the whole body
becomes thinner, firmer, more harsh, more dry, and loses strength
and mobility, and the power of repairing injured or regenerating
lost parts. The muscular system has become so weak as to be
almost useless. The once powerful man, now unable to stand
erect, stoops; the shoulders are raised, and the head falls forward. In walking, the spine is much curved; the aid of a strong
stick or an able arm is required to keep the body in equilibrium;
the step is tottering and uncertain; the hands are unable to
grasp any object firmly — they tremble in a palsied manner if the
attempt be made, and the command over the particular fingers is
very uncertain."

In this picture of old age, some points of which may be questioned, we see plainly enough that very important structural
changes must have occurred in the organism; the source of these
changes lies in the very nature of the nutritive process itself. If
the Repair were always identical with the Waste, never varying
in the slightest degree, Life would be only terminated by some
accident, never by old age. But the Repair is never thus nicely
balanced with the Waste. Moreover, in Food we are constantly
introducing different substances, which produce variations in the
composition of the Blood, and variations in the nutrition of the
parts. These differences accumulate their influence in those
changes named the Ages, and they culminate in the final change,
named Death. The cellular mass becomes *differentiated* into
various tissues; these in turn become differentiated as they grow
and act; and thus it may be said that the very processes of Life
bring with them a gradual deposition of Death.

That Death is really and truly the inevitable residue of the
activity of Life, and that its approach is determined by the rapidity with which developmental changes take place, is proved

by the experiments of Réaumur on insects. He shows * that the
duration of an insect's existence may be prolonged twofold, nay,
fourfold, beyond that of its species; or, *vice versâ*, it may be
abridged, without doing it any other injury whatever, simply by
retarding, or accelerating, those stages of metamorphosis, by
which it must pass to complete its career. In Kirby and Spence's
delightful work we read: "The aphidivorous flies live in the larva
state ten or twelve days, in the pupa state about a fortnight, and
as perfect insects possibly as long, the whole term of their existence in summer not exceeding at the very utmost six weeks. But
one which I put under a glass on the 2d June 1811, when about
half grown, and, after supplying it with aphides once or twice,
by accident forgot, I found, to my great astonishment, alive three
months after; and it actually lived till the following June without
a particle of food. It had therefore existed in the larva state
more than eight times as long as it would have lived in all its
states, if it had regularly undergone its metamorphoses, which is
as extraordinary a prolongation of life as if a man were to live
560 years."** At the moment of writing this,*** I have the tadpole
of a Triton, which was taken last autumn from a pond, and kept
in a glass vessel of water through the whole autumn and winter
in a very cold place; it has remained all this while untrans-
formed; and its "infancy," instead of having a duration of a few
days, has been prolonged over many weeks.

Now it is clear that the causes which determine the accelera-
tion or retardation of Development — which make each epoch of
Life longer or shorter — must be also those which prolong or
shorten Life itself. In other words, Death is determined by the
metamorphoses of Life. And thus, in a certain sense, those philosophers are justified who teach that every organism has an
allotted amount of vitality, which it may expend in a shorter or a
longer time, but which it cannot increase. We can no more live
our Life and keep it, than we can eat our cake and keep it.

In England one person in every 3100 reaches the age of 100.

* RÉAUMUR: *Mémoires pour servir à l'hist. des Insectes*, vol. II.; pre-
face, p. II.
** KIRBY and SPENCE: *Introduction to Entomology*, ed. of 1856, p. 225.
*** January 1859.

Some small minority exceeds the hundred years, and cases of 150 and even of 180 are cited, but the evidence for them seems questionable. Respecting the numerous cases of long-lived people, so often spoken of, it is to be observed that wherever a registration of births has been established, such marvellous examples never appear. In Sweden and Norway we have a striking illustration of this. In one country the cases of men living to 120 and 140 are said to be frequent; in the other they never occur. In the one country there are no official documents to test the age of the people; in the other there is such a test.

I do not assert that there never has been an example of human life prolonged even to 180 years. Let such an example be authenticated, and the physiologist will no more see reason for surprise, than at the child remaining eleven months in the womb, or commencing its teething at two years; for the physiologist knows that Time itself is not a factor in the sum — is not a condition of Life; it is only a mode we adopt of measuring changes. But until such an example is authenticated, we may reasonably be sceptical.

VII. DEATH.— We have seen reason to consider Death as the closing scene of a successive series — the terminal act of Life; not therefore as an antagonist of Life — a negative which destroys a positive — a darkness which shrouds up a light; but the *dénouement* of the drama, inevitable, and indissolubly linked with all that has constituted Life. Death is a new-birth: with it certain forms of existence are completed, and certain others are commenced. It is the *destruction of the organic unity, and consequently of the phenomena which were dependent on that unity.* This definition seems preferable to that which says, "Death is the cessation of the functions of life;" for that cessation may take place in an organism still capable of life, and therefore not dead. The congealed frog, and the dried rotifer, exhibit none of the functions of life; yet they are not dead; the unwound watch is silent, but it is not destroyed.

As there is Life of the parts, of the cells, and of the whole organism; so likewise is there Death of the parts, of the cells, of the whole organism. In each case the destruction of the organic unity brings a cessation of the organic functions.

1°. *Death of the Parts.* — The life of the cell depends upon a twofold movement of composition and decomposition, of assimilation and disintegration, of repair and waste. In the first of these movements there is *union* of elementary principles, and *growth* of the substance of the cell; in the second movement there is *separation* of elementary principles from the existing substance, and this is *decay,* or Death. Thus indissoluble are Life and Death.

Molecular death, or waste of substance consequent on vital activity, is incessant; but the organism lives on, surviving this death of the organs, as the nation survives though men perish daily.

2°. *Death of the Organism.* — Although differing only in unessential particulars, there are three heads under which all forms of death are classed: 1. Natural death; 2. Accidental death; 3. Death from disease. It is clear, however, that whether the interruption of the vital manifestations arise from the gradual decay and obstruction which is brought about by old age, by disease, or more suddenly by wounds and poisons; in each case Death results from the interruption of that *relation* between the several parts of the vital mechanism, which brought all its units into active unity, making each play into the other. In old age this interruption comes on gradually. The old man dies in detail; his functions dwindle; his senses grow one by one less active, and many ordinary causes of sensation cease to affect him. In disease the interruption is rapid; still more so in fatal accidents.

Yet, although the organism may be dead, many of the organs may be living: the interruption may have taken place, and the unity be destroyed, but the units are not destroyed. Hours after a man is dead, his muscles live, and will contract; his glands live, and will secrete; his heart lives, and will beat; his stomach lives, and will digest. * Beard, hair, and nails will grow, and cut surfaces grow together. M. Gerdy says that the head rolling on the scaffold is not dead, for the features can be made to contract, as

---

* In certain fishes, digestion will continue twenty-four hours after death. — CHAS. ROBIN: *Mémoires de la Société de Biologie,* v. 134.

in horrible passion, twelve or fifteen hours after decapitation. Dr. Ure experimented on the body of a man who had been hanged, and frightened the spectators by the sight of this corpse starting up, its features convulsed as with passion and terror, when a powerful galvanic battery was applied.

On the other hand, many of the parts may be dead while the organism continues to live. In disease and wounds this is constantly the case. The negroes on the African coast frequently begin to putrefy at their extremities before death comes on — their limbs rotting, while heart, lungs, brain, and stomach are active.

VIII. APPARENT DEATH. — It is of the first importance that we should be able to discriminate real from apparent death, and that we should have some simple memorable indications which may preserve us from those fearful mistakes of "buried alive," common enough in ancient times, and not wholly unknown in our own.

Writers on this subject are fond of citing the case of François Civille, a Norman gentleman of the days of Charles IX., who described himself as having been "thrice dead, thrice buried, and thrice resuscitated by the grace of God." Winslow, the famous anatomist, is said to have been twice buried. If many of the reputed dead have awakened from their lethargy in time, there is a frightful suspicion that many others did *not* awake in time. It is easy to say that only culpable ignorance, and culpable carelessness, can in our day permit such mistakes; but I find an authentic case so late as 1843, in France, in which a beggar was found drunk, on the road to Nantes, and was mistaken for dead; all preparations for burying him were made, when those who came to carry him away were startled by his opening his eyes, shaking himself, and asking where he was? Nay, so late as 1849, the French Academy accorded a prize of 1500 francs to the essay of M. Bouchut, * the money having been furnished by a philanthropic professor at the University of Rome, P. Manni.

---

* BOUCHUT: *Traité des signes de la mort et des moyens de prévenir les enterrements prématurés.* 1849.

The definition of Death which I have proposed, furnishes the real clue in every case. The common notion that Death is the cessation of the vital functions, is no guide. It does not discriminate between Lethargy and Death. Those who were buried alive gave no sign whatever of Life; and except one little detail, which will presently be noted, there was nothing which could lead by-standers to the suspicion that a corpse was not before them.

Mr. Braid, in his *Observations on Trance*, has collected examples of the Indian Fakeers, which seem tolerably authenticated. "In one of these vouched for by Sir Claude M. Wade, the Fakeer was buried in an underground cell, under strict guardianship for *six weeks*; the body had been twice dug up by Runjeet Singh during the period of interment, and had been found in the same position as when first buried." In another case narrated by Lieutenant A. Boileau in his *Narrative of a Journey in Rajuarra*, 1835, "the man had been buried for ten days in a grave lined with masonry, and covered with huge slabs of stone, and strictly guarded; and he assured Lieutenant B. that he was willing to submit to an interment of twelve months' duration, if required. In a third case, the trial was made under the direct superintendence of a British officer, a period of nine days having been stipulated for on the part of the devotee; but this was shortened to three days at the desire of the officer, who feared lest he should incur blame if the result was fatal. The appearance of the body when first disinterred is described in all instances as having been quite corpselike, and no pulsation could be detected in the heart or arteries. The means of restoration employed were chiefly warmth to the head, and friction to the body and limbs."

Let us now glance at the various signs of Death, and estimate the value of each.

1°. *The cadaverous aspect of the face*, familiar to every one, is by no means a certain characteristic, since it is observed in persons much exhausted by chronic maladies; and, moreover, it is not observed in persons who have died from accident, or from acute malady.

2°. *The coldness and lividness of the skin* are very equivocal

Those who die from chronic maladies or violent bleeding rapidly become cold; but those who die from asphyxia are a long while becoming cold, nor does the body lose its tints for many hours. I have already noticed surprising cases of the body retaining its warmth many hours after death. *

3°. *Rigidity of the limbs* is one of the most reliable signs. It is always observed sooner or later: sooner in those weakened by old age, or long illness, than in the young, or in those who perish from accident, and in those suffocated, especially those suffocated by carbonic acid. It persists generally twenty-four to thirty-six hours; but the causes which retard its first appearance prolong its duration; for instance, after suffocation by carbonic acid it does not come on till about fifteen hours after death, and lasts several days if the air be at once cold and dry. This cadaveric rigidity is to be distinguished from the rigidity of congelation, and from that convulsive rigidity produced by certain nervous states: in the first case a limb or finger is heard to *crick* when bent — which is said to arise from the breakage of little congealed masses; in the second case, the bent limb returns to its original position when the force which bent it is removed, whereas in the dead body a limb once bent retains that position.

4°. *Cessation of the Respiration and Circulation.* — It is worthy of remark that all the ordinary means of ascertaining whether the heart has ceased to beat, and the lungs to act, have little scientific value. You may fail to detect the slightest pulse at the wrist, temple, or chest. You may place a bright mirror before the mouth, and it will not be obscured; you may hold a flame before the mouth, and it will not flicker; you may place threads, or down, on the lips, and there will be no stir; yet the patient may be living. Nevertheless it is tolerably certain that, in the higher animals at least, actual cessation of the circulation must, if prolonged, be regarded as the sign of death. How then to establish the reality of this cessation? M. Bouchut says there is out one test, and that is infallible — namely, *auscultation*. By the aid of the stethoscope the cirulation can be *heard*, when it can be detected by no other means. In the Report of the Commission

* See vol. I. chap. vii. p. 308.

appointed by the Academy, this cessation of the heart's action, as detected by the stethoscope, is considered to be *the* infallible sign of death — and the time which this cessation must be observed may be estimated at five minutes. If during five minutes no sound whatever be heard, the certainty of death may be relied on.

Taken in conjunction with cadaveric rigidity, this last sign may be said to furnish a positive assurance of Death. But in cases where the stethoscope cannot be applied, or where no skilled practitioner is present to apply it, there is one other sign — namely, *Putrefaction.* This cannot be mistaken. It manifests itself at first as a blue-green tint over the skin, *especially about the abdomen*, and soon spreading all over the body. This sign, if preceded or accompanied by cadaveric rigidity, can be relied on as infallible.

CONCLUSION.

AND now, reader, we have reached the end of our toilsome, but, let me hope, not profitless journey. There are many other questions of interest and importance which the physiologist has to study, but they do not fall within the range of common interests, and must therefore be omitted from these pages. My object was thus explained in the original prospectus: —

"No Scientific subject can be so important to Man as that of his own life. No knowledge can be so incessantly appealed to by the incidents of every day, as the knowledge of the *processes by which he lives and acts.* At every moment he is in danger of disobeying laws which, when disobeyed, may bring years of suffering, decline of powers, premature decay. Sanitary reformers preach in vain, because they preach to a public which does not understand the laws of life — laws as rigorous as those of gravitation or motion. Even the sad experience of others yields us no lessons, unless we understand the *principles* involved. If one man is seen to suffer from vitiated air, another is seen to endure it without apparent harm; a third concludes that 'it is all chance,' and trusts to that chance: had he understood the *principle* involved, he would not have been left to chance — his first lesson in swimming would not have been a shipwreck.

"There is a daily increasing desire for scientific knowledge. Science passes from its laboratories into the public thoroughfares. But although thousands are now anxious to understand the chief physiological laws, the majority cannot overcome their invincible repulsion from anatomical details. Many would rather remain ignorant than gain knowledge through such paths. It is believed by the Author of the proposed work that a clear and accurate conception of the chief physiological laws, sufficient for ordinary practical guidance and for scientific culture, may be impressed upon the mind, and illustrated by memorable facts, *without once appealing to anatomical knowledge.* It will be his object to *expound principles* rather than to teach a science; and these principles will be illustrated by the most striking *facts* hitherto ascertained. Assuming the position of a lecturer addressing a miscellaneous audience, he will imagine that beside the Medical Student there sits an intelligent Artisan — beside the Man of Letters sits the Mother of a family; and he will endeavour to be intelligible and interesting to all, while reproducing the *latest* discoveries of European investigators, and the results of *original research.*"

How far this object has been attained, the reader must judge; but I have received such cheering and generous encouragement from the profession and the public, during the course of monthly publication, as fully to repay the great pains and labour bestowed on the work; and I now part from it, and the reader, with reluctance and regret.

INDEX

21*

THE END.

PRINTING OFFICE OF THE PUBLISHER.